The E ation

I, Herodotus of Halicarnass, am here setting forth my history, that time may not draw the colour from what man has brought into being.

The History, Herodotus (translated by David Greene),
University of Chicago Press, 1987

The Ethnographic Imagination

Paul Willis

Polity

Copyright © Paul Willis 2000

The right of Paul Willis to be identified as author of this work has been asserted in accordance with the Copyright, Designs and Patents Act 1988.

First published in 2000 by Polity Press in association with Blackwell Publishers Ltd

Transferred to Digital Print 2003

Editorial office:
Polity Press
65 Bridge Street
Cambridge CB2 1UR, UK

Marketing and production:
Blackwell Publishers Ltd
108 Cowley Road
Oxford OX4 1JF, UK

Published in the USA by
Blackwell Publishers Inc.
350 Main Street
Malden, MA 02148, USA

A catalogue record for this book is available from the British Library.

Library of Congress Cataloging-in-Publication Data

Willis, Paul.
    The ethnographic imagination/Paul Willis.
        p. cm.
    Includes index.
    ISBN 0-7456-0173-1—ISBN 0-7456-0174-X (pbk.)
        1. Ethnology—Philosophy. 2. Ethnology—Methodology. I. Title.

GN345. W52 2001
305.8'001—dc21   00–037502

Typeset in 11 on 13 pt Sabon
by Kolam Information Services Pvt Ltd, Pondicherry, India
Printed in Great Britain by Athenaeum Press Ltd., Gateshead, Tyne & Wear

This book is printed on acid-free paper.

Contents

Acknowledgements

I am very grateful to the Centre for Cultural Research at the University of Växjö in Sweden for providing partial financial support for my professorship at the University of Wolverhampton. This has allowed me generous time with which to work on this text. Thanks to the Ethnography Seminar in Wolverhampton and to the Graduate Seminar in Växjö for listening to and making many helpful comments on various presentations relating to material in this book. Heartfelt thanks to the friends and colleagues who have made detailed and specific comments on many, many previous drafts: Mats Trondman, Phil Corrigan, Huw Beynon, Marcus Free, Chris Rojek, Andrew Worsedale, Chris Barker, Jean Lave, Jim McGuigan, Christina Klosterberg and Helen Wood.

Paul Willis

Foreword

This book outlines an approach to method and understanding in the social sciences, an approach which I've termed the ethnographic imagination. The juxtaposition of 'ethnographic' and 'imagination' is meant to surprise, condition and change the meaning of both. The two may seem far apart, ethnography faithfully reporting 'the reality' of the everyday, imagination deliberately seeking to transcend the everyday. But, actually, for its own full development ethnography needs a theoretical imagination which it will not find, 'there', descriptively in the field. Equally, I believe that the theoretical imaginings of the social sciences are always best shaped in close tension with observational data.

Perhaps I could have called the book *Ethnography* and *Imagination*. But I mean to emphasize the ethnographic as conditioning, grounding and setting the range of imaginative meanings within social thought. Ethnography provides the empirical *and* conceptual discipline. Ethnography is the eye of the needle through which the threads of the imagination must pass. Imagination is thereby forced to try to see the world in a grain of sand, the human social genome in a single cell. Experience and the everyday are the bread and butter of ethnography, but they are also the grounds whereupon and the stake for how grander theories must test and justify themselves. They should be not be self-referenced imaginings but *grounded* imaginings.

The particular articulation of how the everyday and the social imagination are brought together depends on many things, not least the type of research question being asked, what drives the curiosity of the researcher. I will explore some of these in detail, but there is a broad conjunction which provides the main spine for how this book is organized. It underlies much of my own work and is relevant to many social questions and issues. This is the bringing together of ethnographic accounts of everyday life and aesthetic questions. I pose the question in this book: what happens if we understand the raw materials of everyday lived cultures as if they were living art forms?

A biographical vignette may help.

In October 1968 I registered as a PhD student at the Centre for Contemporary Cultural Studies, Birmingham University, UK, to conduct a field study on Biker and Hippie cultures (subsequently published as *Profane Culture*, Routledge). The Centre was in an English Department and I had previously studied English Literature at Cambridge. Newly arrived at the Centre, I was asked to lead an early seminar analysing Blake's 'Tyger, Tyger'. Trained in the techniques of literary criticism, specifically in practical criticism and close reading, I struggled to analyse how the words on the page achieved their effects: 'Tiger, Tiger'... OK... twice for effect, but why 'burning'... that's unusual, tigers don't usually do that,... 'symmetry', OK, but why 'fearful'? Why an industrial metaphor to describe an animal, nature and the jungle? That same night I was using the same techniques of 'close reading' to try to understand the bike culture in the city centre of Birmingham: why the 'cattle horn handlebars'... that's unusual... why the 'chrome exhausts' and 'no baffles' in the exhausts... that's anti-social... why 'no helmets'... that's dangerous... why and how was an industrial product used for meaning-making in a flesh and bone, human world? Almost on autopilot, by chance or unconsciously, there I was trying to use the categories of art to understand an example of lived culture.

Practical criticism and 'close reading' techniques had come both to baffle and bore me at Cambridge. They seemed inturned, narrow and related only to judging canonical hierarchies, displacing altogether the life-enhancing breadth and openness which had inspired me, an unlikely candidate in many ways, actually drawn me into literary studies. By contrast and surprisingly, in the living context of the bike culture these techniques of practical criticism seemed full of life and promise. They seemed to grant significance where condescension had ruled. Almost accidentally and in drastic measure, I had reconnected what had been slowly drained out of literary studies at Cambridge – in a word the *social connection*, the connection with real life in all its tumbling profusion and messiness. At the same time, however, these same approaches and techniques, violently relocated to the social, *also* offered an immediate inoculation, so to speak in the other direction, against the flattening reductions of social science. Further and not least, my version of a transplanted practical criticism offered a productive, concrete and unfussy practice and methodology for the study of the real world. My afternoons and evenings were not so far apart. The dreaming spires and the spiral springs of the motor-bike world could be brought together imaginatively.

That is the same engagement I am trying for now on a grander scale: understanding the nitty gritty of the everyday as containing its own forms of symbolic creativity. Chapter 1 of this book sets the scene and traces through, in an evocative kind of way, some of the implications of bringing together ethnographic and aesthetic categories into the same frame. The rest of part 1 takes up the main issues and develops them in more analytic ways.

Perhaps this is an unusual book; method, theory, substance all in one. I aim to bring together, codify and extend the essential themes and concepts as they have developed in my work over the past thirty years. I aim to present not only a chosen methodological approach (ethnography) but also an allied theoretical approach, and also, overlappingly, theories for and some account of its subject matter, varieties and forms of lived everyday cultures: at school, on the dole, on the street, in the mall, in front of the TV, in the dance club. This Foreword supplies a map, some signposts and definitions, making clear some of the broad-brush assumptions that underpin my whole approach.

At bottom, you could say that in this book I am trying to outline an experimental, *profane* theoretical methodology. Imagine that I am a bit of an academic vandal, in the nicest possible and disciplined way. I take, develop or invent ideas (while immersed in the data) and throw them, in a 'what if?' kind of way, at the ethnographic data – the real world of the nitty gritty, the messiness of everyday life – to see what analytic points bounce out on the other side, pick them up again, refine them and throw them again. The problem with many empirical data, empirically presented, is that they can be flat and uninteresting, a documentary of detail which does not connect with urgent issues. On the other hand the 'big ideas' are empty of people, feeling and experience. In my view well-grounded and illuminating analytic points flow only from bringing concepts into a relationship with the messiness of ordinary life, somehow recorded.

Part of the difficulty in defining what I mean by the *ethnographic imagination*, and its focus in this book, is that, in general, I refrain from precise or neat definitions of concepts. I do not see the social sciences as comparable to the natural sciences (or an early version of them), requiring precision to mirror objectively and as exactly as possible separate elements in nature in order to determine the pattern of their relationships: discovering unchanging laws controlling the movement of atoms. As Blumer[1] says, the social sciences can hope only to develop '*sensitising* concepts' about the social world, approximate conceptions which are rough and always provisional guides to a changing and complex reality. Social science conceptions have to be fluid, not least because the subject matter with which they deal is comprised of, certainly in part, the views and thinkings of social agents themselves, if you like, deploying their own kind of 'sensitising concepts'. Though in much more informal ways, they are trying to understand, for themselves, the world in which they have to operate. Atoms thinking for themselves! Even as they are in some sense determined from the outside. How to encompass this? By capaciousness and imagination, I reply. First step: use broad ethnographic techniques to generate observational data from real life, recorded with goodly inputs from subjects themselves and with sufficient finesse that you are able to register something of the internal 'life' of social atoms. Second step: experiment by bringing this into forcible contact with outside concepts, accidentally or inspirationally chosen, by trying to frame the whole with necessary complexity and to deliver analytic and illuminating points not wholly derivable from the field but vital to conceptualizing its relationships. Of course, the effects can be unpredictable when you throw concepts at things. You might just get shards, useless academic fragments in crazy piles. But the ambition, at least, is to

tell 'my story' about 'their story' through the fullest conceptual
bringing out of 'their story'.

But these concepts which I throw at the data are not about
scientifically understanding how human atoms respond to general
laws. They are fallible, continually revised *approximations* of the
relations of external forces to the interior life and movement of the
atoms. Since these latter are fluid and dynamic and, changing in
their own way, playing the same game, then, perforce, my own
categories, ideas and concepts about them are bound, themselves,
to be even more fluid and always provisional.

There is a further complication. Social agents are not academic
sociologists or organized in obedient seminar groupings, so their
practices of sense-making require some digging out, some interpretation – the further exercise of an ethnographic imagination.
An important line of argument pursued throughout the book is
that embodied 'sense' is often not expressed in language; sometimes, more strongly, it is organized against, or in tension with,
language. Such meanings have to be translated into language.
Furthermore, there are what we can think of as informal traditions
of meaning-making, relating to gender, humour and self-presentation for instance. They are often sedimented in their own ways,
long-running and semi-ritualized, so producing their own long
durees and slow motion logics with respect to how quickly they
can change and react to changed circumstances. The motives,
meanings and lived dynamics of everyday culture are also multi-
fold and organized for different questions and situations, with time
scales enforced by different immediacies: getting to work, holding
a family together, 'getting a life' through and on top of it all. All
these are often unconsciously, chaotically or eccentrically organized with reference to each other, not rationally spoken, so
requiring further interpretation.

Let us move on now to some more specific signposts and definitions. What about my practical methodology? There are many
possible approaches to understanding the field of everyday culture.
My approach foregrounds the experiences and practices of social
agents, sensuously understood and ethnographically studied. But
what do I mean by the 'ethnographic method'?

It is the central spine of an overarching set of techniques, one of
only two families of methodological approaches for generating
primary data about the social world: the quantitative and qualitative approaches. On the one hand, you can send out questionnaires

to generate responses you can *count*, concerning essentially the regularities of what people do – at school, at work, so many people going to the cinema, to the pubs, to the clubs, so often a week, spending so much, etc. This yields *quantitative* findings. On the other hand, you can make direct contact with social agents in the normal courses and routine situations of their lives to try to understand something of *how* and *why* these regularities take place. If possible participating in those activities yourself over a long period and through many situations, you witness and record in detail what they do, their practices in schools, in pubs, in cinemas. Through observation, interview and informal interaction you inquire into the meanings and values they attach to particular activities that are the focus of study, and further inquire how they see them in relation to wider and central life concerns and issues. This produces *qualitative* findings. Any one of the constitutive techniques of this ethnographic range of techniques can produce qualitative data, but it is only a combination of them over time that produces sufficient 'quality' data to generate an *ethnographic* account of a social or cultural form.

More directly, the ethnographic impulse is to be so moved with curiosity about a social puzzle – why do working-class kids get working-class jobs?; why are the unemployed so passive?; is TV an agent of passification? – that you are seized to go and look for yourself, to see 'what's going on' as bound up with 'how they go on'. Physical and sensuous presence then allows observation and witness and the use of five-sense channels for recording data relating to social atmosphere, emotional colour and unspoken assumptions. You can also sense for yourself important aspects of context and of the material and institutional features of the enclosures and regimes through which subjects pass, seeing for yourself how they use and manipulate surrounding resources in their cultural practices. This same physical presence also allows you to interact and to pursue questions and issues related to your puzzle, probing and reconstructing how subjects symbolically inhabit their worlds: what are *their* agendas, *their* de-codings, *their* stories, *their* uses of objects and artefacts.

What about art. What do I mean by it? Why use it? What I have said about fluidity and indeterminacy has to be firmly borne in mind here. What follows are starting points that my own work has developed and extended in ways which stretch my original metaphor, perhaps into unrecognizable forms. Following Marcel

Duchamp, I could simply say, 'Art is whatever I say it is.' Finally, in effect, perhaps that is exactly what I do in this book: report the results and sum of conceptual developments over many years and move way beyond my starting-out points. But I also mean to utilize and lean on the sedimented meanings of art throughout. I know that proclaiming 'life as art' may come across as a cliché and banal. But all labels are or become clichés; that is why they stick. And I want my assertion to raise questions which stick. Essentially, what are the consequences of viewing everyday relations as if they contained a creativity of the same order as that held to be self-evidently part of what we call the arts. What analytic tools do we need to comprehend that the 'sensitising concepts' used by social agents might be indissolubly linked to aesthetic forms of feeling and knowing.

So, to my provisional definitions. Most basically I am using 'art' to specify a quality of human meaning-making. Human beings are driven not only to struggle to survive by making and remaking their material conditions of existence, but also to survive by making sense of the world and their place in it. This is a cultural production, as making sense of themselves as actors in their own cultural worlds. Cultural practices of meaning-making are intrinsically self-motivated as aspects of identity-making and self-construction: in making our cultural worlds we make ourselves. At least for those who have moved out of economic subsistence, perhaps the balance has tipped from instrumental to expressive struggle, so that humans now are concerned more with the making of their cultural world than with their material world. Even in their material struggles for survival, they grapple with choices in 'how to go on', so as to deal with practical exigencies in ways consistent with the maintenance of a viable cultural identity and its distinction and acknowledgement from others.

Crucially, this making of identity is achieved through creative cultural practices which produce something that was not there before, at least not fully or in the same way. With formal works of art as a result, legitimate artistic creativity shares in this defining feature, but not as its centre, only as its regional exemplification and reification. At the centre are lived cultural practices in which this creative aspect is bound up essentially with the cultural birth of the self, knowing the self as 'home-made' difference, however small, from all that has been received.

In everyday life this meaning-making and finding difference become ever more important. The old, 'off the shelf' cultural worlds no longer supply believable practices and materials. Class traditions, work, trade unions, organized religion, the family, parental role models, liberal humanist education – these things no longer believably place and fill identity in connected and homogeneous ways. No one knows what the social maps are any more, there are no automatic belongings, so, more than ever, you have to work for, and make, your own cultural significance.

I come now to the second main element of my provisional definition of art. This is that important and specifically creative aspects of meaning-making are accomplished through *work upon forms*. Meaning-making is not an internal quest, a search for an ever elusive (disappointing if found) true self as an unchanging inner essence or state of being or intrinsic soul. Meaning-making can be considered a work process involving its own kind of labour and expressive outcomes issuing into some kind of inter-subjective space. This work is never 'done': only by expressing themselves over time do human beings continuously reproduce themselves culturally. This process of labour requires, assumes and reproduces a locating cultural world through which self-expression is achieved.

Among other things, meaning-making is a form of cultural production which works upon materials received from this cultural world, remaking them. Formal notions of art have a developed self-consciousness about their crafts upon form, but only within secluded traditions of what constitutes the cultural world and its materials. Everyday cultural practices, by contrast, are unselfconscious and take the normal life world of everyday culture as their working context. There is, therefore, an important contemporary dimension in the provision of relevant forms. This may be in some narrow participation in 'retro' or contemporary cultural styles, or in absorption into some passion – football, Elvis, country and western. But it is also in the ordinary responsibilities of deciding 'how to go on' when 'things have changed so much', how to find moral bearings or criteria for making choices when tradition does not help much but when a range of clues are on offer in a complex and messy web of chats with friends about 'what they're into', TV programmes, soaps, films, ads, talk shows, magazines, songs deliberately played or serendipitously caught, kissing you from the radio. Meaning-making is a 'poetry (that) constructs a voice out of the voices that surround it'.[2]

The third and final element in my specification of art concerns a *social connection*, which is usually lost or suppressed in more formal and textual versions, though often the secret hallmark of great art. This is a poignancy in which social and structural location is articulated not as an 'add on' context but as an indissoluble and internal relation, a quality or property itself, of meaning-making. Social structure and process are encompassed as things to be made sense of, as providing fields of things to be discovered or understood, as carrying their own possible meanings, including ideological presentations, which can be adopted, contested, explained, refused. The combinations here of meaning-making, form and social connection, all condensed, produce elegance and economy deserving the name of art.

The social connection of cultural practices in the everyday is of great importance to the ethnographic imagination and is subject to a particular conceptual development here and throughout the book. The title of this book echoes, of course, that of the famous book by C. Wright Mills, *The Sociological Imagination*. In it he defines his version of this social connection as 'enabling us to grasp history and biography and the relations between them'.[3] I follow this but want both to add some complexity, some middle terms, to this relation, and to be relentless in the pursuit of the *internality* of possible relations and strings of overlapping connection between the creativity of individuals and groups, ethnographically held, and wider structures. Everyday culture is the main middle term that I want to add as mediation between individuals and structures. I see the production of this symbolic realm as in part a result, *upon conditions*, of the creative self-activity of agents, also thereby producing and reproducing themselves. But the symbolic realm also operates at another, connected level, where it is involved, viscerally, in the maintenance and differentiated formation of the social whole or whole social formation, including the reproduction of the conditions upon which 'self activity' originally takes place. Hard as it may be, these are the further threads of hooped strings that I have to pull through the eye of my ethnographic needle.[4]

Part 2 of the book looks at how agents 'self activity' operates, under all developing aspects of my definition, within the new conditions of the commodization of culture and its universal, saturating, electronic mediation. As long ago as 1960 Asa Briggs defined a crucial shift produced by the industrialization and commercialization of the symbolic realm: 'Massive market interests have come to dominate an area of life which, until recently, was dominated by individuals themselves.'[5] This cultural realm, which so interests me, is now thoroughly dominated by commodity production for profit, bringing along with it the attendant commoditization of the cultural forms, relations and services that are the grist to the mill of everyday life. Successive chapters of part 2 deal with how the creative cultural activities of agents encounter this new domination of what was previously 'their own', with how this encounter colours the whole cultural realm and with how this changed realm is implicated in contemporary processes of differentiated social reproduction (maintaining social stability or inciting social challenge). There is no question that fundamental changes in the systems and institutions of cultural provision (the concentration of ownership, globalization, advertising, the privatization of distribution) have fundamentally changed both the lineaments of the cultural realm as a whole as well as fundamental aspects (relations and forms) of the whole social formation. But, crucial to note, from the point of view of the social connection as ethnographically imagined, economic and other forces do not do this directly. The role of the 'creative self activity', ethnographically registerable, of agents continues to be crucial to the indeterminacy and variety of how these technological and political-economic changes pass into (or are read into) cultural and social change.

There is a further point about the operation of the ethnographic imagination when it comes to structural issues. I argue that, like social scientists, social agents are, in their own way, concerned with larger structural questions, only in their case making sense of them as surviving and living out their consequences – for instance grappling with the meanings and effects of the current epochal and global restructuration of economic relations. I want to pursue the subjective fast tracks of experiential response without being overwhelmed by a welter of empirical data. It is necessary sometimes to sum up, or reach for the kernel of, structural form or change in conceptual and shorthand ways. Chapter 2, for instance, conceptualizes state education in a certain way, as embodying individualism and meritocracy. Chapter 4 presents a Marxian analysis of the cultural commodity, which I take as the central 'driver' of the bewildering and rapid cultural change around us. Of course not all 'things' around us are commodities; but many of them are, especially those concerned with sense-making, and, increasingly, the direction of change is that many more will become commoditized or formed in relations very much like them – anonymous production manipulatively organized by strangers for profit. My conceptually presented understanding of commoditization and cultural change influences the analysis of the whole of the second part of the book.

So, if you like, there are at least two types of conception operating in my view of the ethnographic imagination, two types of thing 'thrown at' the messy data: approximate conceptions encapsulating the scope and action of the creative cultural practices of agents, and approximate conceptions of that which, *in situ*, social agents are 'making sense of'. Perhaps there is a triple dynamic of understanding: my understandings of their understandings of an understood (conceptually held) world. Against charges of academicism in view of what my academic vandalism may produce, I can only offer the empirical part of my formulation of the ethnographic imagination. There *is* resistance against pure abstraction in observational data. I ask for patience: the abstract detours may be quite long. But what does not finally help to illuminate the nitty gritty of experience should be discarded.

In this book I refer throughout to my previous work – forgive the immodesty but I am trying to codify and systematize ideas developed over thirty years, ideas often umbilically attached to the ethnographic data with which I have worked. I need a clarity of focus in what I am trying to offer, and I can muster this only in relation to my own work. But I believe that the conceptual developments produced are applicable in a variety of ways to a variety of other empirical works, as well as to works in progress or planned. In particular I refer to *Learning to Labour*[6] as the basic grounds upon which my perspective of the ethnographic imagination in 'practical state' was developed. Readers will need to know the main contours of this book which I shall now briefly summarize.

Learning to Labour reported the results and findings of a long-term ethnographic study, conducted in the mid-1970s, of a group of working-class white boys, members of what I called the counter-school culture – they called themselves the lads – in a working-class comprehensive school in an industrial town of the English midlands. I followed them through their last eighteen months at school and then into work, where I clocked on and worked alongside them, for a week or so, in their different jobs. I did qualitative work, with less depth, on five comparative groups. The puzzles leading me to the field were fairly straightforward. Why do working class kids fail? What is the role of their own culture in their 'failure'? What were the continuities for them between school and work? Not all working-class students failed then, of course, but, then as now, middle-class school students were about six times more likely to go on into higher education than working-class pupils: I wanted to get at the inside story of this phenomenon. I observed 'the lads' around the school, sat in their classes, attended all their careers sessions, accompanied them to a limited extent in their social rounds, conducted regular, recorded group discussions and interviewed their parents at home.

The central vertical dynamic of their lived culture was a vigorous opposition to the authority of their teachers. 'Who are they, telling us what to do when they're no better than us?' The central horizontal dynamic was a rejection of conformist pupils labelled as 'ear'oles' – i.e. always listening, never doing: 'They'm prats, they never get any fun do they?' This rejection was felt as a kind of distinction and superiority. 'We can make them laff, they can't make us laff.' These positions and orientations were enacted and embodied through a strong, rough masculine style, embellished in various ways through smoking, drinking and stylish dressing. Also central to the culture was a devotion to and deployment of 'the laff', a ubiquitous form capable of turning almost any situation into material for jokes and ribbing: 'it's the most important thing in life, even communists laff'.

From an educationalist and careers point of view, the strangest thing about the attitudes and behaviour of 'the lads' was their low interest in, often hostility towards, academic work and the gaining of qualifications. From a sociological point of view, the strangest thing about their culture was the indifference it induced among them to the kind of work they thought of undertaking, in the event ranging from factory work to tyre fitting to brick-layers mate. I argued in *Learning Labour* that their own culture helped induct them, voluntarily, into the low-paid, low-status jobs that most would shun. Their own culture was involved in processes of social reproduction, surprisingly, in more effective ways than any intended ideological mechanism.

The book details some of the horseplay, adventures and confrontations of 'the lads' at school as well as some of their later experiences and cultural practices at work. Though I did not formulate the ethnographic imagination perspective at the time, what was precisely different and fresh about the book was its digestion and presentation of ethnographic, fine-brush data in relation to and through the practical methodological assumptions that the 'anti-social' culture of 'the lads' was creative and craftedly interesting in its own right and contained, embodied and embedded, often highly rational seeds of knowing and analysis about their current and future situations. Here was no sullen defeat, no cultural inadequacy, no simple ideological domination. They were not dupes or zombies. The sheer life, intelligence and wit of their cultural practices had to be recognized. At the same time, it was this same culture that helped deliver them, and those like them, into a life of manual labour (and later unemployment) in ways which seemed quite against their basic interests. There was a tragic irony at the heart of their culture.

There is more of this analysis, and extensions to it, in the book, as well as an update on the current experiences and prospects of those like 'the lads', but this summary is enough to give a context and meaning to early references in part 1.

Part I

Art in the Everyday

1

Life as Art

You were virtually the answer to our prayer, because do you remember, we used to make vague attempts at writing accounts of things we'd done at school, y'know what I mean, we'd had to make an essay...I thought that we were the artists of the school, because of the things we did, I thought definitely we had our own sort of art form, the things we used to get up to.

Joey on what he had made of my presence in his school in a group discussion recorded in the Appendix to *Learning to Labour*

Life as art? Caveats and elaborations aside, this provides a starting point, direction and compass for the ethnographic imagination. It gives a quick and fundamental bearing when you are lost or mired. It also helps to will an ambition to write, that representation should, to some degree, mirror, or more exactly recreate, or more exactly still be continuous with something of the original.

I want to reclaim art as a living, not textual thing and as inherently social and democratic. Art as an elegant and compressed practice of meaning-making is a defining and irreducible quality at the heart of everyday human practices and interactions. It is at the centre of the commonplace human uses of objects, expressive and other, producing and investing meaningfulness in our relations with others and with the objects and materials around us. It is the combination of these practices with their locating relations and materials that produces culture or cultural forms which are the stock in trade of ethnographic analysis, for example school cultures, subcultures, occupational and shop-floor cultures, small-group or individual cultural formations.

Joey offers no finished poems. His poems are situated, performative and embodied in and through his whole social life and activity at school. Maybe subordinated cultural meaning is not an abstract linguistic type at all. It is concretely articulated as that which 'makes sense' in, of and by the connection between different elements of a cultural form or set of practices – action, language, interaction, the use of objects and artefacts, bodily presence, disposition and style, configurations of gesture and posture, ways of walking and talking. Their life artistry – not a mentalized or condensed resistance – is what makes 'the lads' socially distinct, their cultural forms relatively hardy and resilient. This makes them personally independent and difficult for their mental-work-oriented teachers to handle.

I am not proposing here an art of free individual creativity and inspiration, now relocated to the everyday, democratically frolicking in the school, dance club and High Street instead of suffering, lonely in the garret. Against the dominant individualistic view, the creativities embedded in cultural forms are usually collective; where they are individual they can be seen as crystallizations of socially originated forms of meaning. Culture is crucially about identity, but social and positional as well as individual and self-inventing. Cultural identity is certainly about the maintenance of the self as a separate and viable force, irreducible to institutional role, ideological definition or dominant social representation. But the meaning-making involved is not free and open but instrinsically framed and constrained, as well as enabled, in specific and contingent ways, by powerful external structural determinations. It operates within material conditions and given or inherited formations of sedimented or textual meanings. As such the overarching importance, as well as the beguiling complexity, of structural determination has to be mentioned immediately, dewing the breath of ethnographic enquiry into individual or group creativity.

I share an interest in a human creativity which is capable of transcending position and context, but I also have an ethnographically imagined interest in a situated human creativity which exists not despite, but because of, finger printed from the inside by, outside structuration and determination, or which finds a local and lived transcendence in and through a kind of sensuous awareness of contexts, seen and unseen. Animals may suffer their material and social conditions dumbly and certainly without any insight into their causality. But one of the specificities of being human, of humanness, that which must be interleaved through any worthwhile ethnographic account, is that symbolic activity brings some sense of wider positionality and outside formation of the self: an awareness of causation, axis or support of cultural being and consciousness located somewhere other than at the geometric centre of the self. These problems and mysteries specify a humanness for us all just as surely as the physiology of our bodies specifies it, but it is not understood that they are apprehended, usually, not coldly, cognitively and rationally, but affectively, poignantly and aesthetically. My sense of social art is in an important sense just this: the sensuous and affective acknowledgement of the presence of structure, of the lived awareness of invisible as well as visible context, of even a minimalist silence (an empty canvas) speaking for the closing structures around it. These things occurring in a narrow life space enforce an economy of elegance and form, an artistry of controlling an unavoidable 'excess of meaning'. This tension with and connection to a larger stage brings presence and importance. It brings the possibilities of creative 'penetrations' (see chapter 3) and culturally mediated forms of knowing and influencing who you are and where you are, and what kind of person you could or should be.

Of course, immediate poverty or immediate oppression produces immediate suffering, but external powers work more widely and subtly, the small grindings of which are the very business of ethnographic research. Large forces which it seems cannot be known directly or controlled personally produce something of the micropowers of the self. They reappear as small embodiments often in self-hood as resistance to power and, more strangely, through the very reproduction of that aspect of the self bound up with the reproduction of the countervailing powers. 'The lads' made themselves and went into work and so made that world which held the stage for their resistance. They celebrated their freedoms even in the forms of that unfreedom which approached, their artistry the very preparation for its opposite in a life of drudgery and compulsion on the shop floor. Oddly, it can be the contending force which does the work of reproduction. Unconscious formation and positivistic determination would be a kind of

freedom compared with this: the complex, ever shifting, only
partly knowable and controllable, always mediated experience of
seeing into, perhaps as its mechanism or hair trigger, the closing
trap of social reproduction.

The mystery of the relation between the general and the particular encompasses the contradiction that general social forces or
determinations are enacted only through the particular will of
individual agents, even though all or most of them may individu-
ally oppose, seek an alternative to, attempt to exploit in their turn,
or remain indifferent to the whole which they also constitute.
There is somehow a consciousness or subconsciousness (not
Freudian, but a culturally articulated sense or meaning) of the
self as both a separation and a discontinuity – with perhaps
other like selves, a base for a genuinely independent vision – and
also, *simultaneously*, as continuous with a larger, partially alien,
even predatory whole: the self as a spot in the eye of the tiger.

In response to an 'Art Attack', that my ethnographically imagined sense of art ignores essential qualities of rarity and transcendence, I argue that it is not just the elites who have some experience
of the complex and mysterious relations of the particular and the
general. Everyone is involved, and these experiences of the masses
are echoes, though never heard, of distant thunder, of the high and
serious. Selection, distillation and translation produce from common experience the apparent timelessness and transcendence of
textual art – their possibilities to produce inspiration as well as for
distance and reification. But textual art should not become the
false centre. The point remains that there is something rare and
special about the symbolic stresses of the common and everyday
that ethnography so routinely picks up and records. The fact that
these experiences are both repeated and common does not make
less of them, or make them any less human defining. They are an
essential part of the creative finding of symbolic place and identity,
of recognizable time and place in out-of-scale and baffling historical structures.

Experience is the poem

I argue that the *ethnographically imagined* possibility of making
connections between art and everyday life is relevant to all the
social sciences, actually to all ways of making sense of human

place; but it arose for me as a historically conditioned feature of my biographical experience in an early stage of the formation of the British cultural studies tradition as it unfolded at the Centre for Contemporary Cultural Studies at Birmingham University during the late 1960s and 1970s. The contemporary currents of that tradition are flowing away from me now, so the reconstruction of its early history which follows is a personalized, recuperative and in part retrospectively rationalized account of this formation. The early history of British Cultural Studies can be seen partly as the product of a series of shifts or revolutions, associated especially with the work of Raymond Williams, but also with Edward Thompson and (selectively) Richard Hoggart, in the structure of an important strand of English social and cultural thought known as the Culture and Society Tradition.

From the early part of the last century through to the middle of the twentieth, this tradition had been concerned with the relations between 'high', principally literary culture and the surrounding society, understood especially through the pain and massive disruption associated with rapid economic and industrial development during the world's first industrial revolution in England. On the one hand the interest was in recognizing how the texts and artefacts within high culture had recorded and grappled with the significance of dramatic social and industrial change. On the other hand, the aim was to recognize *and promote* the ways in which society was and might be affected by the rich store-house of high culture: how its elite were moulded as well-read (usually) gentlemen and how the dehumanized masses might be lifted to a somewhat higher level of civilization by exposure to what the major nineteenth-century figure in this tradition, Matthew Arnold, termed 'the best that has been thought and said'. A whole liberal humanist educational tradition grew from these concerns, with Arnold himself, in his time, appointed as the first chief inspector of schools in 1851.

Throughout his work, but especially in the early books, *Culture and Society* and *The Long Revolution*, Raymond Williams was the initiating figure and central contributor to a series of arguments which produced what we can think of as a double reclamation and rearticulation of this tradition: a reclamation first of its content, and then of its socio-symbolic form and location. The latter was of the greatest significance to me, and for my ethnographic appropriation of a transformed Culture and Society Tradition.

As to the first of these reclamations, Williams argued that much of the great literary tradition, even if selected by elites and absorbed by them as a constitutive part of their very culture and sensibility, including a felt mission to 'improve' the lower orders, could be seen equally as the property of the non-elite and dominated classes, and therefore available for their own direct social appropriation of oppositional or critical purposes. The Culture and Society Tradition was centrally concerned with an aesthetic and critical evaluation of the human impact of the unfolding of the world's first industrial revolution: bearing witness to the spiritual as well as material depredation of the dark, satanic mills, to the obliteration of the colours and smells of the seasons by soot, smoke and grime (a particular theme of Ruskin, another major figure in the Culture and Society Tradition). Though the stance was conditioned very much by a conservative nostalgia for a disappeared – probably never existing – pastoral golden age blotted out by industrialism, the contemporary concern was very much for the welfare and condition of the new industrial masses. The aesthetic-aristocratic charges against industrialism – ugliness, the destruction of nature, the distortion of human nature – overlapped with some of the feelings and responses of the people inside the mills, who actually experienced their dark satanism. Of course, within the literary tradition there was no basis for collective working-class organization, and no economic analysis of exploitation. Indeed, an antithesis towards political economy held sway, itself a 'plague on the human spirit', said Ruskin. But it could be argued that there was a particularly English qualitative contribution here in the rich depiction of the coloured sensuousness and spiritual resonance, rather than merely the abstract nature, of the devastation wrought by the coming of the new industrial-capitalist social relations. Since the experience of the proletariat, rather than that of the literary and aristocratic elite, was precisely the material through which these transformations were worked, the aesthetic tradition belonged to them also. Workers should read poetry too as a rightful part of their patrimony: in part it was *about* them.

The second reclamation was more radical and, for me, more important because, though never followed by Williams, it laid out a clear basis for a critical and imaginative ethnography of the everyday. Since theirs was the raw material wrought and rewrought by the epochal upheaval of industrialization and urbanization, why not treat the working classes' own experience itself, not poetic representations of it from the elite, as the direct substance of poetic response? Workers had access to their own cultural repertoire; they were their own symbolic resource. They were a site of critical-imaginative meaning-making concerning their own situation. The patterns and interconnections, the symbolic lights and depths, that were articulated in a poem were also articulated in real social relations. Experience could be the poem. And more progressive, liberating and full of light it might be, understood as such directly, rather than filtered through the writings of others, coloured with backward-looking romantic longings for a never-was arcadian past. The symbol-conscious literary critic, then, should place no greater burden of meaning on a poem than on actual lived practices. Literary criticism, as a kind of interpretative ethnography of language, could extend its methods to the real thing in new kinds of open and forward-looking cultural criticism. Reclaim as lived relation not only the content of poetry, but the poem itself!

This was how the weight and significance of the Culture and Society Tradition came to me. This was its concrete, practical bequest to me: to treat living experience and its immediate practices and symbolic materials as a poem. That meant, very importantly, respecting it in its own terms – 'only the words on the page' – and also looking at it very closely for its (important this, too) assumed-to-be complex meanings, and to see that these were produced more importantly in metaphorical, indirect and atmospheric ways than in literal or rational ways.

This double reclamation account of the transformations of the English Culture and Society Tradition is my version of events: a formulation tailored to give a history to my version of how cultural studies led (could have led, or should have led) to its own route of a distinctive ethnographically imagined line of studies. It would not be accurate to subsume the whole early history of British cultural studies under my version of events, not least because of the relative unimportance of anything approaching genuine ethnography to this history. Nevertheless, though none of them were ethnographers, I do claim a provenance from the founding fathers. Throughout his work Williams directs us toward the recognition and study of 'ways of life' rather than, or as well as, textual studies. Famously in *The Long Revolution*, he claimed that the trade union movement should be considered *the* art form of the working class. Thompson similarly lays stress throughout on the rationality and creative meaning embedded in common customs and practices, and on the self-making of living culture: again famously, 'the working class was present at its own birth'. Strangely, but perhaps fittingly, in the unselfconscious descriptive practices of *The Uses of Literacy*, rather than in his conscious theoretical pronouncements, Hoggart gives us the clearest justification for, and model of, an ethnographic-like rich recording and reading of everyday habits, language and customs; in his case, of a concrete working-class way of life in the Hunslett of his childhood.

I have my own subsequent appropriation and critical development of the later history of an ethnographic 'ways of life' model. That is the subject of this book. The whole tradition can certainly be accused of insularity and a restricted vision focused primarily on class, male and white–ethnic relations. But traditions cannot think out of their historical skins, and the practical and abstract points I am learning from and taking forward are eminently transferable to other social and symbolic grounds. This early history, or my version of it, delivers and protects my starting out proposition, that living practices can be approached as if they were art forms. History, or the geological formations of knowledge as I encountered and made sense of them, made and makes this a durable and securely founded, rather than merely idiosyncratic, starting point.

Language and experience

In treating cultural experience as inherently formed through art-like creative cultural practices the ethnographic imagination recognizes that there are few unadorned 'social messages' written on the surface of everyday cultural forms. The latter's embedded and localized meanings work through observable but often non-verbal modes of being and expression – that which only ethnographic techniques can record, so requiring aligned forms of theoretical understanding and analysis. As the next chapter explores more theoretically, the approach to the ethnographic study of culture that I am outlining problematizes the centrality and centredness of language in relation to the meanings embedded in cultural experience.

Meaning is usually taken to reside only in language, the princi-
pal instrument of reason. But is language so transparent in its
meanings? Is it really a singular, unified and hermetic thing, carrying its own specific and unique ability to communicate? At the very
least, I would argue that it is wrong to see language as all of a piece
and consistent in the way it coheres and functions. There is, most
basically, an obvious division between, broadly, literal-analytic
language and figurative, non-analytic language. The former is
more likely to be standardized and instrumental. It is concerned
to show and explain relationships, patterns and relations of deter-
minacy. It is self-sufficient, autonomous in space and time, requiring of the deracinated listener or reader only a commensurate if
scarce ability to reason. You stand back from it, judge it, walk
around it, send it through the mail for others to judge. By contrast
metaphoric language is not standardized and functions expressively – to show feeling, emotion and identity – rather than instru-
mentally. It engages you; it immerses you. It assumes and needs a
receiver placed in space, time and biography. You must use your
own experience of the compared and referred-to thing in order to
make sense (i.e. make your own sense) of the relation embedded in
the figure. You cannot send the whole package of meaning through
the mail, only half of it. Metaphoric language always has, or
always finds, a location in experience.

The languages associated with a particular cultural form – the
'lads' culture, subcultures, individuals swept with a particular
passion – are highly likely to be of the located, metaphoric type.
Further, I would argue that the figures and conceits of a culturally
located language function not only to compare unlike things, but
are integral parts of the meaning of other practices and meanings,
so that they merge into, mimic or complement adjacent elements
of the cultural form. Such language includes stories, jokes, piss-
taking and wind-ups.[1]

None of this is to argue that figurative-metaphoric language is
against reason or the carrying or development of thought.
Certainly, versions of it may seem to be less suited to analytic
reasoning and presentation, but that does not limit figurative
language to non-analytic purposes. Metaphoric language is certainly useful to describe things, but it is also and fundamentally
useful to think with. It clarifies, or perhaps brings to its only
articulation, an abstract idea, or brings out and highlights the

abstract quality or essence of something by comparing it to something else, usually concrete, in the world. Where there may be no alternative expression, this is the most condensed thought available. All language must originate in reference to the concrete, either naming or comparing. However rarefied and developed language is from this point, however fast it approaches escape velocity, perhaps there is no pure unreferential and non-figurative language (higher maths, quantum physics?), no pure thought, no non-metaphorical metaphysics, no language free from social gravity. Certainly great pieces of logic, reasoning and intellectual analysis, as well as literature and poetry, often work in and through a metaphoric mode. Perhaps there is a poetry in all meaning, perhaps ultimately no other meaning than in poetry.

If language can be understood to lie on a continuum ranging from the abstractly literal to the concretely metaphorical, why not extend this register to include the metaphor of the really concrete in the lived and material practices of cultural forms? The embedded meanings of a living culture are merely one step beyond metaphor from the (anyway chimeral) view of language as pure reason.[2] Cultural practices can replace metaphor with the really real, really removing the quotation marks. The elements of a cultural practice mutely 'speak' – clothes, body, style, demeanour, interaction, the use of commodities – of many things, but importantly of the actual social and physical locations of the cultural participants. Part of the ethnographic imagination is to fill in the missing blanks in what is being referred to.

Despite the continuities, the move here towards seeing lived metaphor as producing meaning is radical with respect to its implications for language (see the next chapter). It is not saying that the sensuous and expressive practices of culture function *like* a language, leaving language queen. It is saying that language is part of a continuum of types of human meaning-making, and therefore that meaning is not *contained* by language. Figuration is taken to extremes, to a real picture language, a language you cannot send through the post at all and which is immovable from, only meaningful in, its immediate concrete location: a practical demonstration of the passing of the point at which 'whereof we cannot speak, we must be silent'. To the extent of that real passing, then, cultural forms as unique configuration and presence are also thoughts, ideas, even abstractions – entities that have a mental content which would otherwise find no expression and which has no, or is allowed no, alternative existing articulation.[3]

'The lads' do not say that school is like a prison (actually they do, and are punished for it!), but they demonstrate through their practical artistry all the nuance and contradiction of the special-ness of an institution which exercises compulsion in the name of benevolence. They do not verbalize a reasoned resistance against mental inculcation; instead they manually express a studied pre-sentation of dumb insolence. They do not find logical syllogisms to criticize credentialism; they drive the teachers to distraction with ever more creative ways of playing them up. They do not conduct learned debates on how labour power is or should be moulded in state schools; instead they evince other practical applications of sensuous human powers in 'the laff', in winding up staff and other students, in finding unexpected collective fun and diversion in the driest institutional contexts.

Ethnographic imaginings of life as art deal with both abstract and sensuous forms of knowing and with connecting both. How-ever, the essential and defining interest is with sensuous meaning, in recognizing its critical importance and defending its profane poetry.

2

Form

Music alone awakens in man the sense of music. The forming of the five senses is a labour of the entire history of the world down to the present.

Karl Marx, *Economic and Philosophic Manuscripts*

Cultural practices of the everyday produce meanings and meaningfulness; but what is the nature of the human relationship to the forms – languages, styles, musics, materials towards the informal curations of body and space – through which humans express themselves? In successive transparent waves, do all these materials simply reflect some inner human expressive essence, or, in reverse direction, do the forms, through their own constraints and enablements, somehow condition human potential in crucial ways? My ethnographically imagined emphasis on human creativity, producing something that was not there before, brings some form of agency into the picture, as practices struggling either to control or to utilize the expressive potential of surrounding forms and materials. But the 64,000-dollar question remains: what is the balance between the forms and the practices? Which of these two has the greater formative influence on meanings produced and the formations of cultural identity?

Language and the language paradigm

Language is by far the most important single symbolic form used by humans for expression and communication. But we cannot make and use our own private languages. The English I am using now is a system lying outside me and any other human being. Language systems as independent structures have been massively analysed, and the paradigms developed in the process have been generalized into varieties of structuralism and poststructuralisms, themselves massively influential in all the social sciences. Do any of these developments help to resolve a central ethnographic conundrum: does language make its own meanings forming subjectivity, as actors adopt, often unconsciously, the assumptions of the speaking 'I'? Or can language be *used* by actors creatively and purposively to express, directly and uniquely, their own states of mind, emotions and meanings? Do we speak language or does it speak us?

From the point of view of the ethnographic imagination, structural and poststructural linguistic theories give a disappointing and clear-ish answer. Basically, language speaks us more than the reverse, or at least severely constrains what we can say or express.

Structural linguistic analysis is founded on a distinction drawn in Saussurian structural linguistics: this is between the two parts which constitute the sign or symbol. First is the *signifier* – squiggles, dots or sounds, meaningless in themselves but which stand for something else. Second is the *signified* – the referred-to concept or mental construction (for instance, the idea of a cow), not to be confused (the *pons asinorum* of structural linguistics) with concrete referents (real cows) in the real world. These latter are more or less suppressed or forgotten. Since the signifiers are essentially conventional in language – they are made to stand for things, because people agree that they do – rather than, for instance, deriving from hieroglyphic or picture languages, they could in theory be absolutely anything. They are arbitrary. The concept of 'cow' could be signified by 'xyz' for instance. The variety of different words for 'cow' in the current six thousand (though diminishing) human languages, all perfectly effective in context, attest to this essential arbitrariness. There is, therefore, no necessary connection (perhaps, more strongly, necessarily no connection) between what signifies and what is signified. The signifier floats.

Furthermore, what distinguishes signifiers from each other – why 'love' is different from 'hate' – cannot be, as we have seen, their different *intrinsic* connections to the things referred to, but solely the differences between the types and order of the bits (squiggles and dots) that constitute them at their own level. The alphabet is a kind of digital code through which thousands upon thousands of language signifiers can be constituted, all different from each other. Think of 'love' and 'hate'. These very different words are not distinguished by the very different things to which they refer, but solely by the internal differences of bits of the alphabetical chain they use, letters switched on or off and different orders of letters. 'Love' has 22 letters switched off, four letters switched on and arranged in a particular order. 'Hate' has four letters switched on again, though three of them are different from those in 'love', and it is in this, and only in this, that it is a different signifier and signifies a meaning different from 'love'.

This is an 'anti-foundationalist' or 'anti-representational' view of meaning in language. Meaning arises only within the internal operations of language and not in any reflection or representation of anything prior or separately existing – human states or emotions for instance. The claim is actually stronger: for linguistic theory, many things may exist outside language, but meaning is not one of them. Meaning resides *only* in language, certainly not in any internal human process. Think of trying to express in words the 'love' you have for someone 'in your mind'. Can you make up your own special words? 'Xyz' for 'love'? No! Do the 'right' words come easily? No! With difficulty you choose words which you know are second-hand, and the meaning comes out as stilted or slanted, or much more specific and particular than you intended. To do better you borrow literary fragments from Shakespeare or John Donne: 'my love is like a red, red rose'. But then who is talking, you or Shakespeare? Even in such an intensely felt arena, do we ever really 'talk for ourselves' or have private meanings which we then accurately express in words? Linguistic theorists would tell us that the 'having in mind' bit is not its own ontological or existential thing but only ever a foreseeing, an anticipation, of particular forms of words which only then bring meaning.

Poststructuralist approaches have loosened up some of the rigidity of the internality of meaning in structuralist approaches to language. They show openness to indeterminacy in language meaning – basically, though, from the point of view of its internal instabilities rather than from any identifiable impulse from located acting subjects. A 'subjectivism without a subject'[1] has been added to structuralist approaches to pose the possibility of multiple readings of any given sequence of signifiers and the theoretical possibility of the productive use by social agents of language in 'signifying practice'. The indeterminacies and instabilities of language arise in two basic ways. Firstly the floating signifier is held to summon the unspoken 'other' of any particular signified meaning – i.e. white implies the existence of black. Apparently unequivocal or concrete terms always produce a shadowy or ghostly counterpresence of meaning. Secondly signifiers are also presented as relating to signified meaning on the basis of permanent 'delay' or 'deferral' – any definition of a term, looked up in a dictionary for instance, leads only to another signifier difference, which can be understood only by using the dictionary again to find another signifier difference, and so on *ad infinitum*. It is necessary to open a dictionary to find out what something means, but having opened it you can never shut it. These *still internal* functions of language – the summoned 'other' and 'deferral' – produce an excess of meaning, through which readers and speakers, it is claimed, can, to some extent, enter into a play or game of meaning. However, the point of access and the field of play are always bounded by language with all the limits related to its intractable symbolic structure – still no direct 'reflections' or 'representations' of actors' internal states or intentions, no essential expression of a 'real' you, no meaning outside language.[2]

There has been a quite widespread move in cultural studies and across large swathes of the social sciences to generalize 'language paradigm' approaches, applying them, after Barthes and his opening of the field of semiotics, to other sign systems – photographs and advertising for instance – and now to wider fields of material culture, museums and clothes and even further now into analyses of ethnic cultures.[3] Culture, it is said, 'works like a language'.[4]

All this has great import for the ethnographic imagination. It challenges all forms of humanism by demonstrating how meaning can be seen as externally constructed. It certainly provides a stern warning against essentialism. Even language, the most immediate, familiar and omnipresent form of expression and communication, is recalcitrantly symbolic in having its own logic of form not immediately bendable to the individual human will. It is not transparent or automatically responsive to our every whim. It cannot be used uniquely to make or express unique creativity, or to express uniquely that which is added or not there before. It may even constitute what we take our 'essential meanings' to be. Subjectivity, itself, may be discursively constructed.

Certainly this alerts us to the potentially destructive and containing power of language mobilised in the execution of unequal power relations. Once a type of subordinate subjectivity has been signified from above in language and attached to a social agent, it is difficult if not impossible for them to escape its weight. The litany of subordinating terms – unskilled, unemployed, unqualified, inarticulate, used in different combinations with 'only a worker', 'only a woman', 'only a . . .' – constitute meanings wholly from above, swallowing or expelling all other meanings or rendering unintelligible other more local and embedded alternative meanings generated from below.

The ethnographic imagination must take note of 'language paradigm' approaches, appreciating how language and wider signification processes might work and taking seriously the challenges they pose to other, often simply assumed humanist positions on the generation of meaning. Just *how* are the latter supposed to operate? But taken too literally and projected, as they are being, into a science of the cultural, language paradigm approaches can be very damaging. They do not help but hamper our understanding of the ethnographically imagined sensuous creativity of cultural practices.

The problem is that these formal and technical considerations drawn from a particular domain have been catapulted onto the largest social stage with little regard for the complexities, the dialectics and the transformations between levels and forms, of actual cultural practices and their relations to cultural and social formations. The 'floating signifier' becomes the multiply applicable basis, a metaphor extended to be a science, for a clarion call against all essentialisms everywhere, for instance against those, like Leavis, who believe that a really good poem or word somehow sounds like or umbilically grows out of the original, what it actually means, for instance against those Marxists who believe that working-class culture and organization grow from the classed experience of oppression and exploitation, for instance against black activists who believe black culture grows out of the experience of blackness. Not only signifiers, whole cultures 'float'.

In fact I would argue that the language paradigm provides only half the story for understanding even language use as *located* cultural practice, as distinct from the formalisms of considering abstract language in general or its general use, publically or officially, in the exercise of power. The language paradigm may be positively misleading – especially if it is assumed to be a total explanation, often in practice the case despite protestations to the contrary – as a model for understanding important aspects of the cultural practices of the everyday, in particular the immediate, sensuous and three-dimensional aspects of the crafted use of concrete items, objects and artefacts. These sensuous relations and practices are not comparable to those of language. Their differences reside most basically in the fact that, although all the material things of the human world signify, not everything has the *sole* purpose of signifying, i.e. sending messages, meaning or information to others. Concrete items have their own 'use values', and human relations to them include their sensuous as well as their signifying uses. These sensuous uses entail cultural practices that involve some agency moving around and, with practical knowledge, working on the material world, rather than 'subjectivity' being figured only as an effect or position within generally or abstractly conceived 'discourses', language and other. The ethnographic imagination must be alive to all potentials for profane meaning-making: in forests of meaning, how the wild as well as the cultivated trees are shaken for what might fall down!

The material items and 'use values' taken up into cultural practices must be understood as their own *profane* forms, forms which, while not fixed, are precisely not arbitrary; nor do they have identity only through the articulations of difference in the combination of arbitrary signifiers. They have actual uses and identities – clothes to warm and cover you, musics to move you, the human body itself to house, sense and enact you – before or on top of any capacity they might hold to signify in a message code to others. By contrast, language meaning is only itself; the thing to which it adheres, the code, has only the function of carrying that meaning, in no way other than as a separate form, bearing no other 'use values'. It is necessarily arbitrary and working through difference in having no other concrete anchors. The human *use* of objects and artefacts is not meant primarily (certainly not only) to signify meaning or information in a code to others, but is an immediate means of satisfaction and bodily fulfilment, meaningful as pleasurable or satisfying in producing the fullest direct engagement with

human needs and effecting the fullest expansion of human capacities and senses as bearing ultimately on the formation of a
cultural identity. Of course these bodily uses take place within a
communicative social world, so signification is never far away as
precondition, medium, outcome. But concreteness and sensuousness in location are the anchor. Central is the 'there-ness' of the
uses of forms, objects, materials and artefacts. And while there
may be constraints on their use, concrete forms are not subject to
grammar-like rules of usage or combination. Taste or fashion may
be involved, but their variable combinations are matters of variable judgements, not of following rules. Tastes and their rules vary
at the same time for different groups and over time for the same
groups.

I argue then that the language paradigm cannot help us very
much to understand or record the sensuousness of cultural practices, including the sensuous use of objects and artefacts. Human-
object relations are not only or primarily code phenomena.[5] They
exist in and for a variety of other uses and purposes as well as for
signifying. Remember the *pons asinorum* aspect of structural linguistics' account of the signified: that it calls forth the idea, concept or image, not the thing itself, the idea of a cow, not the real
cows? Well crudely, an interest in sensuous meaningfulness stops
us from crossing this bridge. We are still with the asses, the real
cows, or more exactly, with real coats, real bodies, real musics –
not phonemes directing us towards only ideas of these things, but
the concrete cultural items themselves. They may not exist for us in
human culture outside, or disconnected from, the symbols that
help constitute our idea of them, but nor do they exist only in
language. That material bit which exists outside though indissolubly linked to language, has a sensual and material-structural
presence with which humans engage through direct cultural practices. This sensuous side of lived culture simply cannot be
embraced and presented through a paradigm which denies sensuous presence.

Of course there is the little local difficulty of my language use
now. I am attempting to present the idea of concreteness in a
language form which can represent it only in abstract ways,
through the differences in the chains of signifiers you are reading
now. But when the language paradigm is mobilized, not only to
indicate the difficulty language has in mediating some direct sense

of the original referent, but also to explain the properties of the original itself, then confusion is worse confounded. I try to deal later with aspects of the complex relations of language and non-language meanings. Bracketing this for the moment, we create a much greater and unnecessary burden when we say that the three-dimensional relations of concrete cultures, including the enormous 'there-ness' of the human cultural body, can be understood through modelling them on the abstract parts and functions of language. This is to reflect and assume in the way we are driven to name and talk about a phenomenon in language, the *nature* of that phenomenon. Whatever the difficulties of our language medium, what sense you, the reader can take from this now, it cannot really be the case that 'the medium is the message' in endlessly refracting the same paradigm. Use your imagination, reader! Exercise your experiential as well as your mental powers, pick up the clues strenuously offered here (however communicated), look away from this text, match my clues with your own three-dimensional experience of the concrete library or lounge where you are sitting; these latter things have names which affect how you constitute them, but they also provide the sensuous world which now encloses you. Is this concrete micro-world organized like a language, like the arbitrary signifiers which confront you when you look again at this text?

Coding information through arbitrary signifiers produces, strictly speaking, a string of internal gobbledegook, timeless and history-less in its own terms – try listening to a foreign language you do not speak. The code can be extended through time and space at will. It is certainly incredibly efficient and compresses data with little, through electronic digitalization, and increasingly, negligible physical limit. By contrast, sensuous cultural practices work through their own real time and immediately legible and self-referencing, independently useful forms. Infinitely compressible and history-less gobbledegook is no model for understanding this.

It is particularly and deeply ironic when language-based distinctions are used in discourse analysis as the basis for theories of 'otherness' (gender and race), when their referent, the human body, above all other cultural items so indisputably a concrete somatic presence, is singularly resistant to gobbledegook coding.[6] Barthes said that speech 'smells', still more do bodies. What we know and constitute as the body is certainly and indissolubly linked to our signification of it, but the body also exists as a material and acting entity, both knowing and known in sensuous ways not fully internal to language, often 'knowing' things the latter suppresses, evades, hides or misrepresents. Referring to the five-sensed, in context, living cultural body as a digital 'other' (signifier *difference*) declares a demolition derby on all sensuous specificity. It disavows the point of embodiment as the inescapable and permanent immersion of humans in the sensuous world. Only ethnography offers the possibilities of an embodied set of methods able to observe and record both the obviousness and the complexity of this immersion, but imagination is also needed to harness and develop grounded conceptual forms of analysis and presentation which preserve this distinctiveness.

I would argue that, rather than see all human meaning as modelled on one type of code, we need to see social life as containing many different kinds of meaningfulness, incarnate in different practices and forms, layered and overlapping, connecting up in complex ways. Language is one of many formations which bear meaning and can itself be an instrument of practice, not contemplation, including the attempt to gain control of the world and to share or make available meanings for the practices of others. This includes the attempt to produce states of feeling or awareness in others, in which case language is used as a communicative connection between emotional states. If you like, the music of emotion and knowing sentience must be rendered into and produced again from the digital pulses of language. This is what I was trying to do with my 'use your imagination and look up in the library' example above: sending digital pulses to produce a *sensuous* meaning at your end not reducible to language. This is to see language as one of many meanings systems, as multiple in terms of purpose, and bound up with *practices* in the world, where the point of verbalizing is to *produce effects* for and in other sensuous practices, meanings and outcomes in context. A moment of externality and risk, creating the space for structural theoreticisms and idealisms, is necessary before meaning can be reconnected to local contextual meaning and action. You could say that the whole ethnographic writing enterprise is such an exercise, a struggle against language in language to produce sensuous reconstructions in the reader's mind.

Of course, I can be accused of a naivety and empiricism in trying to grasp and present 'original' forms of sensuous and non-linguistic meaningfulness. But in this book I am not claiming to present reality or the social 'original', only, through the ethnographic imagination, to present something about the possible complexity of meaningfulness and the variety of types of meaning-making and meaningfulness which help to constitute whatever reality may be. Rather than claiming privileged access to empirical reality, I am arguing for the recognition of an ordinary human capacity for creative meaning-making in context. Of course, with respect to meaning, language is a major stake, site, function and mediation. I do not underestimate it. It is my only medium for communicating something about other types of meaningfulness now, to you, the reader. But I can use this medium to argue for the existence, and importance, of other meaning types, as an aspect of, or as a way of understanding aspects of, a complex, possibly never to be known, external reality.

Socio-symbolic analysis

To grasp the sensuous materialism of the human use of objects, artefacts and concrete forms in the everyday we need a model for the generation of cultural meaning which, whil fully cognizant of signification processes, puts agency and a concrete scope for action firmly in the picture. Not allowed for in the 'language paradigm' is the possibility of a local action which makes an observable and cumulative difference to form, materially present and containing sensuous 'use value', expressive and/or instrumental. There is a need to bring a form of humanism, understood as specifiable human practices, into relation with a material structuralism, understood as the properties of form upon and through which those practices have effects. It is very unusual for an attempt to be made to bring the social and the symbolic into a common analytic frame, but it is precisely this that the ethnographic imagi-nation of life as art requires.

The fundamental issue is to avoid what most approaches assume: an 'homoousian' (from the Greek *homoousios*, 'of the same substance') quality in cultural phenomenon. Forgive the neologism, but it matches *homology* (see the Appendix), which I am going on to in a moment, and neatly makes the comparative point. The 'homoousian' assumption is that there is a connecting essence which unites the different forms of the relation between the human and the surrounding symbolic material with which it engages. Essentialist humanistic ethnography runs out all meaning and analysis basically from human givens of some kind; discursive and linguistic-based approaches run it all out from structures. Oddly, 'Audience Studies' which you would think had this problem writ large at the centre of their concerns, almost always fall into one of these categories[7] despite much muddying of the waters.

I propose now a *socio-symbolic*[8] approach which deals with homologies as likenesses or correspondences of structure/form but in essentially different materials – human to the one side, and concrete materials, bearing humanly appropriate-able symbolic form, to the other. In contrast to 'floating signifier' positions, the materiality of form is crucial here. This materiality is obvious in examples of material culture, clothes, room decoration etc. But it is also a necessarily distinguishing dimension of less obviously material forms, such as music, where practices of expressive use, irreducible to notation, have sensuous dimensions and components, from the movement of the ear drum, cochlea and rib cage to the rhythmic movements of the whole body in dance.

In the *socio-symbolic* perspective the human and the material are brought into sensuous relation through human practices of symbolic work.[9] The two sides (and in their different ways, results) of symbolic work – human subjectivity to one side, located and humanly engaged materials to the other – require separate analyses and approaches (or at least the theoretical space and effectivity for such) which can then be brought together with sensitivity both to how they are different and commensurable as well as to how they produce creative tensions, especially through the human *use* of the profane and unprefigurable elements of material forms. It is in this use that we can theorize and locate important sources of human creativity.[10]

'Objective possibilities'

Instead of conceptualizing the concrete materials of the form side of human engagements as containing arbitrary signifiers, I suggest that it is more illuminating and productive to see them as containing 'objective possibilities' – internal structures capable of bearing a broad but theoretically finite range of potential meanings. Understood as 'use values' (both instrumental and expressive) 'objective possibilities' set limits for, as well as enable particular kinds of human meaning-making in specific kinds of sensuous interaction. Meaning does not arise *autonomously* in the possibilities themselves – contrast the 'floating signifier' – but through human *use*, from the interaction of sensuous human activity with concrete materials bearing symbolic form.

The 'objective possibilities' introduce a radically profane and unprefigurable element into human–material relations and into how we can approach and understand them. Although the 'objective possibilities' of particular forms are clearly influenced by their own 'object histories', especially by their commodity history (see chapter 4), and by their previous signification in prior uses, signified meanings, as poststructuralism teaches us, are never fully stable. Meanwhile, their profane and non-linguistic synchronous content and structure, however derived and deposited historically, can be explored through concrete and contemporary exploratory use and experiment, their meanings fixed in new ways. The 'objective possibilities' can also be understood as internally and unstably stressed, posing a wide field of potentials and cross-overs, by differing instrumental or expressive use values within them, facilitating different types of potential human use. A functional item may come into expressive use, according to the conditions of human practices around it.

Bike culture provides a good example. In *Profane Culture*[11] I outlined a *socio-symbolic* methodological approach to the lived culture of the bike boys. My fieldwork took me to the Double Zero bike club in the centre of Birmingham in the late 1960s. The book gives an ethnographic account, among other things, of the dialectical relations of the motorbike with the human world of the bike boys, not least in their finding a non-linguistic masculine expressivity in, and confirmation through, the technical functioning and design of the bike. I identified how similarities or correspondences or 'passabilities' ('possibilities' precisely bringing 'passabilities') between human sensibility and material form allowed the confirmation, reinforcement and development of preferred human meanings and satisfactions. Choosing carefully between different bikes; removing baffles from exhausts; adding chrome; fitting a cattle horn or different-style handle bars; the style of riding; the refusal to wear crash helmets: all these were 'material variables' open to creative manipulation by the bike boys to enhance the expressive meaning of the bike – essentially, rather than sheltering from, opening themselves up to and amplifying *through* technology the raw and elemental forces of nature, the tearing wind, the rushing tarmac. There developed a *homology* between their bedecked machines and their rough, self-confident, raw, nature-defying, masculine identity. The loud, spluttering thumping and banging of the exhausts, as bikers stood by their machines gunning their engines, and the intimidation I felt, as I barely controlled flight reflexes in the face of explosive stationary movement, spoke briefly, but in volumes, about the possibility and effectivity of non-linguistic cultural forms as use, potential use, presence and communication. Generally, oppressed or subordinate groups are more likely than other groups to find meaning in hidden, unexplored or newly stressed 'objective possibilities', or meaning in new, as yet uncolonized or 'meaning-sedimented' items, or meaning in jarring, dynamic use-functions, interrupting the cultural stillness of received forms.

The posing of a social relation between users and material items based on sensuous practices of engagement also raises the possibility that *symbolic work* can produce dynamic change and 'little histories' of choice, selection, intervention and two-way influence – the exploitation by the bike boys, over time, of the material variables of the bike: higher handlebars, more or less chrome, etc. Symbolic work produces the possibility of 'integral circuits' between agency and form. Having itself been confirmed and developed in specific ways, agency continuously reselects and resets the structures of the 'objective possibilities' – so shifting the range of their profane as well as of their intended meanings. This produces further reverse effects on sensibility and feeling and, in their turn, new potentials for concrete human choice and intervention, all in the direction of tightening socio-symbolic congruencies as well as in the direction of producing unprefigurable future possible meanings.

Of course, signification, as in the 'language paradigm', operates throughout. Language helps to set the humanly appropriatable range of the 'objective possibilities' of material form. Cultural practices and the changed 'objective possibilities' themselves help to signify new social meanings, not least through *reactions* to them, such as the moral panics in the case of the bike boys. Both help to signify the 'objective possibilities' in new ways, for instance emphasizing the antisocial nature of the motor bike. But the material *shifting* of the 'objective possibilities' is a question of specific human, not general linguistic, agency. This shifting, as well as producing intended effects, shoves the 'objective possibilities' into new profane and unknowable territory, so producing the possibility of unintended effects on sensibility and feeling, themselves open to creative adoption or refusal seeding further circuits of signifying effects (the proliferation of bike culture into separate traditions). Human/form social relationships produce routine opportunities for their own transgression, in part mediated but never produced by linguistic forms.

Sensuous meaningfulness

The socio-symbolic perspective delivers some key points for the ethnographic imagination and for ethnographic practice. First of all the *particular* nature and types of 'use values' of material forms matter: music is different from clothing is different from room decoration. Functional as well as expressive items (in fact there is nothing used or observed in the world by humans which does not also signify) can generate cultural meanings; especially interesting are the cross-overs between physical and expressive use. The aim is to show the specific ways in which the 'objective possibilities' are not 'floating' but significantly anchored in concrete forms and their existing or possible sensuous uses, activated as human meaning in the work of 'little histories'.

Secondly, I would argue that sensuous meaningfulness, as embodied and embedded in cultural practices, materials and relations, especially in their object-related forms, are relatively resistant to, or destabilize, linguistically borne ideological meanings. Why? Linguistic communication always offers a one-sided bargain to uncoded parts of the self. Linguistic encoding threatens to subsume or even to swallow, whole, meanings as yet unformed but in cultural solution. But sensuously held meanings are not commensurate to start with. Held sensuously, not digitally, they can maintain identity and separateness beyond the colonization of language and provide the grounds for non-linguistic intersubjective recognition of sensuous meanings within a specific cultural world. Sensuous meanings are not only coded meanings, and their coded element is messy and anchored. They are held in homological relation, pre-linguistic but not so unformed as to be swallowed without resistance. Bits of meaning inhere separately in material items or liminally in elements of practice. They cannot easily be invaded or absorbed by linguistic meaning, which fails to encompass them as signifieds to 'swallow'.

Sensuous *socio-symbolic* holdings also offer more guiltless harbour for meanings which are taboo, transgressive or otherwise too heavy for language, for facing out things which named would make you turn your face. Here is refuge for that dark sensuousness which refuses never-ending stories and happy human endings whose enforced though artificial continuities burden 'narratives of the self' with the need for apparently clear meaning, explanation and justification. Without pressing to wholeness or completion, sensuous homological meanings allow a 'reflexive' holding of that which is mysterious and always unfinished, holding up the bleedings away of language and time whose endless slippages and deferrals put sleepless rationality permanently on guard.

Socio-symbolic practices can also overthrow, by physically throwing out, oppressive meanings exercised through objects. For instance, the 'hungry wolves' of young adult independence throw out parental objects in room and personal decoration, emptying themselves as well – all without rhyme or reason (grammar) to adult taste. Without regard to grammar, they devour new objects, changed and rearranged, dialectically self invested, so introjecting new self-made possibilities, still open and playful because uncoded.[12]

Furthermore, sensuous meanings have the potential *in situ* to practically reveal general ideological meaning as partial, by contrasting the latter's sensuous poverty and stasis with their own sensuous fullness and potential for concrete dialectical development. Lived identities offer greater and more testable satisfactions than the imaginary ones. Where ideological or imaginary identities, relations or positions are really lived out as cultural meaning and local embodiment, asked to *move*, then 'reality principles', not least adjacent concretely dynamic meanings, will soon demonstrate their stasis, partiality and inadequacy, so contradicting, correcting or subverting them. Here lies a rich field of play-acting and irony in subordinate cultures, for winking where ideology only blinks.

Thirdly, there are some general implications here for how we understand essentialism. As we have seen, the 'floating signifier' has certainly provided powerful theoretical resources for critiquing all forms of essentialism, to great effect at the level of language as system. But the socio-symbolic model provides counter resources for understanding why real subjects (rather than abstractly animated discursive subject positions) seem so persistently to live and believe in essentialist relations to their own cultures.

To be clear, there are some definite anti-essentialist aspects of the socio-symbolic model. This is, in fact, the whole basis of its distinction from 'homoousian' approaches. There is no claimed prior or guaranteed connection between sensibility and form, which are of discontinuous, not continuous, basic natures. Rather than being mirrors or passive servants of humanly given meanings, the 'objective possibilities' of material cultural items are *profane*, enjoying their own life and history. Similarly there is no assumption, except for the capacity of human meaning-making, about a centred human nature seeking pure expression of itself in the external world. But the way in which specific 'objective possibilities' are taken up, dialectically, through human practice, through use in context, and through 'integral circuiting', do form the *made* basis for an objectively privileged human connection to cultural form, which could be experienced, some way short of illusion or the imaginary, as 'essential'.

The meaning of cultural objects and artefacts arises only in human activation and, therefore, in some sense, does really 'belong' to human practice, and therefore to humans. Trees crashing in the middle of uninhabited forests; from a crashed rocket, taped voices wasted on the airless Martian desert: these have no human meaning, though they have semiotic form. As soon as humans hear or see them, something has passed; they have been possessed, changed, something about them made different from their previous non-human, out-of-human, condition. The steps beyond this, where a human praxis rearranges the 'objective possibilities' of a cultural item, put this psychic ownership on a more specific material footing. Human sensibility has a sensuous, five-channelled, two-way, three-dimensional relationship with preferred cultural items that brings satisfaction and the generation of psychic energy and feeling, which make their own register, in turn, on those items. This is not the lodging of an abstract concept in signifier difference, but a direct and sensuous human fashioning with real results, which may well be experienced as constituting some form of intrinsic connection, or which validates a hopeless striving for it, with sufficient effect to consecrate the effort as its own state of grace. We must recognize the possibility of psychic, culturally 'authentic' connection to material forms, produced through work on them. For instance, in the bike culture it was widely held that real bikers could repair, maintain and stylistically adapt their own bikes. British bikes were preferred, in part because of, rather than in spite of, their perceived unreliability – break down and repair, though not welcome, affording experiences and fateful stories of a distinguishingly authentic relationship to the mechanical personality of the machine. Rich urban bikers taking their stylized, oil-free, machines straight out of the Harley David-son showroom can never be *real* bikers.

Fourthly and finally, these revisionist concerns have implications for how we understand the imperial homelands from which the linguistic model was exported. I would like to make a few explorat-ory observations on how language, itself, functions generally with respect to sensuous meaningfulness and also *within* it as one of its constitutive forms. The schism and variable relationship between the signifier and the signified, between the symbols they constitute and external concrete referents, are claimed as scientific break-throughs which found linguistic paradigm models of the world. But these gaps actually mark out rather simplistic positions on a very human and contingent map of the unexplored territory of the relation *between* language and situated cultural meanings. As post structuralist insights inform us, language itself carries many unsaid 'other' and polysemic meanings. But these have to be understood not only with respect to the internal instabilities of language but also with respect to whole hinterlands of sensuous contextual meaningfulness with which they try, variably, to connect.

Ultimately, language functions as humanly meaningful only in relation to this hinterland – not only the signs but the forests and Martian deserts, all plus active humans. Unless all human meaning is a hall of mirrors with signifier difference reflecting only signifier difference, some notion must be allowed of at least a partially separate human meaning existing and maintained somewhere else other than in language. 'Cow' signifier difference written on the page in front of you may not mean only and always the idea of a real cow – it could be a derogatory sexist term, or business terminology for an industrial plant which produces lots of money. But whichever of these it is to be, that concept needs to have a sustenance separate from language to maintain it for variable attachment to the signifier difference in front of you. I would argue that the general (concrete referent suppressing) functions of language are in a strange, antagonistic as well as symbiotic, multi-pointed and counter-pointed, frequently overlapping relation with socio-symbolic and other (concrete referent promoting) aspects of sensuous meaningfulness. More so in new and emergent language use, in which stable conventions have not yet become established, signifier differences are in a never ending and elusive game of hide-and-seek or touch-and-go with emergent sensuous meanings. Rather than produce their own signifieds from a magician's hat, 'floating signifiers' seek to connect and reveal, even if constituting in new forms, lived meanings in order to make a symbol that humanely communicates. If not in a representational relationship, language has to be in *some* relationship, *some* time, with a meaningfulness which is not entirely internal to it.

Coming so to speak from the opposite direction, I would argue that sensuous meaningfulness reacts like oil in water with respect to especially written or official or formal, if you like, 'incoming', general language. It evades or holds it off, translating it perhaps into the bodily oil of lived presence but ejecting again what is not commensurate or is not sticky. This makes it harder for the differences of 'floating signifiers' to find the specific attachments that they must sometime make. This can be seen as part of the long history of antagonism and dependency between bodily and abstract forms of knowing, between the mental and the manual played out in cultural and everyday arenas.

More specifically, I would argue that the language use, overwhelming speech, which arises *within* sensuous meaningfulness, which helps to constitute it, can be understood as engaged in its own impossible tasks of tying up and clamping down its own 'floating signifiers'. Concrete meanings abhor the arbitrary, which they instinctively associate with imposition. It is one of the reasons why cultural meanings do not easily produce linguistic representations publicly from their own base. The general case for the active nature of socio-symbolic practices, the action of their 'little histories', can also be applied to immediate language use. This is the effort to sink or anchor the 'floating signifier', to

tattoo 'love' and 'hate' on opposing human hands, to make language use as personal as a signature or a fingerprint.

This is a productive way to understand the 'why' and 'how' of
different language register usage. Working-class and subordinate
forms may instinctively see in the 'floating signifier' a source of
mentalism which is ultimately about constraint and control, social
exclusion and excluding the social. The 'sunk signifier' may be an
aspect of how dominated groups seek to make their own culture a
protected zone for some 'essentialist' expression of their own
meanings, especially those related to resistance or survival. To be
clear, the 'sunk signifier' is not a route for a one-to-one representational code to enter by the back door after the 'floating signifier'
has been thrown out of the front door. I am not arguing for a one-
to-one connection of signifiers to things in something called 'reality'. Actually, working-class speech is full of irony, 'pisstakes' and
'put ons'[13] which are about the development and reinforcement of
symbolic systems precisely *not* reducible to material referents and
relations, more a subversion of and provision of alternatives to
precisely this appearance of naturalized connection in official
representations and ideological accounts. The attachment I am
arguing for is between particular signifiers and emotional expressivity, and between signifiers and practical 'pointing' and 'referen-
cing' functions. The 'sunk signifier' is sunk not with respect to
reality, but with respect to sensuous practices. Making words *seem*
concrete, metaphor used for its coming across as real, is the point,
not the truth of whatever it is they are supposed to represent.
Ultimately, of course, as the linguistic model has taught us, 'sink-
ing the floating signifier' may well be an impossible project. But
there are some heroic failures along the way which tell us a great
deal about actual language use differences in context.

Take the case of swearing. Swearing is perhaps a paradigm case
of the 'anti-paradigm' at the metropolitan heart of the linguistic
empire. It is a universal feature of informal culture, particularly
important in its working-class varieties. Swearing can be understood as the formal opposite of euphemism. Euphemism maximally extends the floating power of the signifier, limit-case testing
the artificiality of convention. Swearing moves in the opposite
direction, limit-case testing convention as *minimum* repertoire.
Rhythm, brevity and repetition from a small range, these all
mimic concrete, especially physically aggressive movement, and

limit the scope of convention as well as the number of signifiers available to make autonomous chains of difference. Swear words have particular semantic roots but defy *particular* meaning in their usage, so scuppering the convention of how specific meanings reside in *differences* of specific signifiers. They qualify the whole of speech with the intention to shock or transgress, colouring a larger whole in some apparently *direct* emotional way. Perhaps transgression is the defining quality of swearing. The transgression of conventions of politeness (ironically reconfirming its possibility) seems to deny the very idea of convention, whilst stranding in shock and embarrassment those still constrained by those conventions, a living comparative signification whose signified is disbelief in or scorn for convention itself.

In many languages, perhaps universally, swearing usually involves giving a visceral and physical dimension to the spoken word which seems to produce uncoded moments of physical expressivity akin to spitting. We spit out our swear words, using the tongue-teeth and tongue-lips contacts to deliver the fricatives, the f's and k's. Fuck is perhaps archetypal.[14] Swearing is often directly accompanied by, or channelled by, physical movement and tone of voice expressivity, which anchor and sometimes submerge the 'floating signifier'. While not the best of situations for pondering linguistic theory, violent confrontations demonstrate how inescapable can become the continuities between physical and linguistic meanings systems, with lifted fists and threats – 'I'll punch your fucking head in' – becoming interchangeable.

Though apparently far from the field of poetry, all these things bring out an almost Leavisite quality in foul language. Both fields may share the practical assumption that really living language struggles against its own arbitrary and conventionalized nature. The counter resources of this 'struggle against' cannot be conceptualized, understood or recorded through language-paradigm-based approaches. Within language the 'floating signifier' should be used, not to attempt to explain everything,[15] but to test, qualify and map out particular contextual *forms* and *types* within the rainbow myriad of actual language use.

3

The Social

Of fundamental importance to the ethnographic imagination is comprehending creativities of the everyday as indissolubly connected to, dialectically and intrinsically, wider social structures, structural relations and structurally provided conditions of existence. Structures not immediately and present in the field are undoubtedly 'there' in ethnographically observable relations and sensuous effects. But these relations and effects are too often seen as abstract and one-way 'downwards' operations. The imaginative construction of the everyday as ordinarily including creative cultural practices enforces a reverse impulse, the cusp of where aesthetic categories meet social ones, to explore the ways in which cultural practices make active sense of their structural conditions of existence, even within the context of the evident continuity of social structural formation.

Penetrations

The sensuous meaningfulness embedded in cultural practices must, therefore, be understood as 'sense-full', not only in immediately local terms, but also in relation to social-structural form and location, providing 'lived' assessments of their possibilities *as humanly occupied*. These formations of meaning I call lived *penetrations*.[1]

This is a term that I developed in *Learning to Labour* to identify the ways in which counter-school culture saw through the meritocracy and individualism of schooling, allowing and helping to form realistic lived assessments of the real collective future of generalized manual labour as it confronted such as 'the lads'. Penetrations can be imagined as a means of a culture 'thinking' for its members. Cultures are good for many things: good to communicate with, good to find identity through, good for establishing mutuality and reciprocity. They are good for all these, and more perhaps, because at bottom, they are also good for 'thinking with'. They are not simply autonomously meaningful in an enclosed and cultural world, but meaningful with respect to context. Of course, participants may not appreciate this thinking cognitively, but they do so *sensuously*, in the greater power and viability of their own practices and in a more secure, bodily and psychic sense of themselves in relation to their circumstances and conditions of existence. Penetrations guarantee the longevity of a cultural form.

The ethnographic imagination of creativity in cultural practices assumes a provisional inversion, or degree of reflexivity, in how determination is supposed to flow between levels in human affairs. 'Objective' structural forces are seen not only as determinants but also as sources of what is to be known and discovered in the possibilities of experience. Penetrations designate the contextual and culturally mediated human 'sensing' – in its two meanings characteristic of sensuous cultural practices, simultaneously felt and understood – of wider structures, forms and structural relations, their possibilities and potentials. In its own way, this 'sensuous knowing' is superior to, and can hold off or invalidate prescribed models of how you should act, feel and be in relation to those structures, so also penetrating ideological forms and repertoires.

Partly this is a question also of assessing material / structural situations from the point of view of the viability of playing different options within them. This includes determining the basic down-side limit of what is externally enforced, of minimally meeting it in personally or culturally appropriate forms without suffering the double imposition of living oppression *and* accepting it in the terms of the powerful. Maximally it involves exploiting the space left over for cultural purposes, creatively seizing possibilities and materials in a structural and historical situation, ground small, which have been overlooked by the powerful or which do not appear in ideological accounts.

Blocked from conventional goals, cultural practices extend and develop into areas and into ends which *are* controllable. Cultural practices make creative use of provided services, objects and materials (meant to be private and consumed in line with dominant norms, institutional or commercial) to release their social potentials and produce aberrant decodings, uses and potentials never meant to be there. 'The lads' of *Learning to Labour*, for instance, not only resist the school and give it very minimally its Caesar dues, they also utilize its state-protected freedoms and cast of unfortunate straight men and women to prosecute their very own, postmodern-like subversion and exposure of institutional partiality and contradiction. They also adopt and make creative use of capitalist consumption commodities – clothes, drink, cigarettes – not only to resist domination but to make, project and believe in versions of their own worldliness and superiority. They penetrate the shells of fetishized commodities to find new social use values.

I do not mobilize a sense of class, race or gender humanist 'essence' to found the possibility of penetration. The 'floating signifier' has done for that. But there are other routes to demonstrating epistemological groundings for *difference* from below; difference on your own terms, classified by you, not as a term deviant from the norm, but as the claiming of your own norm, at least for some purposes, somewhere, sometimes. These found the possibility of different articulations to relevant conditions of existence.

Socio-symbolic cultural practices outlined in the previous chapter help to found the possibility of a reordering of social signification. Whereas ideological and official linguistic forms seek to annex all lived meanings to their own powerful constitution of meaning – good citizen, worker, student, etc. – socio-symbolic practices stabilize alternative liminal, uncoded or residually coded identities and meanings. They are held sensuously and practically and therefore relatively *outside* and resistant to dominant linguistic meaning. They refuse to be swallowed whole. 'Integral circuits' open or reinvent what should have been closed by those who 'take the floor'. New or unseen or differently used 'use values' – smoking and drinking in the case of 'the lads' – open up new avenues for meaning and activity showing practical grounds for autonomy and independence.

Penetrative resources and forms also arise from creative explorations and rearticulations of received dominant social codes and representations: working-class/middle-class, black/white, male/female. Binaries can be played off against each other and miscegenated or ironically positioned to reveal third terms. Contradictions, gaps and ill-fitting overlaps can be exploited and levered against each other. This also includes the mobilization of symbolic nuances, differences and binaries picked up in ethnographic accounts but not yet categorized and labelled by theorists. Careless and schematic placement from above produces discrepancies on the ground in which creative cultural practices can find arsenals of semiotic ammunition. Masculinity may be positively coded from above, but it can then become, in exaggerated form, a weapon against class or race domination on the ground. Inappropriately masculine and aggressive female style can challenge race or class domination. White 'positions' can take over black style and language to wrong-foot dominant class relations.

Fun and pleasure are also powerful resources for, and mechanisms of, penetration. Among 'the lads' 'the laff' confronts the power of institutional command, drawing out, developing and reproducing powers and abilities and a cultural world of reference not defined by institutional roles. Informal cultural practices are undertaken because of the pleasures and satisfactions they bring, including a fuller and more rounded sense of the self, of 'really being yourself' within your own knowable cultural world. This entails finding better fits than the institutionally or ideologically offered ones, between the collective and cultural senses of the body – the way it walks, talks, moves, dances, expresses, displays – and its actual conditions of existence; finding a way of 'being in the world' *with style* at school, at work, in the street. The immediate 'own level' success of cultural practices lies not in their critical or penetrative potential, but in the relatedness, the energy, the excitement of a culture's members as they find the most productive expressive relation to their conditions of existence, so finding individual and collective feelings of potency, subject senses of dignity and personhood, subjective feelings of authenticity.

So the sensuousness and embeddedness of penetrations should not be forgotten here. I am not arguing for individual, cognitive critique. Think of experienced pleasure intertwined with cultural practices as a lived out form of indirect or contingency testing of a hypothesis that has not been stated or answering a question that has not been asked. The ethnographic imagination asks the unasked questions – if satisfactions are higher in this set of practices, what does it say about their assumed preconditions? 'The lads' reported in *Learning to Labour* are not directly concerned logically to critique the contradictions and partialities of state schooling; they pursue 'the laff', fun and the pisstake. But these latter things can only flower in the light of a set of lived assumptions about the false promise of schooling, and they daily reproduce a feeling of superiority for 'the lads', versions of how they should use and inhabit their own vital powers. These life forces, engendered, channelled and reproduced in the pursuit of fun, expand and practically run up against what contains them, so further exposing institutional repression as material for penetration. The counter-school culture of 'the lads' is my example in this chapter. What did its penetrations consist of? I argued in *Learning to Labour* that their lack of interest in qualifications dumbly criticized the contradictions of meritocracy and individualism in education, and that regardless of official definition and symbolic labelling their general cultural insurgency explored all profane spaces, potentials and materials in the school for the development of their own cultural world.

Individualistic logic says that it is worth working hard at school to gain qualifications to get a good job. It may be worth while for any particular individual to believe and act on this. But is it logical for *all* individuals in the working class to behave in this way? The cultural responses of 'the lads' remind us that no amount of extra qualification will improve the position of the whole group: that would constitute, in fact, the dismantling of the whole class society. Meanwhile, meritocratic credentialism gives the middle class a functional legitimacy for enjoying their privilege – they are there because they have passed exams – and the capacities of the majority, graded in descending order, are stultified in hopeless obedience to an impossible dream. Prevented from pursuing alternative flowerings of their capacities or subversive courses of growth, credentialism enslaves their powers and seeks to trap them in the foothills of human development. 'The lads' refuse to collude; they play in unconventional ways their allotted hands in the game of their own subordination. They develop their own cultural pursuits and identities, at least avoiding the double oppression of living out subordination in the bankrupt terms of the official routes mapped out for them. From the collective point of view, lived out in the culture of 'the lads', the proliferation of qualifications is simply a worthless inflation of the currency of credentialism, and advance through it, a fraudulent offer to the majority of what can really mean something only to the few. Against the deafening roar of omnipresent individualism, here is a *sotto voce* cultural collectivism whose witness and analysis is always a prime focus for the ethnographic imagination.

The dominant, official, individual logic continues now more strongly to direct feeling and behaviour in schools today, but for many the collective logic also continues to exert a powerful, perhaps growing force, especially worked through a variety of alternative and increasingly commercially and commodity borne cultures.

With no expectation of genuine prospects for personal development, 'the lads' took a pot shot at choosing work, randomly sticking a needle into the full list of jobs available then. They were not seeking the careers counselled 'right job' for the 'right person'. On arrival in work they maintained their sceptical attitude, seeking not intrinsic job satisfaction or advance through merit but a continuance of 'the laff' and 'the crack' in coarse and independent forms of shop-floor culture, continuing to maintain a resistant dignity and practical alternative evaluations of human powers and potentials. The shop-floor cultures they found and helped to reproduce can be understood to contain in their turn culturally mediated penetrations of individualistic ideologies surrounding work and of the condition and nature of labour power under capitalism, limiting the scale of its exploitation, finding outlets for its alternative expression. This laid the foundations for a cultural world of meaning which made the labour process human and manageable from the workers' point of view.

Collective logics and cultures continue at work, but they are increasingly demonized or picked up only as individual pathologies, as 'wrong attitudes' or 'character flaws'. Increasingly, the demand for 'skill' in the new internationally competitive worker is newspeak for requiring compliant subservience in attitude and bodily disposition: in a word, self-disqualification from shop-floor culture. But dumb collective logics remain, driving much of subordinate behaviour, especially in the informal and unsurveilled shadows. Culturally mediated forms of private reservation or withdrawn consent continue to baffle, lighten, or deflect naked power – if not defeating it, still cordoning off some real uncolonized territory. In so far as modern regimes squeeze out these pores of autonomy and independence from the working day, we might expect some transfer of their content to non-work zones and locations, perhaps in heightened forms of 'anti-social' culture and attitude.

Social reproduction

It might seem that lived penetrations heroically dare and challenge the world. In fact their forms and artistry are often the very means through which what they seem to oppose is reproduced. The ethnographic imagination must encompass the aesthetic category of irony when it contemplates the unintended consequence of how cultural forms can help to reproduce social structure. It is crucial and defining to trace through the consequences and outcomes of creativity in cultural practices over time to see how certain preconditions, imposed fundamentally by capitalist imperatives, must be met, though often in surprising form.[2]

Though their resistant, creative and alternative identity-forming capacities and potentials should never be overlooked, there are multiple ways in which penetrations can be implicated in reproducing forms of what they seem to oppose – even as they also condition and change them in lasting ways.[3] Penetrations see into and produce an intimate knowledge of a specific situation and so the possibility of detailed strategies, not only for forms of resistance to, but also for a detailed, highly informed, sassy and creative accommodation *within* that situation. The exercise of a secret and privileged skill to determine the real minimum it may be possible to yield can become a collusive reason, in itself, for yielding: a bird in the hand etc. Penetrations also tincture acceptance and compliance with a compressed dignity, so qualifying the banality of subordination. Some substantial victory in immediate experience, even inversion and a form of superiority can be found within a larger failure. In submitting to fate, at least its face can be marked. There can be accommodation and compromise in the sensuous knowledge that all reproductive victories, at least in their own separated arenas, can be made pyrrhic at a cultural level.

We have to understand the unconscious blindness as well as the creativity of cultural practices. There are immediate and longer-run ironic social dynamics to penetrations. In so far as they make use of existing resources – say race and gender classificatory systems – as raw materials for their own local challenges, they also renew them in potentially more virulent home-grown form. Furthermore, the very success of a cultural form can reinforce the practical turn of its members and participants towards those practices and arenas in which their informal identities seem to flower (what I have termed before 'isomorphism'[4]). 'The lads' go to the shop floor partly to be with their own.

'The lads' provide a paradigm case for the reproductive dimension of creative cultural practices. One might think that their lived penetrations of the circumstances and conditions of their existence and future prospects could have produced refusal or a radical politics. In fact they, and many others like them, go willingly, even for a time in a celebratory way, into manual work – so meeting a fundamental requirement of capitalism not only to produce and apply labour power to production, but also in a way which orients it to continuous exploitation. This transition from school to work, as it is conventionally known, is aided and experientially accomplished through some important cultural continuities, which help us to understand something of the irony of 'the lads'' choices and actions. Their tumble out of (rather than transition from) school, with its adolescent restrictions and atmosphere, is, in part, a cultural vote with their feet for the working-class world of work, for what seems to be its more mature, adult and respectful way of treating them – continuous of course with aspects of their own previous cultural experience. You could call all this a kind of informal pre-socialization process. There is also an enthusiastic taking up of rights to the only working-class inheritance – the wage. Its power releases possibilities for which their own culture has already precociously and only too well prepared them: smart dressing, pubbing and clubbing and cross-town driving.

But something deeper and stranger is going on here which is to do with the culturally medi ated and produced fact that 'the lads' do not even want other kinds of jobs. They see their own job occupancy not as some kind of velvet defeat, the calculated acceptance of a known evil to bring access to other valued things, but as a part of the natural ordering of the world. Why is this?

It is important to appreciate that the anti-mental animus of the counter-school culture, while highly relevant in opposing and penetrating the demands of the school, also continues to orient and help direct the attitudes of 'the lads' – 'like a soldier's courage in the absence of war'[5] – long after the transition and across the board. This 'locking'[6] impels them towards a certain kind of culturally mediated, experiential set of meanings throughout their lives. There will certainly be future situations in which these attitudes and practices produce worthwhile 'pay-offs', but the danger is that the whole world might, henceforth, be divided into two – the mental and the manual. This makes hope for a 'second chance' return to higher education much more difficult and unlikely – the male, white working class continues to return to it less than any other group even under open enrolment schemes. As part of the tumble out of school, their anti-mentalism reconciles 'the lads' and those like them to manual work and often to job hopping between dead-end jobs (now interspersed with long spells of unemployment) for the rest of their lives. It makes all jobs involving mental work, now and for the future, seem to be simply boring paper work – who wants to spend their day pushing paper around, or now, fumbling over a computer keyboard? It can make even the necessary paperwork of their everyday life an unconscionable burden, to be shuffled off onto the wife as soon as practicable.

More generally, this anti-mentalism works against that abstraction necessary to seeing the connections between yourself and those with similar interests in similar sites (as well as the historical connection of sites), and working with them to organize and work collectively for change. The anti-mentalism of 'the lads' also leaves them vulnerable and without resource when they simply cannot evade the operation of power exercised through mental forms at work and other institutional sites. Though it was no direct purpose of the counter-school culture, there is a self-building here of the mental/manual division which is a fundamental feature of capitalist ideological architecture.

Symbolic structures of masculinity in the culture of 'the lads' also operate in a way similar to the anti-mentalism just outlined. Inherited and refocused masculine themes help to embody and give an extra force to their school resistance. Masculinity gives them an axis of power over and exploitation of women, but it also gives them a realistic basis for feeling superior to other less successful males – teachers as well as 'earholes' (conformists). This has a definite logic and is effective against the attempted domination of the school. It gives alternative grounds for valuing the self and a solid, sometimes formidable presence.

But once formed, hard masculine identities and the patterning of social relations which follow prove highly inflexible, intractable and durable. This is perhaps especially so where they have been formed through the contested winning back of identity and dignity lost on hostile and unavoidably 'compulsory' institutional grounds. Masculinity and its reflexes henceforth help to organize the same repertoire of defensive–offensive responses no matter what the situation – as if all social sites and social relations contained some- how a mandatory threat. This produces an obvious danger for women in and out of the home, where a compensatory masculinity may seek proof and exercise of a felt superiority. Shop-floor and manual work relations are suffused with masculinity, which can disavow the pains of labour and blunt the recognition of specifically capitalist forms of subordination. More generally, the world has been divided again into two irreconcilable camps, men and women.

This division is not a mental or a purely formal category: it divides the world into two cultural geographies. The masculine one has its own kinds of routes and connections, activities and values exclusive to that world. An isomorphic masculinity con- nects and finds connection between sites: counter-school culture, the street, the pub, football. The obvious masculine connection between the counter-school culture and shop-floor culture further smooths the path of 'the lads' into accepting the unacceptable, into finding a masculinized dignity unavailable on other grounds. On arriving at work they find value in being with men who behave 'like men', no matter what other sacrifices they make. Concerned with the continuities, transitions, rigours and rites of passage of their own masculine world, they are oblivious to what defines the new world they have passed into as quite definitely less benign than ever was the school.

There is a further twist here. The anti-mentalism and masculin- ity of 'the lads' become intertwined, fused, in their sense of them- selves. A manual way of acting in the world is also a manly way; a mental way is effeminate. These two things reinforce and lock each other into, if you like, a 'market masculinity' on the one hand and a 'patriarchal manualism' on the other – mutually producing a locking of disposition and sensibility, which may, quite literally, last a lifetime. In this final and damning move we can see how, for 'the lads', mental work becomes not only pointless paper pushing but also sissy work. Teachers can be seen as inferior because they are sissies. Even higher paid mental work is not that great, because it is still sissy from 'the lads'' point of view.[7] Exhausting, exploited and low paid, manual work can still somehow be seen in a masculine register as 'manly', in ways which prevent its true brutality from showing through.

These tragic ironies are what make penetrations cloudy, allowing social reproduction its dusty trophies. Orientations and dispositions remain long after the time and place of their formation. The 'unconscious' of a cultural form somehow assumes that all future locations will be like past ones, so determining the same kinds of appropriate response. But oppressive and subordinating relations do not repeat themselves as exactly the same everywhere. Actually, their *total* effect is importantly through the *combination* over time of effects from different sites; from neighbourhood, school, workplace. What is culturally appropriate to one site may lose its oppositional or revelatory power in another, help to reproduce subordination in yet another. Cultural meanings can continue to operate in the same way regardless of time and place, extending therefore into external conditions which were not those of their formation. There are temporal and spatial disjunctions, lacks of fit, between cultural form and material circumstance. These latter have different logics, different time scales, different rates of the passage of time. The symbolic and discursive forms being 'out of sync' with the material ones can lead to a penetration of one set of determining conditions constituting the reproduction of another, or even of the same set later.

The cumulative power of cultural forms over time, therefore, may not be in an aggregation of oppositional force and connection so much as in a disorganization of centred resistance and an unintended and conservative reproduction of given aspects of received social structure and form. This all helps to contribute to a 'teeth gritting harmony', wherein conditions are supplied within tolerances acceptable to the continuing functions and requirements of that capitalist economic system which individual cultures may resist or oppose.

Part II

Ethnography in Postmodernity

4

The Quasi-modo Commodity

So far I have drawn my main examples of lived culture from white working-class cultures and cultural forms. The contemporary cultural world becomes more diverse and changes faster by the day. Creative cultural practices of the everyday continue but now have to be ethnographically imagined in a rapidly changing context, the final surge to dominance of the commodization and electronic mediation of our surrounding culture. The things around us, including the 'meaning materials' available for take up into socio-symbolic meanings, are now overwhelmingly things made for profit by often distant strangers. In a word, the cultural commodity has become the dominant resource for everyday cultural practice.

How has this changed creativity in everyday culture? How have the relations of agency to form changed? What new penetrations might be developing in newly emerging articulations of cultural experience, and how are they involved with different forms of social reproduction? This chapter sets the scene for later chapters to follow up on these questions, by considering the cultural commodity form *per se*, first descriptively and by example, then in theoretical terms. The chapter becomes rather abstract in the latter theoretical section, but this is necessary in order thoroughly to locate the ethnographic imagination of cultural creativity within a conceptually grasped new ordering of signification and of material and sensuous form within the everyday.

Commoditization and electronic mediation have finally and irrevocably changed the conditions under which lived cultures operate, changed the materials and resources of their life spaces. Most of the ways in which we make meanings, most of our communications to other people, are not directly human and expressive, but interactions in one way or another worked through commodities and commodity relations: TV, radio, film, magazines, music, commercial dance, style, fashion, commercial leisure venues. These are major realignments. The general quantitative dominance here is obvious. We spend twenty hours and more watching TV every week, 92 per cent of young people regularly listen to the radio, 87 per cent listen to records/tapes, and three-quarters go to pubs or clubs regularly.[1]

We have a romantic view of a previous organic community, in which people related directly, utilizing local products of their own making. Perhaps that organic community never existed as such. But at least there is an ideal model we can think of, a previous stage at which human relations were more intimately lodged within a sensuous community, at which activities and rituals were formed and informed by care and tradition, including story-telling by known others, and at which objects and artefacts were known, made and passed on by traditional crafts in specific and unique ways. Especially allied with electronic mediation, commoditization is destroying any last material trace of this notion of organic community.

Think of the current changes in English football, its commoditization. Let us take Manchester United and its recent flotation on the London Stock Exchange. If you think of the immediate community, the sensuous community, the local crowd that goes to see Manchester United play at Old Trafford, there are about 45–50,000 warm bodies that can get into the ground. When the club was floated the *Financial Times* reported that the 'fan base' of Manchester United was between 2 and 2.5 million – far, far more than could ever get into the ground.[2] And 'fan base' is very important to financiers and investors, because it is the basis of the stock market valuation – in Manchester United's case about £1,000,000,000 currently. You could say that in the flotation of Manchester United the future purchasing power of those two million fans has been sold as a block on the stock market.

What is it to say that there are two million Manchester United fans? It is to say, of course, that 1,950,000 of them must relate to the club in ways other than the sensuous practices of going along and standing next to the other fans, talking about it in the pub, perhaps knowing a player etc. These fans relate to the club through buying commodities (clubs call it merchandising, selling kits, jackets, scarves, their designs changed as often as possible to maintain revenues) and paying to watch their team on TV. For a long time now, well over half Manchester United's revenues have come, not from gate receipts, but from commercial activities, including the selling of TV rights and commodities literally throughout the world. The overwhelming majority of the fans will never be part of the original sensuous community. Here is the mass commoditization and electronification of 'community' with a vengeance. And the motor is not an interest in extending an organic football community, but an interest in reaching consumers from whom to make profits.

What is true of Manchester United is true of other consumer forms. When you are watching the television you are not expected to be interested in the programme, or that is not the reason the programme makers are providing it: their only interest is to deliver you as a package of consumers to the advertiser. So, exactly like the Manchester United fans, the more people you have watching the more money you can make. There is much talk of digitalization and greater choice. But that does not change the basic argument. As we get more 'narrowband channels', providers can avoid wasting their time on people who may not be fans; viewers can be more certainly sold to advertisers as well as being charged directly. You can target your message. The modern communicative imperative is not to do you good, to educate you, to inform you, to develop you, but to sell your buying power and buying capacity on the largest possible scale.

What of public service broadcasting? Even the BBC now has to act more as if it were a commercial broadcasting company. For instance, a recent internal report, *Reflecting the World*, found that the audience for news was falling; viewers found the old, male announcers boring. The answer? Ship in sexy celebrity figures to read the news, because 'the groups at the bottom are looking for entertainment not information'.[3] When commodity relations become dominant, everybody has to play more by those rules. Non-commodity or quasi-commodity forms have to complete in the same market and try to use some of the same forms to get through at all, not least to justify state subsidy and support. So we are in a commodity-dominated world, where most meaning-making is through commodity objects and relations and where even other kinds of provision are having to take into account, if not quite be dominated by, commodity-type forms.

In my view, getting to grips with and understanding the cultural commodity form is the clue to understanding some of the mechanism behind the chameleon and baffling surface of late-modern or postmodern culture. Rather than simply describe 'fragmentation', 'de-centration', 'uncertainty', 'risk', personalized projects of 'aesthetic realization', a close consideration of the cultural commodity might give access to some of the mechanisms which are helping to produce postmodernity. What grounds and limits are there here for the creativity of the living arts of life? How can we avoid a banal, open-ended and circular humanism as we try to pose and answer these questions?

I argue that the pressing task is to understand the balance of penetrations and reproduction emerging in the new cultural relations surrounding 'meaning commodities'. Crucially important to the ethnographic imagination of life as art is that we recognize and explore the scope of creativity in the *use* of commoditized and electronic materials, their profane possibilities as mobilized in concrete contexts. I shall pursue that in the next chapter, but first it is necessary to clear the ground, to understand more about the *nature* of the cultural commodity, using aspects of a Political Economy approach along with some of the theoretical terms explored earlier.

The basic problem with trying to conceptualize the general nature and potentials of the cultural commodity is that while arguments have raged over its effects – the destruction of culture as we know it against a new 'consumer sovereignty' of choice – very little time has been devoted to analysing the category itself. Either way, it is granted too much unitary power, destroying things or creating things, without a more open and tentative consideration of how its basic forms facilitate the kinds of socio-symbolic engagements only out of which such effects can flow.

Though I accept the importance of a general Political Economy perspective which raises questions about who owns what and how things are produced and distributed, as 'first instance' determinations,[4] I am never convinced that a proven agenda of 'controlling power' at the economic level is worked through convincingly to establish a *cultural* chain of connection between ruling-class interests, institutional practice, identifiable ideological contents of popular materials and ideological effects in 'receivers'. Too often the establishment of an incontestable general case for the *specificity* of economic domination passes for proof of *specific* routes of influence. The question of form (see chapter 2) and the relation to located meaning-making are crucial here, but never pursued from the Political Economy side of the fence. While it is not the focus of this book, I can see the importance of analysing the institutions of production and distribution and their relations to state forms as a basis for developing strategies for counter-influence, limit or control. But the question for me remains: how would greater control *influence* the form of outputs with specifiable results in receivers. We are back to the crucial, pivotal issue of forms and how to conceptualize them. I can also see the importance of research into the creators of, producers of and production systems for cultural materials, whether they be craft or industrial based, into how far commoditization stretches back into the production process etc. But again the pay-off for the analysis must be understanding something about how these factors influence questions of form.

In addressing the question of form in late- or postmodern cultural relations I shall take a route with three staging posts: first, analysing the complexities of form, especially fetishism, in the cultural commodity (this chapter); secondly, examining the creative, upon conditions, uses and transformations of cultural commodities in the everyday (chapter 5); thirdly, following through how this experience relates in folding loops, penetratingly and reproductively, to social structural formation (chapter 6). Adequate answers here would help us pursue more fruitfully all the Political Economy questions outlined in the previous paragraph.

This chapter focuses, then, on the first link of the above chain, digging deeper into the particular nature of the cultural commodity, especially into what fetishism means in this case. For Marx commodity fetishism was at the ideological heart of the stability of capitalist systems, allowing him to make complex, elegant and non-reductive links between consumption, production, distribution, labour and social relations. *Cultural* commodity fetishism, in which communication and ideology are the very material of form, should therefore be of very special interest indeed, generally, to an ideological analysis of postmodern capitalist formations. Yet there has been little or no *specific* theoretical focus on fetishism, little on the cultural commodity.[5]

The commodity form

Of course, cultural commodities have different forms – musical, dramatic, linguistic, visual, plastic – and therefore need specific kinds of textual analysis, which can split easily into rival or alienated camps. But here I should like to consider some of the characteristics which unite different forms of the cultural commodity and which might have produced – as well as profits – new conditions on the other, future side of commoditization for cultural diversity and cultural change. The *particular* nature of the commodity has been passed over too quickly.

Before we get to the special nature of the cultural commodity, it is first necessary to undertake a little exposition about the commodity form in general. The category of the commodity is at the heart of the Marxist system of exploring the inner workings of the capitalist system. It is where Marx starts in volume I of *Capital*, and an analysis of the circulation of commodities opens volume II.

The commodity produced by the capitalist labour process appears on the market, naked, as a simple object for sale. Its smooth surfaces show no sign of the social relation of exploitation which produced it, nor of the labour time embodied within it which gives it exchange value on the market. It might have fallen from heaven. Forgetting its common history of embedded labour in production, breaking off all meaning arising from that, each object seems to be wholly independent and different from other objects, carrying meaning only in relation to possible future individual uses. Commodities are alienated from one another, alienated from prior meaning, alienated from the human processes and relationships which produced them. They seem to exist only in and for themselves; they are fetishized.

But, of course, commodities are in fact produced in a highly specific and determinate set of histories, relations and skills. They have not fallen from heaven. Follow any commodity back to the factory and there is a world of surprise in store – labour expended in complex labour processes; human hierarchies; discipline; sometimes bizarre management regimes of control and motivation; conflict; weariness; often suffering too. These things we know very familiarly in what we produce or provide, but forget in what all others produce. This forgetting produces a fascination in commodities and in their own glistening forgetfulness and mysterious self-absorption. We struggle with our own cargo cultist mentality. Where have these perfectly formed objects come from? There is a mystery about the way in which commodities both contain – because they are produced by – and simultaneously deny – they are only objects – wider social relations and embedded labour. This phenomenon of commodity fetishism is the starting point and lynch pin of Marx's analysis:

> A commodity is...a mysterious thing, simply because in it the social character of men's labour appears to them as an objective character stamped upon the product of the labour...a definite social relation between men...assumes, in their eyes, the fantastic form of a relation between things. Fetishism...attaches itself to the products of labour...value (i.e. capitalist production) converts every product into a social hieroglyphic.[6]

The use of hieroglyph here is fascinating and illuminating. A hieroglyph is a 'picture sign' as in the picture script of the ancient Egyptian priesthood – a system now taken to be difficult or impossible to decode. Marx is saying that the commodity is already a sign as well as a material thing, but one which seems to mystify and obfuscate rather than to communicate, obscuring what made it a sign. The fetishism of the commodity is about and can be summed up as failed communication concerning the commodity's own origin and history and the social relations and embedded labour that produces it. We are encouraged to understand ourselves, our histories and our relations with one another through things which absorp information about them into them. I shall return to these issues later in relation to a discussion of the cultural commodity.

Volume II of *Capital* also makes clear that the commodity form is central to the process whereby capital accumulation is realized through circulation and exchange. Commodities have to be turned back into money, so that the circuit of productive investment can start again. But this is not automatic; there are no guarantees.

There is a devilish risk, which capitalists would sell their souls to avoid, that they may not be able to sell their products, that they may be left with a full warehouse. The characteristic of the commodity which promises, not guarantees, the ability to fly off the shelves is its real or apparent sensuous *usefulness* – what it promises to do or satisfy in human need or desire.

This is a supremely important point when it comes to cultural commodities: the circuit could break down at any point. The risks are more severe in the cultural realm. Only about one in ten films and records make any real money – but all ten have to be made if anyone is to have the chance of making money.[7] Making the cultural commodity as useful as possible is the *sine qua non* of commoditized cultural production. All other norms and social conventions of consumption are to be suppressed in pursuit of use, any possible use – whether in the brothel or in the cathedral of cultural meaning.[8] This all adds to the mysterious and restless fascination of commodities; they are honed, however imperfectly, always in the direction of desire, honed always to the future of individual consumption rather than to the past of collective production. All fraudulent points on the compass of human desire are charted, and at the same time if possible. However brutal may be these insults to refined sensibilities, they also do everything possible to suggest, pump, prime, encourage, even bully into *use*.

The importance of this impulse is thrown into sharp relief when we compare cultural commodities with 'auratic' cultural objects, the artefacts of high material culture housed or performed in subsidized institutions. The location of the aesthetic solely within the internal parameters of the original, unique, authentic artefact; the 'aesthetic distance' necessary to produce reverence; the aesthetic disposition necessary to 'appreciation'; the training in Art History and the liberal humanities needed to place and value objects and artefacts within the Great Tradition; all these things seem virtually designed to prevent profane use, or to socially delimit use within prescribed norms of consumption.[9]

The cultural commodity form

All that I have said so far is true of the commodity form in general. What specifically separates cultural commodities from commodities in general is the particular nature and the quality of their usefulness. This quality is one of actual or potential cultural meaningfulness, the ability to supply expressive resources available for local creative cultural practices ultimately helping them in their roles of the construction and maintenance of identity. The range of cultural commodities, from purely informational goods (linguistically coded) to music to wholly material forms such as clothes, can operate as expressive 'use-values' only to the extent that they are meaningful to consumers; i.e. they communicate as delivering appropriable expressive materials into the latter's cultural practices. But this is to say something very strange indeed about a commodity form. The general form which breaks communication through its very fetishism – concealing its social relations of production, its embedded labour and how and why it was made, for whom and by whom – must in this case and as its first purpose enable meaningful communication. Rather than, or as well as, absorbing information about itself, it emits information.

Furthermore, in cultural commodities there are often evident displays of expressive embedded labour: acting, singing, talking. These things take place over time. The use value of a cultural commodity such as a CD or DVD is not extinguished or ingested with use, so these displays of communicative labour are repeated without diminution. Consumption is experienced through the senses which must be engaged, and through emotional experience over time, 'real time' rather than in single acts of consumption or in the matter-of-fact use of inanimate objects. All this militates against the disappearance of past labour into the fetishized commodity as in the classical model. There is a continuous reminder throughout of embedded expressive labour *in* the commodity.

It is evidently necessary to separate two levels in the cultural commodity form, first its basic 'commodity-ness', the 'bearer form', and second, its cultural usefulness, its 'cultural form'. Marx says that the commodity is, in general, a 'social hieroglyph'. We may say, then, that the cultural commodity is a hieroglyph ('bearer form') supporting a hieroglyph (the 'cultural form') – an enigma within an enigma! The cultural commodity presents itself, precisely, necessarily, as a hieroglyph which must be not so. The consequences of this double, compressed and contradictory symbolic articulation have not been adequately analysed, either for the *complexity* it must bring to an understanding of the cultural commodity or for the possibility of impacted *contrary* decodings of the dual hieroglyphics.

Let us consider, first, what I shall call *simple usefulness*. In a moment I shall look at complex usefulness. The whole point about the second hieroglyph, the 'cultural form', is that it must be inherently decodable, passable or usable within cultural practices outside itself. A potential customer might be expected to be able to imagine the future use values of a 'non-cultural' commodity, chairs for sitting on etc. Such 'use values' are direct and can be understood independently.[10] But the squiggles, dots or sounds of informational goods, for instance, might find no customers! In this latter case it is clearly essential to operate in some kind of linguistic code, which by definition cannot be private, arcane or special. More broadly, the 'cultural form' of any cultural commodity must offer communication as potential use values decipherable by as many customers as possible, bringing some communality, some experience of social connection between them and original message producers as mutual participants in various kinds of communities of practice and meaning. This directly contradicts the cutting of social connection associated with commodity fetishism.

The contradiction I am trying to expand upon is that while cultural commodities are subject to commodity fetishism simply because they are commodities they are simultaneously subject to the absolute need to de-fetishize themselves, simply because they have to offer communicative and cultural use values.

Think of music. It is only within a shared community of communication and affect that specific types of noise can be defined as music and that a giving up and opening of aspects of the spiritual self can be undertaken and experienced as 'appreciation' of that music.

Think of football again. No amount of fetishism will destroy the necessity for an assumption of shared footballing knowledge – rules, clubs, characters, folklores, fan-dom – as the codes of the commoditized text. TV football cannot exist apart from the football community. Commoditization backhandedly recognizes community, however exploitatively, in a way that general fetishism would lead you to think was impossible.

Fuelled by the profit motive, distilled usefulness drives cultural commodities not only to seek and connect with communities of meaning but also to shape and enlarge them in the direction of the greater usefulness (meaningfulness to others) of their own meanings. Classic FM has doubled the radio audience for classical music in the UK at a time when subsidized concert halls are emptying. Pavarotti's World Cup anthem brought a new audience to opera. Classic serializations on TV produce tenfold increases in book sales. The commoditization of Manchester United through TV exposure and the sales of scarves, kits, clothes and memorabilia has produced a community of fans ('fan base' for the stock market and basis of comparative capitalization) of two and a half million – far more than could ever watch a match in a 'real' community gathering. Manchester United plans to start its own satellite TV channel, not least to tap into the huge emerging Asian market for football, so helping to produce an electronic community of many millions more, about forty million according to the *Financial Times* (1 April 2000).

Perhaps Hollywood's commoditization of film is the paradigm case for the turning of cultural artefacts into cultural commodities through the distillation of communicative and cultural usefulness for the largest possible number. Realism is the visual *lingua franca* for reaching back and forth across the commodity form to find meaning and continuity. The rest of Hollywood's filmic grammar pivots on convergent attempts to maximize recognizability and use: human interest; pace; identification; audience targeting; structuring taste and legibility through strong genre demarcation.

The general commodity form then may militate against social meaning, but it needs shared meaning when it wears its cultural clothes. One may just say that capitalist culture is trying not to be capitalist.[11]

The struggle between the commodity and the code

I may seem here to be arguing that usefulness in the case of the cultural commodity, only in the case of the cultural variant of the commodity form, overpowers fetishism. It is certainly important to stress the useful meaningfulness of the cultural commodity at a certain stage of the argument, to underline just what a strange, chameleon and contradictory thing it is. But if the cultural commodity were indeed *all* usefulness, it would in fact cease to be a commodity. The usefulness of cultural commodities cannot imply a sharing of real, authentic, organic community as, for instance, behind our sense of Raymond Williams's 'whole way of life'. Millions of the new Manchester United fans have never visited, and will never visit, Old Trafford. Nor does the special kind of communicative and cultural usefulness of the cultural commodity imply that the consumer knows about the industrial labour processes and the capital relations which produce and reproduce the cultural commodity.

Here we come to the nub of the argument: the final, clinching specificity of the cultural commodity is that its particular kind of usefulness not only must permanently coexist with fetishism but also is profoundly and contradictorily transformed, altered and stressed by it. In no other commodity form are usefulness and fetishism so unifyingly opposed. De-fetishization works against fetishism, and fetishism works against de-fetishism, producing a stable instability in the cultural commodity. This is the elusive quality I have been pursuing, the *particular* nature of the cultural commodity: the quasi-modo commodity. Its two halves are always half-formed, each struggling to complete itself but failing through the ceaseless tension arising from its other half, from which it can never escape. Hardly has any community of meaning held sway than it is extinguished by fetishism, but only by its instant renewal will the *cultural* commodity perform its appointed role.

Unreal adverts surround the shows and films which seem so real; glossy book covers which are nothing to do with what is inside tell you that someone wants to sell to you more than to communicate with you; the way you buy a love song bought from multiple copies in multi-stores tells you it is not really made for 'only you'. The patronizing familiarity and bogus friendliness of the disc or video jockey tells you that he is no friend really. Lines are cut rudely by phone-in hosts, showing you that electronic commodity community is like no real, warm community. Your purchasing power being bought and sold on the London stock market hardly makes a home of a ground you have never visited in Manchester.

There is then a fundamental contradiction and instability in the cultural commodity form. It must seem to offer the shared and communal, while its very form breaks organicism, local connection and local meaning. Lack of social connection must present itself as social connection. This is an intrinsic double naturing of the cultural commodity, the source of its seductive charm. The fetishized fascination in the commodity is brokered through what there is *in it* which leads *out to* community, to communication, to appreciating the expressive labour of others. Here lie clues to the secret powers of cultural commodities, to the inner creative impulses they supply to those who will accept their offer, 'use me but don't possess me'.

Here too, at last, we see why the age of the cultural commodity is also indissolubly the electronic age. The insistent but impossible community offered by the cultural commodity is the false immediacy of the electronic message, best exemplified in the sensuous offer of community in the realist TV image. Reach out to touch its warmth and you find only cold glass. The false, ever hopelessly self-repairing cultural commodity makes its fraudulent offers *ad* electronic *infinitum* in every home. Once set upon the colonization of the cultural realm, the commodity age was fated to develop the electronic image: its own abstract nature made concrete.

It is very important to appreciate that the two halves of the cultural commodity do not lead separate lives. Nor do they simply cancel each other out, as in a simple sum: negative + positive = zero. The 'cultural form' half continues but is destabilized and permanently infected by fetishism, seeking, if you will, the usefulness of fetishized usefulness. Strangely, a crucial point, this can produce unexpectedly productive potentials. Fetishism may truncate meaning, but it simultaneously makes what remains more open, contestable and 'sticky'. Commodity meanings which survive beyond the fetishism are maximally open to finding new articulations, new homes. These provide the basis for possibilities which I term those of the *complex usefulness* of cultural commodities. I shall discuss these latter under the headings of *loss of dependency, culturalization, subversion.*

Loss of dependency

The quasi-modo naturing of the cultural commodity allows social information and cultural meanings to get through to receivers, viewers and users without being framed through forms of social dependency. Fetishism's restraint and half-forming power over its unfetishized other half to some degree strips the guilty baggage of historical connotation from communicative meaning, strips it of limiting and dependence-inducing prior social relationships, including the specification of given, historically accreted norms of consumption and use.

In the dominant register, informational commodity communication is impure and inferior, lacking in seriousness and moral purpose. It lacks the Reithian imperative to educate as well as to inform and entertain. There is, however, a sub-text of advantage unseen to dominant eyes, which allows, in some respects, the freer passage of new information. Remaining communicative, anti-fetishism seeks attachment at all costs, straining itself to the limit to break down all barriers.

The 'authority' of other communication types assumes a deference or semiotic powerlessness in receivers, who are assumed to be subordinate in the social relationship which holds the communication. Institutional-educational communication carries an obvious paternalism, real and implied compulsions. Auratic communications (as in works of art emitting an aura) are explicitly authoritarian, locating all meaning in the text and severely prescribing relevant norms for consumption and decoding. Even 'community meanings' carry a responsibility to those who have communicated or what is spoken of in the immediacy and reciprocity of what is bounded by the sharedness of meaning.

By contrast, cultural commodities make human offers but no contracts. They travel without passports. New contexts really can make new of old texts. The messages and meanings which survive to new contexts are social without being socially overdetermined, without being fixed by the social field forces of their original locations. The possibility of guiltless but still social consumption is born. So only commodity communication offers community meanings without the community. Only it offers the hand of meaning without a stick of authority in the other. Distance and place are abolished in these solicitations. Meanings can carry from the far corners of the earth as easily as they can from around the corner. Manchester United fans in Manchuria. Black R&B makes Liverpool its home. London's EastEnders can live in Manhattan. Brazilian soaps with Italian pasta.

Here is a material base for understanding the compressions of time and space, the disorientations, the disjunctions between 'place' and 'home', the apparently 'free floatingness of discourses':

things labelled postmodern as if that was explanation enough for their being conjured out of thin air.

Culturalization

Particularly in the case of informational or more code-based cultural commodities, the desperate need to find any kind of social connection across the narrow bridge of fetishism leads to a promiscuous displacement of meaning onto as many other bearer forms as possible. This is done to maximize the inclusion of other meanings and potentials for possible inclusion as use values. This can be seen as the *culturalization* of code elements of cultural commodities whereby they are invested with imaginary community or any kind of association with any human activity, value, solidarity or worth, or emotion, including sadness, shock, fear, fun and humour. Pure code signifiers are embrocated in other sensuous values, uses and associations.

Football on TV becomes home entertainment or the conviviality of giant-screen community in pubs and clubs. In news and current affairs, meaning is diffused across as many other uses and categories, across as many implied or imagined communities as possible, to make as many contacts with receivers as possible, beyond that simply to inform. Bridget Rowe, newly installed editor of the *Sunday Mirror*, says 'Newspapers have to be entertaining and different. We can no longer just report the news.' [12] On TV, the newscaster becomes a friend and guide, the programme a neighbourhood get-together with human interest and 'to end with' items emphasizing imaginary solidarity. Ambulance and police car chasing emphasizes human sensation, shock and horror, just in case the viewer's senses have drifted off momentarily during an informational item. Public broadcasting is not exempt. The recent secret report mentioned at the beginning of the chapter, drawn up by senior BBC executives, suggests importing entertainment stars into news reporting. [13] The BBC weather forecast stalwarts are now being dropped in the switch to a 'more entertaining' American format.

Culturalization works in two directions, oscillating between more purely informational and sensuous concrete use values, pulling both onto a central ground of cultural meaning. Culturalization operates not just to 'sensualize' codes, but to drive 'code' into sensuous objects. New branches of expressive community are hypostasized by suggesting fresh, other or more developed social meanings for functional objects, to give other reasons than their immediate usefulness for buying them. This is a driving of an abstract content into other forms to increase their prospects for cultural usefulness: imbuing their use values with communicative and cultural usefulness. This produces a kind of 'semi-coding' in the imbued item – the communicative possessing, literally, of other entities: bodies, practices, things, uses, materials. In such ways cultural commodities find and make new and changing markets out of a previous cycle of commoditization. Commodities become exoticized into a cultural status, bedizened in drapes of a corrupt but still social imagination.

Manchester United has found a new market for clothing and memorabilia. Purchasing any car is also to purchase a 'life statement' and putative membership of some kind of community as well as a means of transport. Trainers trade on the meanings and values of marginalized and minority communities, including their real and potential opposition to that capitalist system which supplies the trainers – 'the revolution will not be televised' (Nike advert). Perhaps the whole of the modern advertising industry is about seeking to further imbue or culturalize objects which may have only limited functions or physical uses to associate them with other meanings, to make them to some degree expressive. Under modern conditions, perhaps, there are no non-culturalized objects, that is objects that signify only their own direct physical or subsistence use values and satisfactions. The culturalization of commodities is now a condition of our culture and how we make sense of others and ourselves in it.[14]

The desperation to make code more sensuous, sensuality more coded, places the expressive human body at the centre of commodity culture. The body is, so to speak, the smallest community of meaning and communicative practice, the immovable material resting place for the possible lodgement of fraudulent community. This is part of the somatization and individualization of meaning in an emergent, more body-based structure of feeling. Unconsciously and blindly, not willed or knowing, the commoditization of communication seeks to embody usefulness in as many body-oriented and immediate ways as possible. Commodities insinuate themselves into the interstices of daily life, in and around the somatic natures and tactile presence of the human body. Commodity-related meanings are therefore likely to be tied up with libidinous meanings in complex ways, both as a materialism of desire, what actually turns you on, and as a projection of the self as materially desirable to others. The marketing and design of the culturalized use values of fashion, glamour, life style and hygiene products invite us to sell ourselves like commodities to each other – in actual use tempered towards enhancing the sensuousness (usefulness) of actual warm bodies in real relationships. But remaining fetishisms add distance and exploitation to personal relations, a mystery and objectification never to be fully overcome but which, in its own way, may aid desire.

Culturalization and the culturalization of the body aid in the globalization of commodity culture – culturalized 'semi-codes' travel where purely linguistic ones cannot.

Subversion

The double enigma of the cultural commodity form produces a struggle not only of one part against another – commodity as usefulness, commodity as fetishism – but also, as we have seen, *within* the 'cultural form' part itself. The effect of the 'bearer form' (the fetishism of the general commodity form) on the 'cultural form' is to partially fetishize and distance the latter's internal forms. Of course the 'cultural form' element of the cultural commodity cannot be completely fetishized, otherwise it would not communicate. But the instability between the forms gives a good 'nudge' *within* the commodity or text to reveal its fetishistic nature, so subjecting even its surviving meanings to irony, relativism and even subversion. Football fan-dom can never be the same after the flotation of Manchester United. Though the 'usefulness' bit of the argument and the balance of contradiction should not be forgotten, nor how this produces its handmaiden of realism in the textual register of commodity forms, it should not be forgotten that fetishism loosens again the frames of realist representation. Viewers, listeners, dancers may be presented with the familiar and knowable, but the commodity form ensures, both internally and externally, that it can never be taken as authentic and original.

The 'productivity' in reception of *simple usefulness* in texts may be along a grain of realism and realist decoding. But the *complex usefulness* of cultural commodities also offers the productivity of immediate subversion. In the days of representative innocence the experts could have fun dissecting how the rest of us were manipulated semiotically. But now these simple investment returns to an elite have been crowded out by the speculations of the mass. We are all practical experts on mythologies now, on how to read with cultural literacy, on how to take the broad hint when the adverts inside and outside texts tell us that nothing is real. When there is no one left who believes what he or she is told, there is no point in deconstruction. Realism subverts realism in the quasi-modo commodity relation. Realism may try to outrun the subversion in plot jumble, fast cuts and short sequences, but is doomed by fetishism to stay cyclically revolving ever more visibly in its own phantom, the condition of capitalist culture.

Cultural commodities and cultural practices

My case is that within the general cultural commodity form there is an inescapable tension, a sprung bow of exclusion and possibility. In a sense there is always, so to speak, 'half' of a communication longing for attachment to 'half' of an imagined community to make it whole, meanwhile attempting all possible strategies to induct real connection across the impossible divide of fetishism.

Adorno argued that the collapse between art and life in modern cultural relations meant that there was no critical or creative room left for 'imagination and reflection'. Strangely, though cultural commoditization does certainly help to bring art and life closer together, fetishism ensures that there is a continuing gap to be closed or narrowed between artefact and contemporary use. Here is space aplenty, not for a transcendental, but practical 'reflection' as a sensuous rearticulation of form to the chemistries of everyday life in sensuous practices of de-fetishization (see the next chapter).

Meanwhile, commoditization produces an ever wider field of now virtually environmental meanings, objects and resources of a special kind. These are a distinct category of things in the world: not codes, not 'not-codes', but 'semi-codes' one way or another attached to other sensuous use values. They are sensuous expressive forms, with the body and somatic forms of knowing at their very centre.

Cultural commodities have a striking suitability, or elective affinity, as raw materials for socio-symbolic practices explored in the previous chapter. Those strange things, through whose fetishism capitalism organizes its social relations, in this case speak, inviting a lived and critical double take – some awareness of labour, communication and community – on that capitalist reification which they also represent. Their 'objectness' and 'nonobjectness' are simultaneously emphasized. Cultural commodities thrash around to find and attach themselves to different, partial, submerged, non-coded or semi-coded forms, developing hybrid use values, appealing to some kind of shared meanings. As will be explored in the next chapter, they meet half way cultural practices themselves concerned with sensuous, non- or 'semicoded' meanings and meaning-making, eluding the closures and encapsulations of linguistic communication.

The internal 'signs' of the cultural commodity are not, therefore, simply 'polysemic' in an inert kind of way. They are internally dynamic, internally contested, internally tensed, in ways which incite a response: to repair their wounded meanings, to find impossible wholeness. The internal textual contradictoriness of cultural commodities can operate as a predigestion of meaning which induces the same processes, but now in the real digestion of social meanings in actual receivers, listeners, viewers etc. Cultural commodities are pre-loaded with an expressivity, stickiness and guiltlessness which orients them seductively, even indecently, for inclusion in the dense localness of lived cultural forms. There is an unholy fit between commodities struggling with their own fetishism and varieties of exploratory cultural practices seeking embedded communication. Unfettered by historical norms of consumption, culturalized codes are more likely than pure codes to be taken up into sensuous cultural practices. The culturalization of physical commodities changes their 'objective possibilities' by fusing or suggesting new relationships between kinds of usefulness, bringing coded or expressive elements into possible engagement with sensuous practice. *Homological* relationships allow a holding and fashioning of human interest and identity which is itself not fully formed, not coded, or fully coded, but which is not lost, running away into the pores of everyday life to one side, or swallowed up, whole and signified, in pre-set subordinating ways by linguistic forms.[15]

The 'one-way' communicators should take more care in their choice of material for 'silencing the masses'. Dominance may not get its own codes back again, or identities forged submissively in the tracks of its linguistic powers. Instead of the masses being 'voiced' with the dominant word, they may be 'bodied' with subversive sensuous meanings. A further twist is added when ravenous commercial producers take up 'street meanings', in part or in whole, for another cycle of commoditization, mediating a complex quasi-alternative meanings system presided over by an uncomprehending, even if dominating, capitalist communications system. Hardly the silencing of the lambs!

5

Penetrations in the Postmodern World

I argued in the previous chapter that while cultural commodities are provided in vertical relations of capitalist logic, they must be formed and made available in socially horizontal planes of prior communicative meaning and symbolic appropriation. In this, they contrast with (now barely imaginable) non-cultural commodities, which can hope to offer immediate, physical and intrinsic use value. The *usefulness* of cultural commodities, the precondition of their profit-making potential, must be with respect to their specifically human role within communicative and cultural meaning systems which are inherently social. Fetishism may wound, for some at its heart, the genuinely social in communication but usefulness forever just holds off the *coup de grâce*. Meanwhile, promiscuous usefulness offers imaginary possibilities of completion to all and sundry. No matter how estranged, here is a first symbolic glimpse of post-scarcity society, of supply in excess of need. Destroying the reverence with which symbolic forms are viewed for a practice of profane use is the backhanded cultural contribution of commodity production.

But, fraudulent and imaginary as commodity culture and communication may be, the situations and contexts where they are received and used – materially 'attached to real conditions' – by active and creative human beings are far from fraudulent or imaginary. Family, school, work, non-work, scarcity – proffered

official models for all their subjective inhabitation – are continuous, if always changing, sites and relations which have to be made
sense of as a *living through* in varieties of informal and local
cultural production. Class, folk, gender and ethnic cultures, the
un-self-recognized folk arts of daily life, now the informal uptake
of the wild yeasts of commodity culture – all these contain
resources for dealing with these exigencies and also, grittingly,
for meeting and reproducing their structural imperatives.

Of course cultures are in flux as never before. They certainly do
not line up in neat rows any more – being > social being > culture >
consciousness – producing solid blocks of working-class or middle-
class culture. And commoditization and electronic mediation
supply ever more varied symbolic grain to the mills of daily meaning-making. But though the changing, gravity-defying nature of
contemporary cultural resources and processes makes cultural mediations harder to stop and name, the constraints, necessities and
imperatives of structure and place remain to be *lived* and *embodied*
somehow. Coming adrift from traditional social moorings is not the
same as 'the cultural' finding escape velocity altogether from 'the
social'. The post-postmodern task, especially of the ethnographic
imagination, is to analyse and depict the practices through which
the structures of discourse, culture and communication find *new*
articulations with, or dialectical uptake within (finally helping to
constitute them) the structures of material and institutional life.

The problem is that we are stuck, necessarily, with the old
categories and measures (community, responsible communication,
collectivity) when we try to trace and comprehend the contours of
emergent forms, forms which are actually more likely than ever to
be precisely and ironically *embodied*, floating perhaps, but not
from the body and sensuousness. They will not be susceptible to
being easily verbalized. They may be multiple and not connected
up in geographically and socially connected wholes. The problem
is that we do not understand the grammar of the new diversity and
embodiment as meaning-making from below.

Cultural practices

The historical explosion in capitalist material production which
came from the freeing of the power of labour from feudal

restrictions, by turning it into a commodity bought at 'exchange value' but exploited for 'use value' (unrestricted by custom, tradition and dependence) is mirrored by a later informal and intrinsically more democratic explosion of informal cultural production. This is made possible through the productive use of meaning commodities, themselves now bought at exchange value but exploited as use values in their turn, unrestricted by the customs, traditions and dependencies of auratic or institutional cultural relations.

Immediate qualifications are necessary. None of this is to argue that all is for the symbolic best in the best of all possible cultural worlds. We are still no nearer to true depth in usable information for all, no nearer to genuine understanding of other cultures in context, no nearer to the democratic control of the agendas and material production of cultural resources. The strange and alienated democracy of signs which feed the informal production of meaning was born contradictorily out of an undemocratic communications market (concentration of power, rising accumulation etc.). Certainly the rise of an alienated semiotic democracy is no more about economic democracy than was the rise of political democracy – there a thousand signs fired at us every day from advertisers, but you try firing back just one! Put up one humble fly poster and you will find yourself fined and reporting to the local police station every week! Still, the daily circulation of usable symbols and the daily scope for creative meaning-making as ordinary events should not be invalidated simply because they do not fit our pre-commodity dreams of collective control.

Symbolic work

I introduced the term 'symbolic work' in *Common Culture*[1] in order to disaggregate my larger notion of cultural production by focusing on the *active* and *productive* nature of cultural practices involving consumption, usually seen as passive, manipulated or mechanistically reflecting the cynicism of how what is consumed has been commercially produced. In one way or another, many of these practices can be seen as attempts to make whole or bring coherence by attaching the fragments and flows of commodity culture to situated personal and collective meanings: to de-fetishize cultural commodities in context. In part, symbolic work can be seen as the combination of sensuous cultural practices through which socio symbolic meanings are produced, practices which search out 'objective possibilities', loosened up and made more sticky by commoditization, and adapt them dialectically in relation to sensibility, passion and disposition (see chapter 2).

Symbolic work is comparable to but less alienated than wage labour. It involves elements of Marx's famous humanist portrayal of work, with the humble architect first raising structures in imagination, but is a form of self-realization, pace Marx, which takes place truly 'when the worker is at home'. Historically commodity production may have driven out from the labour process the skills and craft prides which it welcomes back again, but in the outside world of (productive) cultural consumption.

Symbolic work concerns symbolic understanding and manipulation, meaning and sense making – if you will, a centripetal force to place against the now mandatory decentredness of the subject.[2] As in the material capitalist labour process, production takes the form of the transformation of commodities – their productive consumption through the expenditure of human labour power (but expressive not instrumental) to produce expanded value. This expanded value arises from the productive exploitation of the use values of commodities and takes the form of an expansion of that use value, making the cultural object more useful, especially in connecting general alienated and fetishized meanings and cultural possibilities and converting them into local, specific contextual meanings and embodied satisfactions of a kind which were not available before. This can be seen as an increase of use value over exchange value in the commodity, as a conversion of estrangement into belonging, as the decommoditization or defetishization of the commodity.

Inauthenticity has become a supposed hallmark of postmodern times. Certainly we have seen the in-built inauthenticity resulting from the desperate internal struggle between fetishism and communication in the cultural commodity. Applying symbolic work under specific conditions to these materials offers some possibility for the return of a kind of authenticity, of a practice of appropriation that finds and binds to real conditions some of the loose multiple ends of chaotic postmodernism.

Many cultural commodities, such as CDs, are not diminished at all in consumption. So there is no lessening. Indeed it can certainly be argued that in the case of cultural commodities all consumption involves addition: symbolic work creates new value as mooring and socio-symbolic articulation, some of which is realized in visible forms. One such visible form is the change and transformation of persons, the development of the expressive self and its greater use value as a dynamic symbolic force. Another is the greater value (as embodied labour time increasing potential use values) of cultural objects once embedded in real practices and concrete contexts – their selection, combination and recombination in personally appropriated fashions, musics, styles.

The 'realization' of embedded value is often in the form of informal exchange – the passing round of technical equipment for sensuous use: DIY products, mastermixes; off-air tapes, copies, pirates, ideas for dress, recombinations of styles and new appropriations. The scope and importance of these informal exchanges among young people should not be underestimated and is a main vector of their chosen interests and activities. Just as Marx insists that exchange is the *sine qua non* of surplus realization, so the manifest evidence of exchange and realization in the informal cultural sector clearly demonstrates a *prior* process of real value production. The informal circuits are evidently driven by the value at stake, just as is the formal commodity circuit but without the 'money moment'. Symbolic work produces multifarious forms of new value unseen by the formal world, but continuous informal exchange demonstrates their existence.

The existence of this value is most conclusively demonstrated, perhaps, by the way in which the capitalist cultural commodity circuit keeps dipping back into the streets and trawling the living culture for ideas for its next commodity, its next circuit. Capital's cultural producers remorselessly ransack the everyday in their never ending search to find, embody and maximize all possible use value in products. Informal symbolic production is precisely what attracts them, even as they neutralize it by relaunching it into commodity relations.[3] Evidently the formal circuit would not keep returning to the streets unless it found real value there. This is the capitalist attempt to realize the value of informal production in the traditional capitalist form of money. This has not been adequately factored into the political economy of the circuit of capital.

The concrete practices of symbolic work can be understood through two constitutive sub-categories: selection and appropriation. My examples in the following sections are drawn from *Common Culture* (see note 1).

Selection

Commoditization produces literally a global range of symbolic and (relatively) freely hybridized and open-to-hybridizing materials. Symbolic work includes the selection of objects and items from countless possibilities, and their placement in personal *mises en scene*, in precise micro-circumstances, material and symbolic, of use and consumption.

Though it is certainly an important influence, falling sales of singles demonstrate that the top twenty does not determine current youth taste. So, there are five decades of rock and pop to be selected from. Selection requires a practical knowledge of that musical history. There is also a material and active side to the work of selection which should not be overlooked. In any music shop there is focused activity: young people reading notes, listening to CDs, searching for CDs. There are also now a large market and many outlets for second-hand vinyl records. Many young people explore the history of rock and pop. The role of material technological practices should not be underestimated. Cheap tape recorders and tapes have made it very easy to record off-air, easy also to tape material off friends' records, tapes and CDs. 'Writer' CD machines and down-loading from the Internet add new possibilities. This is bringing the software music publishing industry into a crisis of copyright.

In style and fashion, the same fundamental point can be made. Constructing personal appearance is hard work. Despite commoditization no two people look the same. Shopping is extremely hard work. You have to window-shop to decide what you like. More widely, you have to image-shop from magazines, TV and films from clubs and pubs and from people walking down the street. Inside the shop you have to negotiate with sales staff, try clothes on, make quite complex choices about what suits you and what does not, judge whether, in your opinion, the sales assistants are both competent and truthful. Finally you have to make an opportunity-costed decision to spend finite amounts of cash or undertake credit burdens. Having bought the clothes, the business of after-care and modification constitutes its own clear work of control and maintenance.

TV watching is usually taken to be the archetype of indulgence – couch potato, passive reception. But TV watching is actually a highly active process. People select and argue about the selection of programmes. They select within programmes as well as between programmes, since their eyes are actually on the programme being watched for only about two-thirds of the time. The rest of the time they are talking and arguing, between themselves or with the TV or both. They are also selectively critical, but not as in the literary criticism of the university seminar. They pass rude comments about the clothes or physical features of actors and presenters, they take the mickey out of their accents and mannerisms, they shout and spit out Anglo-Saxon and politically incorrect denunciations of those with whom they disagree. They select their meanings from the many available.

There is a material dimension to selection here too. TV is not simply about off-air broadcasting. It is a screen-based technology with many associated actual or possible cultural practices involving selection and control. Three-quarters of VCR owners use their machines to 'time shift' off-air programmes. While TV companies spend fortunes hiring programme controllers to schedule material and hunt their golden 'inheritance factors', young people especially are routinely turning this gold back into lead by the technological alchemy of their own time shifting, their own selection and control. It is possible to select and control your own symbolic resources by using your video machine to time shift programmes and make your own viewing schedule, as well as to select within programmes by scanning, freezing, replaying, speeding images back and forth. At last there is a practical way out of the imposed linearity of narrative forms.

The makers of cultural messages communicated through the cultural media understand very well that there is symbolic work in reception, and that particularly the young are adept at selecting and 'reading' messages. Adverts now routinely invite the audience to work within an assumed general and contemporary cultural literacy. Adverts interconnect different media, different films, different stars. They comment ironically on other advertisements. They work on the connotations of rock classics in new and surprising contexts. They set up puzzles, puns and riddles; they leave the dots to be connected up by the listener or viewer. One can see the same with the range of new magazines, especially those for young women. *Just Seventeen, Mizz* and *Sugar* are very clearly not arranged in an old narrative sequence with a paternalistic and positioning editorial voice. The items are broken up. They are not meant to be read in sequence. Only by going through the text yourself and connecting it with the pop cultural universe and your own experience of it can you hope to find meaning.

Appropriation

Selection merges into and is perhaps always part of the second major form of symbolic work involved in creative consumption, practices of personal and or collective *appropriation* of images, materials and meaning for personal use and meaning-making. This includes the locking and mooring of the 'objective possibilities' of selected items to the sensibilities and interests, hopes and passions, dilemmas and fears of their users. Homologies can be developed in 'integral' ways (see chapter 2) through further selection, within and between items, and through their material and symbolic manipulation and modification. If physical *objective possibilities* cannot be changed, self-representations and projections constructed out of them can be used in similar dialectical ways. New crystallizations of subjective feelings and dispositions provide the bases and means for new action to select and adapt the objective possibilities of preferred items. Think of children's play as the father of the man. Children make upside-down chairs into castles or ships, they rename toys, they animate dead objects with imaginary life. In adult life the much fabled tendency to repetition and standardization in cultural commodities, the multiplication of the simulacra, meet a counter-tendency: their differential use in practices of symbolic work. In use all things are different, the same things made diverse and multi-faceted through the human work of appropriation. Commoditization aids this by providing cultural items, literally now from a global range.

In *Common Culture*, a young English woman explains that reggae music is 'heart music' for her, a means to express and reflect her deepest feelings and sympathies, which nothing else provides. A young white man describes how the musical expression of 'sufferation' (oppression) taken from Bob Marley had helped him to name, to comprehend and to come to terms with his own unpleasant school experiences. In these two cases no other means (formal, educational, traditional) had enabled them to put a handle on and to come to terms with their own experiences and feelings. A creative taking over of a different geographical, race and class experience from half a world away – through the commodity form of music – had allowed them to seize symbolic control over their experiences and an experiential control over a symbolic form.[4]

Appropriation also occurs when cultural practices combine or recombine selected items helping to produce something new. Cheap tape-recorders and cheap tapes have made it very easy to tape off-air, easy to tape off friends' records, easy to copy tapes at will, easy to circulate them informally. Many young people make their own 'theme' or 'mastermix' tapes, organized according to their own interests in tempo, beat or genre. Here lies one of the causes of the copyright crisis affecting the music industry, and so a public as well as a private challenge to commodification.

In style and fashion, symbolic materials are not only selected from a pre-set range, but also appropriated in combination from different ranges, from different fields and from different times (second-hand markets, retro-style, cross-dressing), according to personal meaning and the development of meaning in everyday life contexts. Outfits are assembled from diverse sources, thereby overcoming the routinized or commoditized meanings in any one of them, a hybridity also strangely encouraged by their very commodity form. The same female outfit may, for instance, include a Tshirt from a sportswear shop, Doc Martin boots from an Army and Navy store, a male jacket from a second-hand market and smart trousers from Next.

Personal clothing statements are also statements about, or experiments with, possible collective affiliations and personal identity. Only those ignorant of, or growing up before, the explosion of subcultural style can be innocent about how they dress, imagining themselves, somehow, to dress to 'keep warm' or to be anodyne 'smart'. Young people know there is an inescapable social meaning in clothes usage. Outgoing messages produce socially franked incoming messages. One young woman calls clothing 'costumes'; and she tries on different costumes in different situations to test out other people's responses. In general the line between paid work and leisure and attitudes towards both are drawn by and through clothing.

All of this is not simply about a greater facility with code, with manipulating the hieroglyphics of style for its own sake, though it is certainly that in part; it is also about cultural practices of sensuous usage to 'hold' personal meaning as an aspect of identity. As one young woman says, 'If I try something on and I know I like it, then I know I'm that kind of person.'

Commercial producers certainly understand these practical skills and the symbolic work accomplished by consumers far more than most educators and policy makers (the entrepreneurial cultural bourgeoisie ahead of the institutional bourgeoisie). Modes of address assume and leave space for the appropriations of consumption – fetishism imagining de-fetishism. The cultural entrepreneurs leave the dots to be joined up, or even recoded altogether. This is the only way to 'read' youth magazines (*Just 17*, *Mizz*, *Sugar*) which do not provide sequenced arguments and items on an omniscient editorial voice. All the time they look outwards to, assuming knowledges of, the modern community/electronic cultural landscape.

Realism may be a dominant form in visual communication, but there is a genre of tabloid 'TV gossip' journalism which is devoted to important aspects of practical deconstruction, to how the realist image is fabricated – gossip about stars moving, what they are paid, production problems and accidents etc. These invitations to deconstruction are taken up in daily life, with a discussion reported in *Common Culture*, for instance, about Bobby's famous return to *Dallas* being determined by the actor's sudden availability even though it led to an absurdity in the narrative structure. This general capacity to detach and take apart some of the elements of realism makes all textual meaning relatively 'up for grabs', open to personal taking over for internal symbolic purposes.

Appropriated items can be detached and creatively applied to a consideration of real-life issues and dilemmas. The young man taking over 'sufferation' as an appropriate term for his own experience also changes and reorganizes that experience – in this case finding a new way to understand schooling as a historical institution and social force, rather than just as an apparently random and disorganized site of his own personal suffering.

A discussion among groups of young women starts from a consideration of Mary's turn to prostitution in *EastEnders* and soon develops into a discussion about their own lives, taking the provided representation into their own experience as template and tool. When might prostitution be justified? Is prostitution immoral? Is it a question of personality or situation?

Romance in stories, magazines, TV and film was appreciated for itself and to an extent in the realist mode, but their evident artificiality was also a spur to disagreement and elaboration of personal experience and difference. Endings are not usually happy. Romance dies in the grit of the everyday. Sometimes men needed 'a good kick in the donkey's' to prevent their romantic interest turning into or being unmasked as a cynical trick to 'get what they always want'.

There is another point to be made about dominant realism. Not only do consumers separate image from reality, but through the work of appropriating texts and applying them to their own reality, they learn something about their own reality – that, never mind the texts, reality itself is composed partly of representations, of how we pose the meaning of our own and others' behaviour to ourselves and others. The materials for this representation to ourselves may be provided, but they can also be to some extent controlled: refused, elaborated, made contextual, run in parallel, played off against one another. Provided forms are all grist to the mill of daily meaning-making. We know the grist, but underestimate the mill! An accumulation of appropriated materials becomes a horizontal currency of informal life and understanding carrying embodied meanings quite different from the apparent 'vertical' meanings supplied, for instance by realism. Nor am I indicating here an accumulation of multiple static moments derived from an encoding/decoding model. The decoding 'moment' is also part of a connected dynamic practice of symbolic work, which changes, so to speak, the possibilities for all other moments of decoding. Signs, symbols, meanings, images, catch phrases and styles are not simply decoded; they are appropriated and circulated, applied to new ends in context.

These abstract points are perhaps most graphically and concretely realized in the case of the informal circulation and new production of musical forms. As we have seen, the humble tape-recorder is used to produce mastermixes for circulation among friends, to detach music from its vertical moorings in the music software industry. In twin-deck form, the tape-recorder is also at the heart of the DIY musical phenomenon, in which, with other technologies of the home and private consumption (turntables and amplifiers), it is used as part of the technical means for producing informal, 'living-room', scratch, rap, house, rave and dance music. The musical resources of the record industry are selected, taken over, broken down, appropriated and reassembled into new forms, which are informally circulated within developing musical and cultural communities. Of course, the whole commoditizing process has dipped back into DIY music, so already changing its meanings, as well as priming future possible informal circuits.

Imagine a multiplicity of different circuits all combining at different stages, and DIY music can stand as a material model for the general symbolic possibilities for the de-fetishization of cultural commodities in the hidden labours of informal culture.

Social becoming

On the edge of new sets of social relations we interpret them according to the old. We shall not find collective certainties in what would now be the provincial idiocy of homespun searches for the authentic and the organic. New cultural practices will provide no holy ground for the 'common good' to stand on, no protected space for 'old times' rationally to work through and throw off the temporary plague of commodity fetishism.

I am not in the design office of the world – nor are you. Were we really the gods of our old paper conceits we surely would have fashioned differently: fashioned for a world of citizens, not consumers, for buying and selling to be subservient functions, not the very conditions of our existence, for the efficient meeting of real need, not the inflaming of extravagant desire. But these are backward-looking dilemmas. We need new ways of understanding the 'revelatory' qualities of informal cultural production.[5] This will not be, indeed if it ever was, in the form of any one settled set of discursive representations wholly opposing, or taken to oppose capitalist relations. Rather than look for better, other or different whole representations we may have to look for eruptions in the very materials in which representations are shaped, to look for refusals, subversions, ironizations of received forms. Cultural practices rather than finished consciousness have to be the ethnographically imagined stuff of embodied social vision.

Grounded aesthetics

The cultural practices of creative consumption burst the category of the passive receiver and *penetrate* possibilities for the de-fetishization of cultural commodities and the relocation of their social meaning. Varieties of artistry in lived cultural forms exploit the intrinsic contradiction that, even though (perhaps because) commoditized meanings are fetishized, they are actually highly suited to forms of sensuous meaning-making. Living cultures which derive their meanings from the specific relation of parts rather than from concentrated linguistic expression are well poised to mine the potentials and socio-symbolic possibilities of culturalized codes and culturalized material use values. Lived cultural forms accept the invitation, overlooked or refused by others, to promote the internal tendency of the de-fetishization of the cultural commodity into an external reality of real social de-fetishization, of an albeit alienated social art. Lived cultural forms complete some strange new communities of meaning under the noses of an uncomprehending, though presiding, capitalist system.

In their untutored rejection of 'legitimate culture' and associated liberal education forms, and in their turn towards cultural commodities, breaking their fetishized shells, popular cultural practices also make a parallel penetration, or mute critique, of formal textual aesthetics.

The traditional or institutional aesthetic has been firmly reified and cut off from human process: it is 'in' things – paintings, pictures, texts, scores. The protective and supportive nineteenth-century institutions have produced this execution of meaning in their promulgations of 'aesthetic distance', timeless objects and breathless auras. High art objects say: 'appreciate, not use me'. Against this, the grounded aesthetics of informal cultural practices put sensuous human activity at the heart of things in the multiple performances of consumption rather than fixed performance to score. They exploit rather than stand aloof from the imperative feature of the cultural commodity: 'use me'; 'use me', perhaps for solid bodily holding of alternative identity and sensuous knowing. You might say, contrastingly, that bourgeois culture has always been tricked by its own enigma, seeking escape from alienation and fetishism in romance, in changelessness, in the still world of auratic objects.

It may be the very homelessness and dirtiness of informal cultural production (reflecting the alienation of the commodity) that guarantees its perpetual motion and inoculates against the creeping auras of things insidiously absorbing the human properties which made them. This immanent critique is, in different form, the stock-in-trade of textual modernism for most of the twentieth century (bricolage, surrealism, deconstruction). But modernism as textual formalism preserved in institutions functions to reproduce social and cultural divisions and to make cultural elites socially unconnected – to widen the gulf between mental and manual labour. In practice, symbolic work functions *sensuously* to break down that division from the manualist side.

Expressive labour power

The development of an expressive labour power is the precondition, medium and result (in more developed form) of symbolic work. Its practical and experiential exercise demonstrates the almost infinite range of potential application and extension of human powers. Here is a sensuous basis for 'sensing' that not only is the capitalist purchase of labour power for a low fixed price an unfair exchange, but also that its repetitive and disciplined instrumental use limits rather than extends human possibility. The inhuman use of labour power in wage labour implicitly counterpoints its expressive use in 'leisure'.

Even if it is mediated through commoditized relations, the exercise of expressive powers is an impulse towards seeing and needing others as expressive selves in mutual pursuits of intersubjective recognition, so embodying, if not expressing, a wider critique of how vertical structures seek to make us treat each other like objects to control. Further, the processes of detaching signs, symbols and materials from provided vertical channels for lateral use and circulation and for the expressive 'holding' of meanings provide a resource against instrumental domination exercised through abstract reason and mentalized communication. Think of communist Russia. The linguistic discourses placed everyone, described 'reality' and subject positions within it, but cultural and material practices, especially linked with the use of Western commodities – Young Communist League badges with pictures of John Lennon on the back – maintained another meanings system which finally helped to overthrow the communist 'regime of truth'.

Abstraction and intellectuality are the key characteristics of the much commented on rise of the 'weightless economy' and the 'knowledge/information society', in which expertise takes on ever increasing importance in the regulation of modern individuals[6] abandoned in seas of detraditionalization. On their own linguistic grounds, forms of subjection and placement arising from abstraction and intellectualism are difficult to oppose. But grounded aesthetics, sensuously held alternative meanings and expressive labour power all provide implicit alternative meanings and positions, so evading the tendency of verbal discourse to make the self merely an artefact of external control systems. If there is only meaning in language, then 'governmentality' exercized through linguistic means can slice through the social like a knife through butter, but if there are other 'sense-making' materials and practices to work through, then there can be resistance to the knife of mental domination.

Semiotic differentiation

There is a bursting of categories intrinsic to the possibility of the functioning of expressive subjects, an outcome as well as a precondition for post-commodity cultural practices of informal meaning-making. This is a bursting of the unitary social subject *from within* – a move towards what can be termed the semiotic differentiation of the subject, a lived out sense of artifice and construction.

I would argue that in a newly emerging 'structure of feeling' there is a tendency for lived relations to reflect and develop the instability of the cultural commodity in a very widespread sense of inauthenticity, a feeling that everything is fake. No one believes anybody else any more. Even when they are not fetishized to begin with, communications can be fetishized from below. Just because you understand a message does not mean that you should believe it, still less obey it. There is a suspicion that all communities are half made, that communities presenting themselves as real are thereby attempting some manipulation or fraud. Just as weddings are now organized to ensure the best possible video of the happy occasion, and bringing home good holiday snaps is proof of the good holiday, all 'natural' communities and communications somehow only exist in the future or in projection. The plague of inathenticity both determines and limits the hopeless search for the real, but meanwhile teaches scepticism concerning the viability of imposed social meanings.

Popular cultural texts are internally aware of artifice. On top of their natured fetishism, they tell of their own construction in an almost Brechtian way. Self-conscious cleverness, punning and cross-references to themselves and between genres make up the very stuff of, for instance, modern advertising. It is no particular feat any more to be able to spot artifice in representation and the ever delayed arrival of whatever 'reality' might be. As advertising differentiates its markets, so it differentiates different kinds of ties of the symbolic to the real. Advertising provides different, conflicting and cross-cutting appeals or 'hails' to the subject also providing different and conflicting views about what different products can do for whom. In the practical recognition that not all claims can be true, the semiotically differentiated cultural subject is born or strengthened.

Not only this, but advertising for the same classes of product changes over time ('You must have the new improved...') and contradicts itself, so further teaching about variable desire rather than about fixed need. New products betray old products which were advertised as originals, for example the fiasco over Coca Cola's launch of the 'new coke' a few years ago. New (soon to be false) meanings usurp previous (therefore false) meanings all the time. Newly peddled desires negate old 'authentic' positives every day. But subjectivities are not reassembled every time a new product appears, and they are differentiated with respect to representation. People do not believe everything they see and hear, so they are under permanent pressure to assemble a semiotic working world and its possibilities for themselves, to make new orderings of personal signification as ordinary events. Especially for subordinate groups this is likely to take place not only abstractly through the reordering of signs but through the sensuous and practical de-fetishizations of cultural commodities in concrete local cultural practices of socio-symbolic meaning-making. But even these practices can never provide the more 'organic' connection of pre-commodity cultures. This is enforced by the continuing fetishism of the cultural commodity. Irony pervades even the most 'down home' use of what can never finally be 'at home'. The eternal dance with irony maintains the role of artifice.

'Body out' social classification

Cultural commodities have a special relation to social representations. Pre-existing social representations are meanings systems, and therefore find their way into, indeed are always already part of, 'meanings' commodities. Race, class, gender, sexuality, regionality, age – these are now perhaps mainly carried through and depend for their reproduction on the medium of the cultural commodity and electronic communication. Cultural commodities are ever more honed to the sensuous, to the tactile and to the micro-emotive, adapted to the direct sculpting, changing, projecting of the human body and its intimate styles of being and relating – all resting on forms of social classification.

But subversion (see the previous chapter) within texts and artefacts can produce a subversion of received social classifications. Embedded in cultural commodities, social representations are equally subject to the latter's internal contradictions, 'double naturing' and instability. The continuing fetishistic bit of the cultural commodity form here operates to limit and disturb the meaning content of social representations, sloughing away the naturalness of their origins, preventing a naturalization in their destinations. At the same time, a vast array of 'culturalized codes' and 'culturalized commodities' produce embedded, semi-coded use values related to gender, ethnicity etc. These may recycle aspects of received stereotypes and classification, but they do so chaotically, multiply and in separated chunks. These are 'up for grabs' in new socio-symbolic assemblies of meaning, posing the possibility of new styles and articulations of identity. This allows the possibility of personal constructions of identity in relation to social classification, so to speak 'body out', not 'society in'. Being sexy, sexual and desirable as chosen exercises of personal power is a different thing from externally imposed prescriptions and proscriptions of sexuality and gender. A somatic 'holding' of meaning can resist or ironically embarrass external domination and positioning.

Take the case of the apparent transparency and user-friendliness of Hollywood films. These may naturalize and circulate traditional representations of social identity, but these things (like the commodity) can never be whole. The 'other side', the fetishized side, of commodity meaning can subvert the social representations it carries. This gives 'the space' for informal cultural practices to find and make varieties of different meanings and their own embodiments of form, for identifications to slither or find unexpected channels, not least in partial or whole support for the 'bad guys' along lines of class, gender or ethnic loyalties.

Systems of social representation are not clapped on from above and riveted by realist texts, trapping social subjectivities underneath. The age of commodity domination has brought all kinds of defeats, disruptions and distortions; but it also makes unstable the received systems of cultural identity and social representation, rendering them up for potential mismatching and rematching. I am not disputing that oppressive meanings may be reproduced and emphasized in advertising, for instance, but equally the latter may open up a field for construction and creativity. Informal cultural practices and varieties of symbolic work may not be able to generate wholly new ways of being black or female or working class, but they can resist the old ones and innovate in the reassembly of the available 'bits' thoroughly stirred up by commodity relations.

The mobilization of a commoditized masculinity can resist or embarrass class or race domination; the mobilization of a commoditized femininity can resist religious ideology or gender domination. Once embarked upon, the rematrixing and re-permutation of systems of social representation offer almost endless possibilities. They offer demythologizing and re-mythologizing of meaning systems to combat patterns offered downwards from ideology or hegemonic manipulation. New mobilizations of representation may be 'dirty', rather than politically correct. They may be packed with ironic and unintended consequence, but they make old-fashioned – and repressively reproductive in their turn – traditional class and gender cultures and race nationalisms.[7] Currently, there may well be more progress on cultural mixing and hybrid ways of living in the popular classes than in progressive intellectual classes, the latter 'feeling' things only with their heads in dry mantras of race, class and gender, divorced from any ethnographic imagination of their sensuous wrigglings and interminglings on the ground.[8]

6

Social Reproduction as Social History

Varieties of informal cultural production and reproduction produce 'long tides' of influence and form beneath the surface waves of visible social history. For instance, the type of reproduction and voluntary application of labour power to the least economically favoured manual occupations is of critical significance to the whole of society, to the nature of its lived cultural forms and to the 'fixing' of other fundamental relations, including male/female, mental/manual and black/white. Particular uses of, and meanings derived from, cultural commodities and electronic communication now colour the whole of our lives in ways which, as we have seen in the previous chapter and as we shall explore in this one, change how crucial aspects of the social order are penetrated and reproduced.

Fundamental economic and social changes since the mid 1970s, when *Learning to Labour* was researched, have certainly made the reproductive balances of British society more jagged, cynical and unstable. Whether for the fraying edges of a still-dominant traditional reproduction or for the loose ends of newly developing ones, a central question concerns how far inherited social themes and divisions will find continuing mutual restraint in lived cultural forms. Capitalism may be glad that the dragon of working-class culture and solidarity is slain, but what dragon's teeth have been sown?

Modernist sources of social stability

I caught 'the lads' of *Learning to Labour* at the end of what was perhaps the last great golden period of working-class cultural coherence and power in a fully employed Britain. At least 'the lads' all got jobs. That is not so for their counterparts now, both in the UK and in other industrial societies. For one major change affecting the male working class has been the massive rise in unemployment, and particularly youth unemployment.[1] Since the early 1980s youth unemployment rates in the UK have hovered between 20 and 30 per cent for the white male working class; much higher for the unqualified and inner-city dwellers; higher still, by a factor of two or three, for black groups.

So manual expectations of a wage have been removed for substantial groups of the working class, the *threat* of its removal made a permanent condition for all workers. To comprehend the impact of this fully it is important to see that the wage is not simply an amount of money. It is certainly the only naked reward for labour under capitalism, and so provides access to cultural commodities and services and to the creative forms of the cultural practices explored in the previous chapter. But the wage is also the crucial pivot for several other processes, social and cultural transitions quite unlike itself.

Most importantly, perhaps, the wage is still the golden key (mortgage, rent and bills) to a personal household separate from parents and separate from work, from production. The home is the main living embodiment of the labourer's 'freedom and independence' from capital – apart from engagement in wage labour, of course, which is the price of the independence of the separate home. But this price really does purchase something. The household is an area of privacy, security and protection from the aggression and exploitation of work, from the patriarchal dependencies of the parental home, from the vicissitudes of the market place. The separate home is still a universal working-class objective, and its promise of warmth and safety more than offsets the risk and coldness of work. Waged work is still the key to its opposite. No wage is no keys to the future.

The loss of the male wage also interrupts the main form of the social and cultural preparation for a working-class transition into the separate household in our culture – the formation of 'the couple' and the preparation for the nuclear family. Gaining access, and giving access, to the male 'family wage' is still one of the important material bases for the courtship dance, romance and love-pairing ideology.

To get out of the parental home on the best terms and to think about starting her own family a young woman needs the greater earning power of the male wage (still on average about 60 per cent more than hers). For a young man to make ends meet, with all the additional expenses of a separate home, he needs 'free' domestic labour to realize the maximum value from the subsistence commodities purchased with his wage. This gives an affective scope for female deference to, admiration for and emotional sustenance of the male, and for the male care and patriarchal protection of the female.

There are also very important cultural and subjective transitions associated with being in the realm of formal production itself. Despite the hardships and sacrifices of modern work, there is, nevertheless, a kind of enfranchisement into a general political adulthood associated with going to work. This is much more than the possession of the vote once every five years. It is a direct personal involvement in the day-to-day 'struggle against nature' to provide for human wants and needs. Of course, domestic work and production is very important and has been underestimated, but the dominant, collective mode of production is the capitalist one, and it is anyway permanently invading and commoditizing domestic functions. Even if you are the weaker and exploited partner in that capitalist production, you are still part of the drama, part of the associated power struggles, part of the main material way in which we make ourselves and our futures.

Partly this is a question of democratically sharing in some of the powers of trade unionism. But it is also a question of sharing in some of the cultural practices, informal creativities and 'secret' struggles for control at work. Workers in groups continuously seek to produce their own cultural world at work addressed to, or having the effect of, among other things, humanizing production and exerting some control over the pace and organization of work. The grain and daily fabric of work consists of the hourly battles and negotiations with supervisors who are trying permanently to wrest this power back, or, through modern employee-centred techniques, trying to colonize the informal world and make it function in line with management ideology and purpose. Also, those in work know how things are made at a material level. They have experience and practical knowledge about how the world goes on 'behind the scenes'.

These real and contested social relationships and experiences are necessary to the development of an adult and worldly view of social relations: knowing how to place and judge people; knowing who is likely to be against you, who for you; knowing when to speak and when to be silent; knowing what makes things tick. These experiences and struggles also supply social contacts and successive social relationships which help to build up a sense of the social and cultural geography of the locality, town or city.

The wage, therefore, also enables a series of cultural enfranchisements on top of entering into the world of consumption. It brings a sense of self and maturity which is achieved through insight and experience rather than through the mere acquisition of years, or through someone else's say so, or through an institutional 'certification'. Youth unemployment brings broken economic transitions but also broken cultural, social and political transitions. A variety of other transitions, or perhaps now, cycles, are emerging in practical state-sites for the ethnographic imagination and explored in various ways throughout this book. For the permanently unemployed, though, old transition points have become permanent states of social pain.

In the UK we have been suffering from these broken transitions for two decades, and it is still the case that no new transitions or alternatives have been forged for the long-term unemployed. Redundant skills, energies and passions have not found new objects and outlets. It is almost as if workers were stuck with the negativity of their own essence: what is the point of a working class without work? The sufferings of being without a wage are compounded by denied access to the world of self-construction through creative uses of purchased commodities. In terms of the processes discussed in part I, it is not so much the case that unemployment has ushered in a new set of lived penetrations and attendant *reproductions* as that the old processes continue but have been thrown into permanent crisis – truly the teeth grittings of a much less harmonious social balance. There are still plenty of male working-class kids like 'the lads' who are willing, perhaps more willing than ever, to take on exploited manual work in the same masculine and anti-mentalist ways as before: evidence itself of the inflexibility and long duree of locked cultural forms. But there is not enough work to go round, so many are left in suspended animation. The lucky ones, at least to start with, feel grateful for any work, though job insecurity, or the deceptive lure of job hoping as an antidote to the wearing down of repetitive or heavy labour, threatens at any moment to freeze-frame their limited joy. Nevertheless, simple gratitude and escape from vertiginous despair have become very important reproductive mechanisms for those finding or holding on to work.

It is a measure of the severity of the worsened conditions of (especially the lower strata of) the working class that the flat plain of what was formerly a qualified and honourable defeat – voluntary entry into manual work – is seen as a golden age and that any kind of work entry has been raised to the very pinnacle of aspiration. Making conditional what should have been a birthright, working-class kids now have to aspire to their own necessary status! Pay cheque slaves, celebrate your chains! Or the prospect of them. Obedience and conformism are necessary not just to gain qualifications but to work at all.

A succession of training programmes and special labour market measures have attempted to bridge the gaping holes left by the collapse of the old transitions. Most recently the New Deal[2] programme for young people in the UK has been presented as the centrepiece of New Labour's 'third way' policy. In all programmes work experience is a central mechanism jammed in to maintain work socialization or, as I would say, to keep barely understood processes of reproduction functioning intact. These are toothless and motionless cogs unable to take up the spin of previous cultural processes, and the central dynamic of access to a decent living wage is not on offer. Nevertheless, despite widespread discontent with schemes there is surprisingly little outright opposition or social refusal. This may be explained in part by some bleak, inturned and individualistic additions to the reproduction repertoire whereby individuals blame themselves for their lack of work and for the lack of success that scheme attendance brings. Individualizing and internalizing a structural problem, they reproach themselves, one by one, for their inability to find work. Having been given so many training opportunities to develop their own individual employability, and having being told repeatedly that finding work is a question of permanent individual job searches, it must be their own *individual* fault when they cannot find work. Quite apart from the institutional encouragement, self-blame is always an insidious and treacherous possibility once a major crisis hits a collectivism which does not understand the full structural provenance of its own forms and conditions.

There may be new 'under-class'[3] cultural forms developing – exaggerated, and not yet so discontinuous with basic working-class-inherited forms and experiences – in which 'work refusal' and 'scheme refusal' do protect its members from the unreasonable and profoundly contradictory official expectations of (hopeless) permanent job search and from the dreadful contradictions of maintaining a life-long, always forcibly suspended, willingness to work. Such refusal responses penetrate that, at a collective level, schemes and training are mainly solutions, not for their trainees, but to the state's need for civil order and to employers' needs for a flexible and expanded supply of labour, with individuals competing against each other, so increasing the motivation of all and holding down general wage levels. Refusal constitutes a kind of inchoate recognition, a general class suspicion, a kind of somatic scepticism about all mental/linguistic messages and their locating institutions, that 'expert' control systems are about adapting individuals to structural processes and requirements through an *appearance* only of responsiveness to the individual and individual need. Refusal is a 'stop loss', stoic defensive position against mistrusted and opaquely clever institutional regulation. It maintains an almost unconscious collectivism of manualism as a last bastion against all exploitations executed through mental forms.

For those who refuse to join state schemes and/or the legitimate labour market, 'blagging' from parents and others, 'black' work, crime, drug dealing, prostitution, varieties of hustling and benefit fraud offer some income, as well as entanglements with youth justice systems, the prospect of criminal records and even custodial sentences with the subsequent exclusions they bring from the diminishing hope of formal work. But the freedom of the streets seemingly may offer an attractive alternative to the mental and physical incarceration of endless state schemes.

Single, unemployed women headed households can also find a practical logic in the manipulation of an increasingly mean and coercive state into the minimal provision of housing and the sub-minimal meeting of daily and generational biological reproduction costs. This penetrates 'the trick' of how the social costs of replacing future factors of production (preparing labour power) are shuffled off onto individual, overstretched, underpaid and both parent working families. At the risk of penury, increasing vilification and the playing of various victim, deviant or dependent parts, it is still possible for single mothers to explore, creatively, how it may be possible to turn the welfare state safety net (designed for those who fall, temporarily, from the conventional routes) into a net of alternative possibility, in which to weave new kinds of transition into adulthood when the old ones seem truly dead.

Under conditions of chronic unemployment, it may be functional for social stability that a slice of the young and potentially most disruptive of the unemployed of both sexes should withdraw themselves into more or less self-pacified positions, excluding themselves permanently from the labour market, so withdrawing from it seeds of non-cooperation and rebellion. Ideological projections of an under-class and its degeneracy, and the mounting economic victimization and attempted restigmatization of single mothers, may also provide an object lesson *pour encourager les autres*, and putative grounds for compensating feelings of superiority for those massed ranks just above them who struggle on in all-working households surviving at subsistence wages. But this is a raw and open form of reproduction very different from the more settled, if mystified, forms uncovered in *Learning to Labour*.

The crisis of masculinity

There are important consequences and implications for gender forms, identities and relations arising from the changes in and unravellings of inherited forms of social reproduction. In particular, working-class masculinity may be losing its traditional moorings in the churning currents of economic change. The rapid diminution of manual work generally available but especially the loss of work and the wage for very substantial and concentrated groups may have profound consequences for the traditional senses of working-class masculinity.[4] Masculinity is becoming disconnected from labour and from the staged postings of traditional transitions. The sense of being a man has been tied up historically with doing, and being able to do, physical work. This is, in part, because of some of the direct and sensuous qualities of traditional work – its heaviness, difficulty and dirtiness. The toughness and strength required to 'do the job' can both obscure economic exploitation and be the basis for some dignity and collective identity which partially reverses the conventional ordering of class and status. It allows some active and positive accommodation within the worst term of the mental/manual split. There can be some masculine pride in manual work. It can be superior to sissy and paper-pushing work.

But work also supports masculinity in less direct and 'physicalist' ways. The possession of the wage itself and involvement in the 'mysteries' of production can bring a 'secret structural guarantee' for masculinity. There was a long struggle by male trade unionists in the nineteenth century for the family wage, one that could support their wives and children at home if necessary. On average, male wages in the UK are still about one and a half times greater than women's. The importance for a man of being the breadwinner runs deep in traditional working-class culture. What we can think of as 'breadwinner power' is one of the bases for the still unequal power, status and cultural relations between men and women both in the home and out of it. It is the breadwinner who must be cosseted, fed well, laundered and rested, so that he can return to work tomorrow to bring the bacon home again tomorrow night. It is the breadwinner who brings home mysterious bits of things, 'foreigners' to enchant (especially the male) children and who 'knows someone' who can get or fix this or that. It is the breadwinner who brings home exotic tales in safe dinner-time intimacy from the dangerous and exciting external world of power, deals and wealth creation. 'Respect me for what I do, know and make, not just for what I am' is the secret guarantee of production for masculinity. Compared with this, domestic work in the home is seen as mere maintenance rather than invoking the power of production: it reproduces what was there before in a very homely circle of a small world unconnected with the weighty world outside.

Of course, work and the wage is not an unmitigated 'good' for working-class men. I am exploring some of its gender meanings under capitalism rather than voting for it. Especially in modern production processes, work can be boring, repetitive and mindless, as well as heavy, difficult and dangerous. Work takes a physical toll of health, safety and mental balance. No amount of 'masculine definition' can render this something else entirely. Often there is an element of self-sacrifice in men's attitude to work – a slow spending of the self through the daily cycle of effort, comfort, food, sleep and effort. But the sacrifice brings the wage, which keeps the home fire burning, and, besides, 'the kids will have a better chance'. So there is dignity and meaning even in sacrifice. Also it gives a kind of emotional powerhold over other members of the family who do not make the sacrifice.

I am arguing that the disappearance of work, and particularly of manual work, and the wage produce a very particular crisis for traditional working-class masculine senses of identity and meaning. Their bases are removed or broken. There are no chances even to make the sacrifices, no dignity from that. One possibility is simply depression, disorientation, personal decline and pathology. Routine suicide stories in the papers now read matter-of-factly 'depressed about being unemployed...', 'fed up with being skint...'. Unemployment is certainly one of the causes of an alarming statistic: in the UK, now, men under 25 are four times more likely to commit suicide than young women, and their life expectancy is fully five years lower than women of the same age.

But especially for young men, expecting perhaps but not yet having experienced this pattern of sacrifice-reward-dignity, there are some other possibilities. One form of the resolution of the 'gender crisis' among young men may be an aggressive assertion of masculinity and masculine style for its own sake. If the essential themes, values and personal identities of masculinity concern toughness, resilience, personal power and the expectation of respect, and if they are no longer supported by 'the secret guarantees', then they must be worked for and secured through more direct display and the making of 'home-grown' transitions and rites of passage. Male power may throw off its cloak of labour dignity and proletarian respectability with possibly dire consequences, especially for working-class women. This may involve a physical, tough, direct display of those qualities not now automatically guaranteed by doing productive work and being a breadwinner. 'Dare to say I'm not a man!' 'Respect me, not for what I do, but for what I am!' Setting their own tests and standards for 'being a man', phalanxes of unemployed and other men in the subsidized gyms are perfecting their biceps, 'six packs' and body contours, working on if not with the body. This has a logic of its own and certainly exposes the paucity of other rites of passage and of other safe tracks of identity testing when a job is not available.

Toughness in varying combinations with age and ethnicity has always been part of the youth cultural and school-yard landscapes

and there is a renewed panic in the UK about male, white, working-class academic underachievement. Recently the Chief Inspector of Schools in England expressed concern about this group,
linking their underachievement to the possible emergence of an
anti-education culture and to the disappearance of relevant work
in some local labour markets: 'is it that employment prospects for
boys are bleaker than they are for girls and that there is no
motivation for boys to work?'[5]

Since many young men are trapped in the overcrowded homes of
their parents by their inability to move, through lack of a wage, an
assertive and aggressive style may also lead to much heightened
family tensions and difficulties. The dramatic rise in homelessness
among young men in the UK is a measure of these and other
generational conflicts in the pressured home – from which the
fledglings cannot fly in the usual way.

Some (especially young) men, long-term or chronically unemployed, may be caught up, experientially, in an impossible social
contradiction. In part, the puzzle of the astonishing longevity of a
tough manualized masculinity can be ethnographically imagined in
part as the stubborn, blind wisdom of somatic opposition to the
omnipresent mentalism of expert control systems, linguistically
executed, which cumulatively and irredeemably place unemployed
working-class males materially and ideologically at the bottom.
Masculine hubris helps hold up the internal barricades, with so few
other supports, against internal acceptance of the current forms of
the ancient stigma designating the 'undeserving poor'. Yet this
general critical impulse, short of intermittent struggles with repres-
entatives of regulating expert systems, has no concrete and local
'other', no faceted and locally embedded themes, with which to
intertwine or express itself to produce a concrete and viable postindustrial individualized subjectivity. It may be that late modern
manualized masculinity can find embodiment only in the body, not
in what it does or achieves as a socially articulated cultural practice.

For men, there are no unequivocal biological triggers to set off
socially expressive courses of cultural and sexualized genderedness
and associated cultural practices, like those available to women
through childbirth, breast-nurturing and evidently sexually explicit
features of the body. If there is no immediate, only an abstract,
'other' with which to expressively intertwine, local strategies for the
ritualistic confirmation of masculinity may be essentially pointless
and self-defeating. There is nothing for such rites to express except

themselves. If masculinity can never survive as a separate essence, then free-spinning manualized masculinity turns only in its own suffering, even if, by that, expressing a universal one. Trying to express itself from a position of subordination and superfluousness, masculinity may ultimately deepen the in-turned trappedness of that social condition which it unwittingly expresses, sealing a monopoly on gendered hopelessness. Sometimes working-class unemployed white men seem to be stranded in a 'non-discursiveness', pathological rather than sensuously compensated, with no narratives, such as are available to women or minorities, about why they are where they are, who to blame, and how to get out of their situation. Gym culture man needs to find some 'other' to reveal practical ways out of the involuting tautology of an identity project which proclaims masculinity for masculinity's sake.

This may well be too pessimistic. My general position on human creativity enforces an optimism of the will. Ethnographic research will show the way by working through different imaginings. For some of the reasons analysed and outlined in this book, there is a general cultural turn towards the body and towards bodily and sensuous expression. Working-class and subordinate cultures have always tended to trust the body rather than the word. Working-class men may seem well placed to adapt to a physically based masculine expressivity. Perhaps they may really be able to convert male working-class culture to individual body culture. Their economic downfall having removed the luxuries of their own exercise of the 'male gaze', maybe some unemployed working-class males will find it better to strive to be the object of the gaze, finding or making sexualized features of the male body to enhance 'allure' to economic and social ends. Perhaps it has to be that gender relations are turned upside down at the weakest point of material male power. But where the gender game is so turned, young men may find their unlikely way into a male 'beauty trap'. For so long stung and trapped by the barbs of the whore/Madonna double bind, women might sting back at last with some binary barbs of their own: 'toy boy / useless boy'.

The currency of a tough masculine expressivity clearly has some worth if its hardness can be underwritten with some other value. Interestingly, some young *middle*-class men adopt aspects of a working-class style with which to enact their material power. Young working-class and unemployed men may also enjoy a transient prestige of macho 'street cred' before it is clear that they are transiting to nowhere. Of course pursuing criminal, black market and hustling careers provide destinations of a kind, money and also open vectors of activity and meaning which are materials to masculinize as a particular kind of style of being in the world. More generally, creative consumption of cultural and culturalized commodities can certainly generate wider circuits of informal meanings, new social threads and sentiments, new vectors of and for male expressivity. Lack of cash is, of course, a major bar for the long-term unemployed. For many the continuing problem is simply the difficulty of practically identifying and pursuing other ends and objectives to be worked through and expressed as a *kind* of masculinity: being a certain kind of man.

More speculatively, and not in my view likely to be more than a minority response, it could be that the forcible unlinking of a certain traditional male working-class identity from manual work and the wage, and from the pattern of dignity and sacrifice involved for men in wage labour, may bring about an experiential questioning of that traditional form of masculinism and its assumed divisions of labour. This could lead to softer and more open versions of masculinity and to a more thoroughly equal sharing of domestic duties and child care, for instance.[6] If there are no rewards associated with a traditional masculine interest and identity, no pay-offs in anti-mentalism, then certain educational and political potentials may also be opened up. However, the formidable cultural obstacles should not be underestimated. For instance, in the UK, mature, white, working-class male students have the lowest take up of second-chance and life-long learning opportunities within higher education.

Gender fortunes have varied greatly during the upheavals and new patterning of crisis and tension in forms of social reproduction over recent decades. Where un- or semi-skilled male manual workers have been the unequivocal losers, the picture is not so clear for working-class women. Though often part-time, low-paid and insecure, there are far more jobs for them. But female unemployment certainly persists in large concentrations in the older industrial areas and in social housing complexes everywhere in the UK. The picture is varied. On the one hand unemployment may well bring a deepening of domestic duties and oppression. The traditional roles of housewife and of child-care and child-support may not be broken but strengthened. Indeed, a much higher level of domestic production of value may be necessary anyway because the cash income into the family does not meet the market costs of subsistence and reproduction. Unemployment tends to cluster in particular families in particular areas and on particular estates. It is not uncommon for social housing estates to suffer from male unemployment rates of 60 per cent or more. Often it may be only the mother who is in (part-time) work at all, so that increased domestic production falls squarely on her in the 'second shift' and also, early on, on daughters – often while they are still at school.

It may be that the disappearance of the role of the male as future breadwinner fundamentally alters the sexual and romantic relations between the sexes. If, for a young woman, there is no longer a realistic prospect of gaining access to a family wage, or to a transition into a separate household through this earning power, then the material base for the courtship dance and the passive and subservient respect for the more skilled and power-ful man may also disappear. One feasible way to 'get your own place' may simply be to get pregnant and to rely on the state to house and support you. Though becoming increas-ingly difficult and full of its own traps, this strategy also gets you off the unemployment register and out of the indignities of suffering increasingly coercive training and work experience pro-grammes.

More positively, child rearing at least offers a clear role for unemployed young women. The work of meeting the needs of a dependent offers a purpose, and sets of instrumental and cultural practices involved in mothering form the lineaments of a life: a transition of a kind into adult status. Despite the economic hard-ships and constraints, past and future, and whether or not it is chosen by some as a conscious strategy, pregnancy certainly widens the practical, cultural and dynamic fields of choice. Com-pare its possibilities, for instance, with the dull stasis or stationary spinning facing young unemployed men. Though increasingly under threat from varieties of 'work fare', it is still a recognizable 'career' to become a 'welfare mother' in state housing. The addi-tion of a man to this arrangement, apart from for the necessary procreation, may simply be an economic and social disadvantage. The prospect for men of becoming apparently useless, except as sexual appendages, is unlikely to increase their own self-respect, already challenged on other grounds. In the UK now, only a small fraction of families in social housing are traditionally nuclear, and over 70 per cent of tenants claim social benefits of one kind or another. The social housing sector has come into a very particular relationship with new gender relations and family forms, even though its housing stock, developed mainly during the 1960s and 1970s, is overwhelmingly designed for the traditional nuclear family.

Again the possibilities here are open and contradictory. There is no clear pattern yet. The changing terms of romance and the growth of single-parent households may induce a passive dependency on the state, and an acceptance of an isolated poverty. But single-parentdom and a greater power on the jobs market, when and if work is pursued, may provide the grounds for a real independence and emancipation for some working-class women, now much more completely responsible for their own destiny than men. They may also be the grounds for a working-class gender politics around equal opportunities, equal pay, child-care, housing and other state policies. Such developments certainly constitute an exposure and implicit critique of the 'gender power' of men as based on their possession of a wage and may lead to a further demystification of love, romance and 'the perfect couple' and to stronger and more independent and creative forms of femininity.

Postmodernist sources of social stability

As fraying traditional patterns of social reproduction find tense new footings ever more grittingly in changing conditions, new forms of reproduction emerge, intertwining with new cultural forms and cultural relations. For the employed at least, and contradictorily for the unemployed, the ever increasing importance of consumption against production, the generalized commoditization of culture and fermenting cultural practices in relation to them have produced new fields for the play of penetration and reproduction.

One of my basic arguments is an ironic and baffling one: that reproduction follows, strangely, in the footsteps of creativity. What are some of the unintended and socially ironic outcomes associated with the creative use of cultural commodities as outlined in the previous chapter?

The leisure society

In general, the sheer symbolic energy, the apparent pleasures and enthusiasms which surround consumption in commodified cultural relations, have helped to shift the 'structure of feeling' in modern societies. The communications and meanings of traditional and 'responsible' bodies have been displaced or sidelined. Public broadcasters, state agencies, political parties, public institutions, schools, galleries, libraries, all have lost respect and purchase in telling you how to live the good or proper life. They seem boring and somehow judgemental, so that even their emancipatory (human, critical, independent) meanings seem to belong to a duty and worthiness as defined by others. Quite generally, society is mapped and understood more in terms of its leisure and expressive relations rather than in the more centred terms of its work or economic relations. Stress, suffering and even deprivation are seen more than ever as matters of personal and private troubles, calling for individual adjustment and modification, essentially separate from the fun-lit uplands of the consumer society, where everyone belongs, even though many are indefinitely delayed in their arrival there. Life is about fun, not work.

This can rose-colour general perceptions. There is a kind of binding into a determining set of conditions which, protean or chameleon-like, seem to offer some degree of particular space and advantage, as well as constraint and pressure. Finding some community of transcendence in musical or dance experience, finding a sense of who you are through stylistic experimentation, finding satisfactions 'in the crack' with your mates in pubs and clubs: all these things seem to have been offered as positives, or at least benignly allowed to occur, making human and bearable, even obscuring, what might otherwise have been hostile and unwelcoming.

'The Revolution will not be televised' (Nike advert) – strangely capitalism has developed new forms of accumulation based on a kind of symbolic anti-capitalism, taking its cues from the streets, stealing semiotically from already economically dispossessed and deprived communities. This dislodging and generalization seems to offer a safe distinction of resistance to everyone. Everyone resists and is voiced or allowed a space. But when everyone resists, nothing is opposed. Expressive resistances can run themselves safely out on their own circular tracks, founding serial difference rather than located opposition. The psychic pleasures of transgression are enjoined without crossing real lines of engagement.

I am not proposing simply a 'magical resolution' here, with consumption values duping innocent ideological dummies. In their different ways, all these forms of widened consumption really have opened up new areas and made possible meanings and creativities not understood, even if managed, from above. They have provided the grounds for penetrations which foster feelings of authenticity, identity and advantage, especially in comparison with proffered official and ideological roles.

Cultural 'wetbacks'

Mexican 'wetbacks' swim across the Rio Grande to work in the US for subsistence wages. Of course they are exploited, but from their point of view they are far from fools. The dollars they earn in the US are worth far more when sent back home to Mexico than ever they are where they earn them.

Many people now, but especially the young, are the cultural 'wetbacks' of the consumer society, putting up with the unacceptable at work in order to gain access to cultural goods and services, psychically worth much more to their informal cultural practices than ever they are worth in the above-ground economy. Instead of valuable dollars, they send valuable cultural commodities 'back home', where they find and make greatly expanded human value: 'music is the most important thing in my life'; 'I know I'm that kind of person when I wear something I like'; 'going out makes life worth while'.

We can also see here the power of the double oppression that unemployment brings, especially for those from poor households in which income, space, mobility and commodity deficits cannot be made up by parents or others. They are not only without money, not only without the things money can buy; they are also excluded from the possibility of the informal production of meaningfulness and identity in relation to the creative consumption of cultural commodities.

These dual worlds of counter-posed formal (wetback world) and informal (back home world) production,[7] of differently understood and differently deposited kinds of value, can produce some strange effects: the experiencing of the same things differently. Though something to be coped with and setting the material frames and possibilities of life, waged work, along with its sacrifices, disciplines and solidarities, is no longer the central axis of existence or meaning with all else its humble servants. To exaggerate to make the point, waged work, in its turn, can become a humble servant to keep another kind of production running smoothly.

The reproductive consequences of these impulses can be profound. The traditional divisions, ideologies and oppressions arising from the capitalist mode of production do not read through in the same way into the world of informal symbolic production. Indeed, far from paid work relations and wage-labour oppressions needing to be ideologized through those central categories of the Marxist system – labour power as a commodity like any other, a fair day's pay and freedom and equality under the law to sell one's labour power to the highest bidder – they may simply be suffered, without ideological adornment, as the necessary price of entry to the informal world of production – the means of recreating the power of non-alienated labour. Not freedom of contract and equality under the law for the wage labourer, but freedom and equality for informal expressive work.

Not to be overlooked either is that the production of expanded *expressive* labour power through the productive consumption of cultural commodities – more forming now for many than schooling or family – is also simultaneously the production of labour power available for application to the formal capitalist labour process. This is possibly a volatile expressive labour power which may be too developed, high-aiming and restless – surplus in its personal meanings – to fit in with the technical and repressive disciplines of the labour process. On the other hand the very mode of its production produces an inbuilt tendency to limit or sideline explicit dissatisfaction or practical discontent or unruly behaviour at work. At the same time, whole branches of industry and new branches of industry – particularly the consciousness and cultural sectors – require exactly such expanded-value labour power and may have little hope of garnering it in sufficient quantity from the formal educational sector.

Fetishism and invisible symbolic work

There is abundant evidence in *Common Culture*[8] of the vitality of cultural practices involving symbolic work, assuming, utilizing and reproducing strengthened forms of expressive labour power. This is one of the experiential bases for the development of cultural identity, in different ways, explored throughout this book and for the reproductive effects tentatively outlined in the previous section. All that is noted there may have been worth the price if there were a self-recognition of the processes and practices involved. There might then be a basis for moving through transitional moments into a more social and reflexive self-consciousness. As it is, there are reproductive losses all round.

Symbolic work and expressive labour power are theoretically imagined terms for ethnographic reconstruction and understanding. They, or similar notions or significations carrying the same weight, are not part of the vernacular of lived culture, though, I argue, their presence is visceral to its impulses and passions. Very important reproductive effects can be seen to flow from the *invisibility*, especially, of the category of symbolic work within those practices of which it can be seen to be the drive and motor.

This is aided by some very important general and ideological meanings which define only paid work as real and which emphasize the importance of measurement. Only that which can be measured can be paid for, so rendering it real work. Further, a very important inheritance from the Protestant work ethic concerns a cultural deposited meaning that work is serious, difficult and unpleasant – the opposite of fun.

Cultural practices involving symbolic work can be precisely seen simply as fun or play acting or pastimes involving passive and lazy consumption. For instance, groups of women go out on shopping expeditions to nearby towns thinking that their main activity is shopping, whereas their humour, interaction and excitement show that they are producing the main event for themselves. Shoplifting as a disease may be a desperate attempt to recreate this community, only without the people, so revealing in pathological ways the general *absorption* of informal cultural production *into* the commodity.

This is crucial: its invisibility makes it possible for symbolic work to be seen as part and parcel of what is purchased, not least for the simple reason that related cultural practices cannot take place without the purchase of, or access to, the cultural commodity. Without any popular analysis or tradition to provide a counter view, satisfactions arising from informal cultural pro-ductivity may seem to arise *from*, rather than merely in relation to, the system of provision. While the creative de-fetishizations of cultural commodities are individual and group accomplishments, they can be mistaken for things that have been purchased as part of the sale of the cultural commodity: consumers unconsciously pay-ing for the product of their own labour. This is perhaps the real and final source of the mysterious allure and fascination of cultural commodities: buying your own bottled praxis![9] But if you are buying this social effect, not making it yourself, it is not then yours to extend to the understanding and mastery of wider social and structural processes.

The new, postmodern fetishism may concern precisely this: the absorption of social labour and social relation into the commodity, not from its historical conditions and practices of production but from the surrounding practices and conditions of its consumption. Labour is fetishized not so much in being seen as a commodity like any other to sell on the labour market (the classic Marxist ideological effect)[10] as in its informal variety being invisibly sucked into the fetishism of the cultural commodity itself. This produces fetishized effects, destroying senses of process, practice and connection arising in and from human activity. This renewed fetishism of the commodity can be seen to produce a tendency in lived culture against social awareness, criticism or solidarity such as might have, for instance, produced demands for better conditions and materials for those very practices of symbolic work.

Taken in the other direction, renewed fetishism relates directly to questions of modern social and cultural identity formation. Here, instead of being absorbed into the commodity, symbolic work can be seen as being absorbed into a reified self-identity. Symbolic work is mistaken for the internal and given qualities of the person. While actually the result of cultural practices with symbolic work at their centre, identity is here taken to be a separate, intrinsic thing. This can be thought of as a fetishism of the self. Rather than as a product of labour, identity is felt as a question of immediate discontinuity, of distinction, of intrinsic personal difference, even election. Being cool, stylish, defiantly masculine, 'hard'; being a 'street revolutionary', a clubber, an alternative type; knowing your way around – street-, music- or media-wise; endless permutations of these and others; all can be experienced as qualities of individual authenticity and specialness. Creative consumers feel the control of what they buy, own and use as a psychic state, not a quality of their own labour. This increases the vulnerability of the products and styles produced by informal symbolic work and cultural creativity to be recommodified by capital in what seems to be the only legitimate field of work and production. Individualization is a pronounced feature of late modern societies; yet it is produced not only by ideological and institutional processes, but also from below by the fetishism of self-identity absorbing the symbolic work which makes it.

The variable, expanding and creative nature of expressive labour power may have become a template for judging, sensuously, the uses of instrumental labour power in the enforced speed-ups and intensifications of modern work.[11] This may well be an area of great potential future disruption and disturbance to capitalist labour processes, as well as a potential basis for collective organization around newly found common interests. But, for the moment, the invisibility of symbolic work destroys the basis for this comparison, while its real requirements (access to cultural commodities) underwrite a matter-of-fact acceptance of paid work. Consequently, expectations for satisfaction and self-development in paid work are often downgraded instead of upgraded.

Renewed fetishism along the axes discussed here can be seen to make its own contribution to the mental/manual divide. Selves and identities are extended and made more symbolically creative, but they can thereby lose the means of, or interest in, making connections with non-present others, making it harder to take the other's role, or swap or imagine other parts. Though the hieroglyph of the cultural commodity may be de-coded in immediate context, renewed fetishism lives to break off wider contact and communication, so that the abstract means of the connection of common sites and interests is being eroded in commodity culture. Increasingly, distant realities do not seem to mean anything unless there are experiential, sticky commodity bridges to them. Some things cohere; others drift loose. Some things are fun and engaging; others are distant and boring. Increasingly, commodities grant or withhold visibility.

Cultural production makes a cultural world but it does not make a perfect world, one which matches, penetrates and controls its conditions of existence. Social reproduction certainly functions through the ideologically laden nature and organization of those conditions, but it also functions through a dissonance or asymmetry between lived experience and the self recognition of its own practices. Cultural production is not self conscious enough to know how to know in its head what it 'knows in its bones'. So the creativities of informal meaning-making with commodity forms can act more generally to help deepen and to reproduce the overall mental/manual division characteristic of capitalistic societies. You might say that this could be understood as a final victory of commodity fetishism, as an ultimate loss of depth and connection, an eventual disorientation and de-stressing of social meaning no matter what the mediations or mechanisms. But the particular mechanisms, the particular reversals, the particular creativities cannot be forgotten. There is an essential openness here, necessary even to understanding closure, which maintains a tension in how the practical de-fetishizations of cultural practices might operate in any particular area, and what their outcomes might be in the future under different social, political and educational conditions.

7

The Ethnographic Imagination and 'Whole Ways of Life'

The ethnographically imagined constitution of everyday life, containing creative cultural practices comparable to those of artistic production, especially in their generation of poignant and crafted meaning, has similarities to some of Raymond Williams's conceptions and approaches, even though the latter were not ethnographically based or realized. In Williams's famous formulations, 'culture is ordinary'[1] and should be understood 'as a whole way of life'.[2] There are, however, significant differences. A view of creativity embedded in everyday cultural practices is less general, more troubled, less benevolent than Williams's view of 'ordinary', 'whole ways of life'. It is based more on specifically observed particular mechanisms, contexts and materials – school cultures, the use of cultural commodities, the meanings of unemployment – rather than on assumptions or assertions about a generalized cooperative essence (usually white and male) that guarantees working-class culture, difference and integrity. I am also less sanguine than Williams about the status of the final results of the meanings and practices of everyday creativity, less sanguine about the centredness and clear-sightedness of the humanism involved. There is no guarantee of an essential or automatic morality or goodness in the meanings of daily life, simply because they are oppositional, alternative or different.

In earlier traditions within the Culture and Society debate, intellectual work enjoyed a crucial and pivotal role in the interpretation of the everyday, living culture of the masses. As Williams observed, 'there are no masses, only ways of seeing masses', and intellectuals were the crucial mediators of this seeing. At one pole the masses were considered *backward*. They were degenerate, drunken, undisciplined hordes in need of civilizing guidance to bring them *forward*, to a settled place within the rhythms of the dominant modern order – moral, social, political, economic. At the other pole the masses were seen to contain *progressive* social bases of alternative – cooperative and mutual – social organization and vision. They were not the problem, but the solution. They were not human baggage to be dragged forward into modernity, but the means of thinking and reaching a higher social order. They contained the resources to resist and challenge the dominant capitalist order in principled ways, which, through the long march of history, would eventually replace it with something better. Either way the masses were certainly a problem for capitalism.

In general things now look very different. More or less everyone agrees that, in their contemporary clothes of 'popular culture', the cultural activities and experiences of 'the masses' work more or less, and in one way or another, in capital's logic.[3] Instead of challenging or interrupting it, the cultures of the masses support the capitalist order in one way or another. There are no large jobs of 'seeing' any more, no prospect of a modernist programme of univeralism and integration, with intellectuals in the vanguard. Intellectuals seem redundant. There are many responses to this situation, many cultural 'gardening jobs' for intellectual workers, if they can find a paymaster, or allotments to till, besides the large factory farms of bureaucratic employment, in and outside the state.

The rise and influence of postmodernist conceptions of the world, and their own ways of 'seeing' what are some real and profound changes, make it even harder to see whole, unified, 'ways of life' as the object of study. For the young especially, enmeshed in the electronic threads and the teeming illusions of the postmodern world, there seem to be no whole connected cultures any more. They may be positioned by structures, fragmented and complex, but they are positioned in many more ways by imaginary relations and manipulations. Young people may be placing themselves not so much by neighbourhood, work and family, as by leisure, media, style, music, travel and peer group. Certainly commodity and electronic desires circulate much faster than the old community meanings, but as working-class cultural representations themselves reach a semiotic escape velocity to join orbit with the general sign system, who would anyway voluntarily choose to be the signifieds of negative 'old-fashioned' signifiers denoting trappedness, limitation and subordination: signifying difference only as inferiority. You could also argue that working-class subjects, with less possibility of escape into the auratic and timeless world of bourgeois culture, know very well about 'floating signifiers' in their practical cultural activities, having been forcibly taught by experience – of work, coercive state regulation of unemployment, living commodity culture – that 'authentic' communication is impossible. Perhaps it is only some leftist cultural commentators who still hanker after the old certainties associated with working-class 'whole ways of life'.

From the postmodernist point of view, more choices seem to be available than can be made. Real choices are irreversible so seldom made. In the world of circulating representations there can be ever changing and reversible symbolic investments, in meanings rather than in materials, in possibility rather than in possession. Increasing density of representation and possibility speeds time up. Decreasing density slows it down. Time is slow in the old worlds of school and work. Time is fast in the new world of electronic and commodity leisure. The structures of the codes which regulate the flow of time and information have eclipsed the structures which regulate economic position and inequality.

But accepting some of this does not mean that concrete economic and social positions and locations have disappeared, or that symbolic materials are not used to understand them, only that the articulations and relations are changed so that we cannot look for homogeneous 'whole ways of life' any more. Williams's original definition concerned 'the theory of culture as the study of relationships *between elements* in a whole way of life. The analysis of culture is the attempt to discover the nature of the organisation which is *the complex of these relationships*' (my emphasis).[4] In the current situation we cannot expect to understand the concentration of all such relationships, ethnographically bundled into single concrete sites – maybe it never was possible, and Williams, of course, never attempted ethnographic field work. But surely it is possible to concern ourselves with more than one element at a time – which narrowness is the besetting sin of postmodernism and how the several current strands of Cultural Studies have parted ways since Williams's time.

The ethnographic imagination should concern itself with the relations within and between at least three 'elements': creative meaning-making in sensuous practices; the forms, i.e. what the symbolic resources used for meaning-making are and how they are used; the social, i.e. the formed and forming relation to the main structural relations, necessities and conflicts of society. Of course, there may be no authoritative guides to the unmediated reality of the 'structures' of the social, not least because they are a dialectical ensemble of the continuous trafficking of all the 'elements' (see chapter 3), but the point at issue is not the analyst's direct view of what the social may be, but the theoretical capacity to register, and a sensitivity and openness to, an interpretative understanding of how the symbolic forms and lived practices under study 'understand' ('live out' practically and sensuously) their social and historical location. The holistic question is not to ask for an explanation 'from the outside' of how all the parts fit together, but how, in this instance under study, is the whole challenged or strengthened, how the forms and the social connections operate in this case. There may be no overt social challenge or rebellion, but an equally interesting question is: how do these things *not* ordinarily occur? As Mayhew long ago observed, 'When times are quiet, things are brewing.' For me, the point of Williams's definition encompassing 'elements' and 'relations' is precisely that the social should not be allowed to escape.[5] It may be somewhat pruned and much harder, perhaps impossible, to pin down, but there is a limit position which enforces some analytical social depth on the study of culture.

Social class

It is in these ways that I would want to approach the continuing importance of social class. However, first let me clarify that I see

symbolic work as always having been part of working-class cultures, as part of how identities and traditions were formed. Most
often it was and is not self-recognized and is absorbed into other
things: work activity, the development of instrumental labour
power, naturalized gender and ethnic forms, home life, general
forms of practical common sense. What has changed in the contemporary commodity-culture period is that there are now many
more (commodity) materials fed into the mill of symbolic work,
which itself takes place more than ever before at 'leisure' (or at
least at non-work) sites – this is a symbolic work mistaken now to
belong somehow to the glamour of the objects or texts themselves.
There has been a shift in the centre of gravity of 'identity work',
from production to consumption sites, matching the same economic shift to the consumer in postindustrial society.

These changes can be exaggerated, or seen in too linear a fashion. Certainly work itself, but also training programmes,
'schemes', the welfare apparatus and schooling, all leading up to
work, are still, in some sense, the most important sites of activity
and experience for most people. In the UK the economically
active percentage of the population has never been higher. It is
more or less impossible to maintain an acceptable family living
standard unless both parents or partners are in work. Work,
school, training and the state have to be negotiated in ordinary
experience, every day. Even as other areas of life become more
glamorous and energizing, the problems of getting and maintaining a decent, reasonably paid job are probably greater than ever.
Quite apart from surviving the poverty, the problems of remaining
outside work on a 'welfare holiday', free from state-imposed,
work-like disciplines and responsibilities, are increasing by the
day.

But work, school, neighbourhood, home, peer and leisure
experiences do not stack up in neat cultural columns any more,
each 'element' reinforcing how the others are understood. Workers
may be hostile or indifferent to their manners, customs and cultures being bundled together, or seen only as working-class pursuits and life-styles. So the crucial questions do not concern the
disappearance of the working class as an economic category also
indicating a concrete field of constrained experience.[6] In terms of
exploitation and relations to production and surplus, what Marx
called the social inequalities 'growing directly out of capitalist

production', perhaps there has never been a more clearly marked out proletarian group – and on a world scale, perhaps never larger. There is no question that work relations and work-like relations, contacts and disciplines continue to structure huge swathes of human experience. But human passions and interests have shifted, their locating sites have changed and the symbolic grist going through their 'meaning-mills' is different and much more varied – all to some degree at least displacing, counterpointing, releasing, changing, compensating for paid work experience. The crucial questions concern how new cultural experiences and prospects, expanded and various forms of symbolic work, relate to the continuing 'culturally empty' but continuingly highly pertinent economic categories of class and production. Here I do not see the possibility of complete disarticulation, the 'production' and 'consumption' pieces of 'fractured subjects' never meeting. Nor do I see the possibility of new perfectly formed wholes linking 'elements' in a straight line: 'I'm a worker, watch Coronation Street (an English soap set in a traditional working-class neighbourhood of Manchester), go to the corner pub or Bingo hall for the crack with my mates, and see X character in such and such a TV series as reflecting my life.'

Perhaps it is a mistake to consider that class was ever such an important and profound category for explaining and organizing the empirical detail of lived experiences and concrete identities and relations. It has never explained 'most' about a person, but has always been a conceptual as well as an empirical category denoting forces and relations which provide the dynamism, tensions and contradictions that drive the direction of change in empirically observed aspects of lived cultures and relations. For instance, if you were asking questions to find out about the identity of someone you had never met, you would probably not first ask about class; probably you would start with gender, then perhaps age and ethnicity, then even perhaps whether he or she was nice or funny or good to be with, or 'what are they into?' Class would be somewhere near the rear, or assumed in asking about occupation. I am not arguing that any of the former are more important than class, only that we may need to understand types or hierarchies of importance. Non-class categories may tell you more empirically about a person, but they do not 'move' or develop by themselves. To understand principles of change or how those categories combine and develop over time, to make sense of the picture, to historicize it we need the dynamism of economic relations. To be crude, class explains more about them than they explain about it. Socially received and atavistic, often still unnamed or analysed, categories provide the sea, class the currents. Class and productive relations and commodity production provide nodal points of influence, confluence and change that allow us to organize and see the empirical 'wholes' in more ordered and interlinking ways.

These nodal points formerly concerned perhaps manual wage labour and masculinity, spatial concentration, white collar/blue collar, work/leisure, collectivity. The point of a class perspective now may not be to look for 'new' working-class cultures, but to understand the strengthening or emergence of new nodal points. Rather than concern only material resources, ideological relations and spatial arrangements, these may now also concern the conditions of cultural practices: different relations to language and to embedded forms of sensuous meaning; different access to and different types of relationships with resources available for symbolic work and for the development of the expressive self. These developments do not yet lead to clear patternings of self-consciousness and sensuous collectivity, with attendant collective interests and politics, and so are much harder to recognize. In practice we still often use the old legible patterns. Where a specific empirical attempt is made to map new cultural change we find chaos and fracture. But the toeholds of ethnographic imagination exercised through solid field work, may reveal more sensible pressure points of difference and convergence, which one day may be connected up into new, coherent, empirical maps. Though in some sense still 'classed' and 'non-accidentally' related to economic forces and arrangements, these new maps will certainly not look like the old two-dimensional and homogeneous ones.

Methodologies of field, theory and writing

There are a variety of particular methods relevant to ethnography and the exercise of an ethnographic imagination. Central are field techniques as a direct contact with, and observation of, human subjects, the essential source and grounds of the testing of 'new' knowledge. But the ethnographic imagination is relevant to the production of all kinds of intellectual work. Non-field-based writing and intellectual work can certainly inform the crafts and methods of ethnography. More generally, purely theoretical work can respect the space for subjective moments, illuminating, with respect to them, structure and structural formations. I have written about field methods elsewhere, but will summarize some of the main points here in the light of the postmodern and poststructuralist critique of ethnographic methods as constituting rather than reflecting their subject matter. I shall conclude this section with a consideration of the problems and opportunities of writing associated with a *positive* view of a self-avowedly artefactual and theoretically formulated attempt to re-create the creativities of human practice in context.

In terms of direct field relations, I have long argued for a form of reflexivity, emphasizing the importance of maintaining a sense of the investigator's history, subjectivity and theoretical positioning as a vital resource for the understanding of, and respect for, those under study.[7] But I have never argued that direct engagement and interaction with subjects can hope to produce, somehow, a 'picture of reality', or that having been in the field bestows an ethnographic authority which gives a hot line, or a guaranteed 'truth connection', to something called reality. A very important consideration for me here is that the preparation for and entry to the field is, unrecognized or not, some kind of intervention into debate, an attempt to grapple with a puzzle (How *do* working-class kids get working-class jobs?), whose temper and pace leads you to want to encounter others who bear moving parts of the puzzle. This brings along with it, implicitly or explicitly, some sort of 'theoretical confession',[8] a world view within which the puzzle is meaningful. This ethnographic imagination takes us very far from an empiricist standpoint or a self-assumption of a general ethnographic authority.

Of course, the point of engaging in field work, what impels you to face its difficulties, dilemmas and jeopardies, is to give yourself the chance of being surprised, to have experiences that generate new knowledge not wholly prefigured in your starting out positions.[9] But it is in many ways the 'theoretical confession' and type of originating puzzle that set up this possibility. You cannot be surprised unless you thought that you knew, or assumed, something already, which is then overturned, or perhaps strengthened, or positively diverted, or fulfilled in unexpectedly elegant ways.

Ethnography is the sensitive register of how experience and culture indicate, as well as help to bring about, social and structural change, but that change has to be conceptualized in ways not fully contained in ethnographic data themselves. The trick is to bring that 'registered experience' into some relation to theory, so maximizing the illumination both of wider change and of the ethnographic data.[10] Often implicit and 'on the hoof', the constant reformulation of ethnographic imaginings is the hallmark of effective field work. To repeat and clarify: the original elements of a 'theoretical confession' are not tightly structured positions looking merely for exemplification (the hallmark of pointless field work, merely the flip side of empiricism). They are the nagging issues which drive a curiosity within an overall theoretical sensibility of a particular kind.

Developing answers to evolving questions, reformulating implicit and explicit hypotheses or hunches, requires an openness (short of empiricism) to experience and data, some understanding and recording of the 'rough ground' on which research subjects stand. There is always more in the field than can be explained by existing answers. The ethnographic point is precisely to pick this up as the relevant material, always in excess, for possible (no guarantees) creative and unprefigured answers to crucial questions, in readers' heads as well as in the ethnographer's. But I insist that this pursuit of the 'open arts' of ethnography is undertaken to discover materials of relevance to basic questions within the cultural world and ethnographic imagination of the ethnographer. It is that such materials are yet to be discovered, the *specific* theories yet to be developed, which makes it necessary to have the widest and loosest, 'hunch-driven', definition of 'relevance', not that there should be no questions, nor that the world can somehow be directly presented. This 'rough ground' can be experienced and recorded only through a degree of sensuous immersion in the field, bringing aspects of the researcher's sensibility closer to, or clarified in relation to, those of agents. This is the material of 'thick description' and the recording in their 'practical state' (as they come to you) of relations and binaries which may yet have no name or attendant theoretical explanation, but which twitch somewhere as relevant on the theoretical radar and offer fertile clues for advancing understanding and for deepening your appreciation of the relation 'between elements'.

A further important focus of field interest in the ethnographic study of culture concerns recording and analysing the uses of, and meanings attributed to and derived from, objects, artefacts and texts within the life spaces of agents (see chapter 2). The point is to avoid a direct analysis of the 'meaning' of these things in favour of a more modal analysis of the type and scope of their *possible* meanings. Specific textual meanings gleaned from a direct analysis are evidence only of the researcher's own sensibility–object relations.[11] Though it is complex, the analysis must proceed through an attempt to understand this relation as it holds for those under study, proceeding through the subjective meanings and observed activities of agents to one side and a more formal, general analysis of the 'objects' to the other, paying attention to how their 'object-ive possibilities' or potentials hold, return, interrupt and develop meanings attributed to them, and to a consideration of what scope they hold, and through what mediations, for agents to change internal aspects of their structure.

Observation and participation are crucial, but a central ingre-dient of all field interaction is, of course, language. Though inevit-able, it may seem odd and contradictory that an approach trying to attune itself to sensuous and bodily meaning has to use lan-guage as the primary means of exchange in the field. But remember that this is not a question of using language as an abstract system, but of language use for a purpose in concrete contexts of location and human action. Field situations remind us again and again that there are several kinds of uses of language, only one end of the spectrum concerning the attempt to communicate abstract senses of meaning, value and orientation. Most useful are the more embedded and expressive forms of language, including the 'sunk signifiers' of culturally specific use, and the narrative forms of self-presentation by which agents become their own observa-tional ethnographers supplying data about non-linguistic forms, activities and events. Of course, there are the mediations, again, of how sensuous meaning and activity is rendered in language and of how agents select and filter their accounts through personal memory, but these biases are also sources and clues for interpretation. Linguistic representations by agents have to be taken along with data derived from different statements from different people or from the same people over time, from observa-tion and the interpretation of structural location, as well as from activity, bodily demeanour, style and the use of objects and artefacts.

Of course, the biggest language question of all concerns its uses in the 'writing methodologies' of final write up. Language can never be a mirror of reality, and, as I have outlined, the final written account can only be a product of the researcher's own sensibility (including its forming puzzles and theories) as it encounters another set of practices and practical theories among agents. This is not to lessen the literal importance of 'record'. Most would agree that there can be some consensus about what is 'objective' in terms of the external description of things. So the ethnographic account should be as rigorous as possible, recount what happened, where and when, record regularities and ensure the accuracy of transcripts and of the detail of descriptions of events and the uses of objects and artefacts. But the subjective evaluation and meaning of these things by agents, their perception and evaluation of others' evaluations and the meaningfulness held in complex juxtaposition of practices and ways of being cannot be recorded in the same way as facts. Reality itself, in the life world of agents, is composed of the fluid relation between representations, practices, juxtaposition of expressive forms, circumstances and experiences – there is hardly a solid 'original' to reflect!

The problems of the relation of language to experience are addressed from different angles throughout this book. They are especially acute in the case of the field write up. The materiality, sensuousness and simultaneity of agents' experiences and their holding of meanings or meaningfulness implicitly, or 'in solution', and in relation to preferred cultural items and in complex *in situ* relations to different types of language use, have to be rendered *completely* into the linguistic form of a continuously written text. How to form and use the written word so as to produce, in the reader's mind, the complexity and 'there-ness' of the quite differently, and in many ways antagonistically, formed original is indeed a formidable challenge. It is a multi-layered and complex task in which there can only ever be variable and partial success. Representation is always selective and transformative, putting the original in terms of something else. But this is not a roadblock to productive communication about the ways in which human beings produce their social reality. The constructedness of representation can be worked for its strengths: to produce desired ends, to influence the thinking and feelings of others, to make them critically reflect on representations which they have previously taken at face value. I am certainly open to experiments in writing, or adjuncts to conventional writing, which are intended in any form – 'it's right if it works' – to achieve the above. For me this should not be in hiding or destroying 'authorship', but, to the contrary, in taking seriously its aims and responsibilities somehow to communicate its own grounded imaginings.

I think it simply has to be admitted that the point at which an objective recording of consensual facts must give way to an attempt to communicate internal and subjective states and sensuous meanings borne in cultural practices and contexts constitutes something of an impasse and deep uncertainty for all ethnographic writing. If it is never passed or surpassed there is no 'quality'. But very often one can only say that it is has been achieved, not *how* it has been achieved for purposes of replication. The aim must be to produce an 'Ah-ha' effect in the reader, in the 'experience' of the reader. Grounded imagination is essential to these moments when new understandings and possibilities are opened up in the spaces between discourse and experience, at the same time deconstructing and reshaping the taken for granted in a particular response to the shape of a phenomenon, as well as transcending dichotomies which normally separate the elements you are trying to relate.

Of course, I understand the contradiction here: how to use the chains of arbitrary signifiers that constitute language to invoke concrete forms and sensuous meaningfulness in context. There can be no simple or formulaic answers here, no unproblematic ways through the impasse between objective and evocative writing. But I do have two sets of relevant comments.

First concerns recognizing and using the creative and evocative role of theory. Just as theory is part of the preparation for and an activity in the field, so it is part of the writing process, not as a separated and settled QED section, but as part of the adventure of the unfolding of the whole, how the ethnographically grounded imaginings develop, change or find confirmation through the course of the study. In some of the best ethnographic writing theory is mainly beneath the surface, informing but not interrupting it. Direct 'experience' can never be named empirically but it can be evinced in a passion for the invocation of complexity positioned simply in concrete forms, showing for instance the grain of experience in poignant dialectical relation to wider structures, or in holding and exploring a fascination in the conundrum that people feel themselves aesthetically to be 'free' even as, somehow oddly heightening it, they know in their social bones that they are not. Though there is a role for abstract argument, the general theoretical interest should be a quality of the direction of travel in the whole empirical sweep of the writing. The train may keep stopping at differently interesting places, but it must be on an unmistakable journey, though the final destination may not be marked at every station. This is a communication of a continuous sense of wrestling with a problem, of answering a puzzle step by step rather than all at once, of presenting 'clothed hunches', of connecting up unlike things in open and experimental fashion, of meeting imagined objections, of trying to persuade though the reader is never sure of what exactly. In such ways can be communicated something profound about the field relation itself and about *all* experience – that it is an unfolding journey over time, always contingent on the local landscape, always embodied, always occurring in order, even if accidental. Theory must connect and explain the relation of elements, but it can re-create, in second-order ways, some of the same properties and uncertainties of what it seeks to evoke.

Secondly, I would argue that it is sometimes desirable, perhaps at the stickiest moments of the impasse, to attempt to creatively evoke aspects of the 'original' through the shameless use of creative language forms – if you like, and certainly within my own ethnographic imagination, reflecting (certainly respecting) the 'original', not slavishly or empirically, but in the complement of a vaulting ambition to crest peaks in a different order of creativity. Especially when it is trying to be scientific, linguistic communication usually flattens rather than evokes phenomena, so artifice to the limits of language is sometimes necessary. Written art is needed to re-create living art. Art reproducing art! Indeed, good ethnographic writing appears to be somehow continuous with the original, not through ever extended techniques of validity, but through this honest lying. Exploit it! This can be the *only* means of presenting the 'rough ground' on which agents live and move, showing the complexity of lived relations and forms for which words and theories do not yet exist, but which somehow, in practice, and in the practical relations of the field, connect up some of the important elements that interest the researcher. So rather than shy away from, there are moments when writing *needs* – as the only possible form of putting the subject of study 'on the table' – metaphors, figures, literary turns, connotations, allusions, theatre and drama. Of course, there are no guarantees here, and forced artifice may simply lead to absurdity. But the ethnographic text which does not sometimes risk being over the top will always be under par.

Cultural politics

Of course, there are academic concerns of institutional and 'subject field' position and survival, inescapable questions of personal reputation, influence and competition, but how to socially justify the various costs and risks involved in imaginative and grounded ethnographic construction becomes a tricky issue when the pay-offs for anyone fall far short of what Williams envisaged: the ultimate grand march of the working classes to the hegemonic realization of its mutual-cooperative ideal in a new kind of society. Why bother? What's the point? Especially given the sometimes antagonistic and always unequal relations between concretely expressive and linguistic forms, why try to translate (betray?) the secrets of lived culture?

First of all, with a twinge of embarrassment, I say, 'Because, it is there.' Human existence and human forms of life exist in amazing variety, and part of our make-up, or 'species being', is to be active and expressive, as I have argued in this book, and most active in those expressive cultural practices that help to make our own sense of our selves. An inevitable part of this sense of self, because it is not fixed but reproduced through self-expression, is an expressive curiosity about our own formation. The making of the self, the human meaning-making, is the 'there-ness' that is there to be studied and is its own justification for study. The first responsibility and justification for the ethnographic study of culture is simply that it should properly do its own job of presenting this meaning-making, as fully and as well as possible at the highest level of achievable quality, methodological, theoretical and textual.

Secondly, ethnographic cultural study can bear witness between the multifarious cultures and cultural practices which make up the broad human field. This is a question of making a contribution towards the ongoing 'human dialogue', of widening the whole field of human discourse, solidarity and self-understanding. This is especially important during periods of very rapid social change, such as now, when we need to maintain some 'other' against which to judge dominantly directed and recorded current trends. Of course, it may be responded and will certainly be argued, 'Who are they to talk, taking on the responsibility for others?' 'Why take their word for it?' 'It's presumptuous for anyone to talk except for themselves.' All true; but this is where the point about quality comes in, and the utilization of, rather than an impotent suffering from, the artefactual and deeply theoretical quality of writing. No ethnographer should say, 'This is how it is', or 'I know better than you do about your life.' The point at issue is whether understanding and human empathy are increased or not. Adding to the 'human dialogue' is not to add better photographs or to make further unreflective claims about Archimedean truths. It is to widen and deepen the always contingent and reflexive body of knowledge about humankind by sieving knowledge and imagination through a tight focus on the specifics and groundedness of how humans use resources for meaning-making in context.

Thirdly, there is a crucial point in this human dialogue concerning inequality. The ethnographic study of culture has a general role to play in pointing to injustice and in contributing to, maintaining and extending norms of social justice and human decency. There are specifically internal connections here for a perspective attuned to the lived penetrations of social agents, i.e. understanding what *in situ* practices themselves 'say' about social justice. Where there is alienation from the written word, and formal linguistic expression, and where cultural practices speak to, but not of, their conditions and emergent relations and possibilities, there is not a removal of, but a more complex responsibility on those who can speak. This speaking is not one of displacing the indigenuous 'voice' but of 'voicing' its otherwise silent body. This must be done in the spirit of respecting, recording, illuminating and learning from forms of sensuous subordinate meaning-making and self-making, even as they may be distorted and constrained by their unpropitious conditions. This has an at least potential role to play for those under study in helping them to develop a self-awareness of collectivity and in helping to release the sensuously held contents of their own cultural forms in ideas and languages less antagonistic to them and their interests than are the dominant ones. This is to give them a potential power in the politics of 'naming', for the deployment by them of discourses and signs growing out of their own expressive cultures rather than struggling always as the losing partner, subject to the constructions of others' discourses *about* them. The *in situ* and local development of language might allow self-analysis to open up the invisibility of symbolic work and thereby offer opportunities for the redirection or limitation of the reproductive consequences of lived penetrations. This is to give a *modus operandi*, a real content, a catalyst,[12] to otherwise potentially vacuous notions of consciousness raising. At the same time, it may be that the legitimacy of 'the academy' can be used to put other namings into the circulation of 'official' discourses, so interrupting or denying the smooth functioning of expert government regulation and the legitimization of inequality.

Fourthly, the ethnographic study of culture has an important role to play in the development of theoretical understanding, especially in periods of rapid change, when some of the basic shifts in structures, social relationships and 'behind back' social change have not become directly evident. These changes may first manifest themselves in 'raw' subordinate experience and practical theorizing, in which social agents are forced to live, experientially immersed, in these new relationships. Emerging themes in cultural relations, changes in how class, gender, ethnicity and sexuality operate and articulate with each other and their conditions of existence, appear first in 'experience' as new kinds of satisfaction, or new kinds of desire, or new kinds of survival, presaging new kinds of identity – remaining to be worked up into new kinds of collectivity with their attendant interests and politics. The point of an idea is to put us in touch with, and give us a way of talking about, a previously cut off or new area of experience. It is now more than ever time for ethnographic antennae to be raised to detect and formulate these changes in the wind.

Cultural policy

Though we are in a period of rapid and profound change, it is not one of epochal resistance or of new social vision, so political questions for the moment concern *policy* questions, often micro, though one of the criteria for deciding whether to get involved, how, when and where, might be for the 'accelerator' effects they may have on larger issues – for me, for instance, the prospects for increasing self-recognition and the development of informal *symbolic work*.

At bottom, I am interested in exploring the potentials of opening up some new kinds of 'public sphere', within the cultural realm at least. These must be tuned to, rather than against, the emergent and existing conditions of culture for the majority, dialectically understood, recognizing the ubiquity of popular culture but discriminating 'common culture' from it, especially along the lines of 'grounded aesthetics' and the concrete *in situ* uses of cultural commodities. Older notions of 'public sphere' were always implicitly linked to the activities of minority groups and culturally aloof, oddly clothed, at least for their critical and avowedly democratic adherents, in the backward-looking forms of basically aristocratic aesthetics. Looking forward really entails treading where we might not have chosen to be: traversing the grounds of commodity culture.

Neo-liberalism seems to be dominant everywhere; the market has won, it seems. But the roles of the state, government and public policy are far from dead or redundant. In fields of penology, welfare reform and labour market policy, the state is more present, active and directive than ever. Within the cultural realm the state provides an infrastructure, from education to arts subsidy to legal frameworks, which is vital to commercial production. Just as neo-conservative programmes are developing policies across the board in order to intervene in and direct the production of instrumental labour power among subordinate groups, why cannot progressive forces, using the still considerable 'good will' funds of social democracy, argue for and develop cultural strategies so as to intervene and develop expressive labour power along the existing vectors of its current but invisible forms?

Taking political economy seriously in the cultural realm is not just a question of tracing and attempting to influence the linear determinations which flow from the private ownership of the means of production and distribution, maintaining public service alternatives wherever possible. It is also a question of how the commodity form is imprinted, from public service provision also, dialectically within the forms of lived everyday culture. Rather than try to know the beast, and its ecological niches, too often the impulse of cultural policy or critique is to try to heave the smelly backside of commodity production out of the sweet-smelling cultural realm. 'Culture jammers' and 'ad busters' deface adverts and put up web sites mocking or subverting famous brands or products. Anti-corporate storm-troopers staged a carnival on the streets of Seattle when the World Trade Organization met there in 1999. Access driven arts administrators torture themselves figuring out how to hypnotize TV couch potatoes into the stalls. Of course, public-sector provision has to be supported at all costs. It guards ancient treasures, keeps open poles of possibility and experiment and supports non-profit-driven forms of working and knowing in ways that production for the market would never countenance. But these are options within a defensive war of position. New forward fronts must be opened beyond the old trenches.

Here it is important to stress the grounding distinction between popular culture and 'common culture' – distinguishing between the things themselves and their uses and creative de-fetishizations in ways continuous with older forms of folk, regional, ethnic cultures etc. We must find footings for supporting and developing 'common culture' while remaining distant from populist celebrations of popular culture.

The market provides most of the materials for the practices of 'common culture', but it remains true that many young people's cultural development remains fettered by a lack of access to the materials and means of their own culture. There is subsidized access, unused by the majority, to legitimate cultural materials in museums, theatres and art galleries; but why not also make institutional provision for the wide cultural activities that have meaning and relevance to 'non-public', 'beyond the institution' majority groups. These latter could facilitate in imaginative ways 'common cultural' pursuits, supplementing them with forms and processes designed to bring out the invisibility of symbolic work in their cultural practices. Why cannot we think more seriously about the non-market provision of market or market-like cultural goods and technologies, which are equally sexy and sticky, encouraging processes of creative control and de-fetishization, but in circumstances where the symbolic work involved has a greater chance of self-recognition and self-realization and development in its own terms, a greater chance of demanding wider control over its own conditions and materials of production?

An important point about the textual production of culture is that within everyday experience it is difficult to draw hard and fast lines between conventional notions of consumption and production. In fact, the move to concrete textual production often comes through creative consumption. The motivation, confidence and sense of do-ability arise, in the first instance, from seeking to copy what has been enjoyed. Most pop musicians begin their activities as fans and create by copying sounds from records, tapes and CDs. Active consumption of the cultural media leads many young people to want to produce their own videos, films, cable programmes and photographs. An interest in contemporary dance and the performing arts is engendered through a creative relationship with musicals, pop videos, popular drama and soaps. An involvement in fashion and design often starts through an enthusiastic participation in the consumption rituals of subculture style.

Perhaps the consumer/apprentice way of learning can be seen as the normal way of 'learning art', certainly before 'the academy' and written notation, as well as in all folk societies and folk arts. The rigid and hierarchical distinction between production and consumption is the historical aberration, not the norm. Perhaps we now have conditions, oddly worked through the dialectics of fetishism and de-fetishization, for the emergence of a new electronic 'folk age'. New kinds of institution and the processes and activities within them might aim sympathetically to oil the wheels, smooth the experiential paths, connections and 'movers' between consumer and producer roles. Elsewhere I have explored some of the practical dimensions of pursuing these policies along lines of subsidy devoted to 'common cultural' rather than high cultural pursuits.[13]

Some of the older collective institutions may be declining or feeling increasingly limited in what they can dare to experiment with culturally. The seeds of new ones are growing and blowing. Meanwhile, other older institutions are developing and changing. For instance, there has been an astonishing growth and change in the institutions of higher education in the UK. From a baseline of about 5 per cent thirty or so years ago, 30 per cent of 18-year-olds now expect to continue to higher education, and there are projections that this will rise to 50 per cent. Apart from white working-class males, there is also a continuing strong flow of adult students into higher education, 'non-standard' students comprising 40–50 per cent of the student bodies of at least the non-elite universities.

These institutions are becoming peopled with new kinds of student. As the transition from school to work continues to be elongated and reconstructed, or infinitely postponed, there are similar developments across the whole spectrum of institutional provision for young adults. Of course, practical, applied and technical studies are the main instrumental focus, but there is also a demand for, and a curricular provision for, Social Studies, Sociology, Media Studies and Cultural Studies, all expanding or adapting to try to cope with this new array of student types, in one way or another, packed into state institutions. With personal histories and contemporary realities involving a variety of lived cultural practices, many students very often feel that their own experiences are unrecognized in curricular, teaching and learning practices. Their cultures seem to be invisible, or, like coats in winter, to be dumped at the class-room door. Ethnographic accounts, scripts, texts and stories could have a role to play here, meeting the experiences of students, releasing a recognition of their own symbolic work and developing a recognition and respect for other kinds of symbolic work in other forms of life. The ethnographic provision of examples of concretely articulated abstract ideas may also provide a base for a serious consideration of theoretical and comparative modes of thought. Cultural practices are, in effect, learning practices and can be connected and mobilized as such. Of course, there is always a risk of alienation when approaching the mental contents, relations and implications of ethnographic texts; but once a mental spark jumps between life forms and abstract categories a new kind of educational bridge may be opened up over the fetishized chasms between mental and manual forms.

The treason of language?

The ethnographic imagination, its researches and writings, hopes to render into language that which is formed partly as an escape from language, mentalizing the body again. But it does this for a purpose. Human development is about the attempt to control and direct human powers. The ethnographic imagination takes on a small part of this, recognizing everyday living arts and guarding against the ironies and unintended consequences which can flow from them. There are many problems in attempting this, not least in rendering the meanings of others into ethnographic linguistic forms. But spelling out the mental contents of penetrations and verbalizing the possible reproductions which flow from them, while inescapably linguistic, also bring opportunities for knowledge, self-knowledge and control, chances to mobilize the art to shame the reproduction, chances to make feelings think, to make beauty a cause for justice. Only by linguistic translation will the hidden processes of symbolic work gain recognition and self-recognition, so opening processes of self-making to more conscious control and blocking the effects of powerful new ideological roles granted by the renewed fetishism of commodities.

Verbalizing sensuously held meanings does not necessarily stop them from existing, or displace them, any more than an abstract understanding of the body or mind stops *them* from existing. But the relationship changes. Instead of such changes being 'behind the back' of lived cultural forms, why not attempt to make them more legible and more controllable? In taking up the job of writing, the ethnographer is trying to turn a possible local treachery into the means of a wider emancipation – the success or not of which is to be judged ultimately by the quality of the writing. This is the 'Ah ha' effect which in part depends on how far writing explicates its subject by going through and expanding on the *fullness* of the original by internal reference to wider questions.

The ethnographic imagination has to try both to fully respect sensuous meaning and to surpass it as an 'adding to'.

Appendix

Homology

The notion of socio-symbolic analysis was first developed by me in my PhD research, and it provided the framework, organizing basis and chapter headings for the written thesis (1972, Centre for Contemporary Cultural Studies, Birmingham University) analysing the role of music and drugs within hippie culture and of the motor-bike and music within bike culture. The published version, *Profane Culture*, presented the ethnographic data from this thesis in a direct form, 'de-theorized', with the *socio symbolic homologies* framework removed into a 'Theoretical Appendix'. The main term of my socio-symbolic analysis, homology, appears in the subsequent Sub-cultural Studies literature, often referred to, without reference to me, as deriving from Lévi-Strauss, even though I undoubtedly introduced the term into the debate. I have no memory at all of deriving the term from Lévi-Strauss, and have subsequently found in his work not a formal or *specific* category, but an occasional and general adjectival usage relating to similarities or 'symmetries' (which does have a formal usage) between external symbolic systems. In fact I do not consciously recollect from where I derived the

Thanks to Phil Corrigan and Mats Trondman for comments incorporated in this piece.

term homology (or indeed any of the other associated categories), though its most likely source is collective discussions at the time in the Birmingham Centre of Lucien Goldmann's specific notion of homology between literary forms and the commodity market (*Towards a Sociology of the Novel*). I have never seen any prior usage (to mine) of the term to designate a type of relation *between* subjectivity and external form, rather than solely within the latter as in the Lévi-Strauss and Goldmann examples.

While the notion of homology has figured in the subcultures literature, my related notion of 'integral circuiting' has been wholly ignored. Indeed the homological position has been criticized widely for its supposed inflexibility and fixity, making it relevant only to the study of allegedly static working-class cultural forms, such as the Teddy Boys, which, it is claimed, in contrast to the Punks, for instance, show no dynamism, artifice or irony in their cultural practices or creativity in finding new uses for cultural materials. Notably by Dick Hebdige,[1] 'signifying practice', borrowed from post structuralist linguistics, has been promoted as a superior paradigm better able to deal with these latter things. Leaving aside whether working-class cultural forms are indeed so lacking in irony and artifice (the Teds and their blue suede shoes?), the socio-symbolic model and especially its category of 'integral circuiting', which brings about basic homologies, are precisely about an 'anti-structuralist' concern with creativity and with movement and change. Unlike the linguistic-based models which are said to have superseded the homological approach, socio-symbolic analysis stresses *concrete* historical practice in relation to *profane* materials and is diachronic rather than synchronic. In many ways this makes it better placed to trace the creative dynamics of cultural creativity. Furthermore, that which, it is claimed, only signifying practice can conceptualize – subversive and shocking cultural forms such as the Punks – can easily be presented in the terms of integral circuiting. Previous uses and significations of the 'objective possibilities' of any cultural item have an effect on their availability for contemporary uses, not only for conformist but also for subversive ones, where strongly historically formed homological meanings are 'integrally' placed in new homological relations to produce shock or confusion in others or to signify an anarchy or refusal of meaning, as for instance in the Punks' use of the swastika. Equivalents of 'semiotic disorder' (also Dick Hebdige) in lived cultural forms can perhaps be more effectively understood through homologies. The exploitation of the internal stresses of particular items, the instability between their different expressive, affective and functional 'objective possibilities' and their 'profane' material presence, dynamically explored, in intended and unintended ways through *use*, allows homologies to be developed in material but still unprefigured and creative ways, switching within and between 'objective possibilities' (compare the safety pins and bin bags of Punk culture). It is also crucial to remember that in the socio-symbolic perspective, the internal and external rearrangement of objects is possible in a way not allowable under the grammatical rules pertaining to signifying practice. Of course, for socio-symbolic analysis these subversive moments cannot last, because they either fade or are taken up into new stable homologies.

Two important issues deserve further mention. One concerns the status of socio-symbolic analysis with respect to issues within the philosophy of science, which the dominance of the linguistic model has brought to particular prominence. My approach here could be considered a linguistic imposition on the external world, imposing on it structures which belong to my discourse rather than to it. I would argue here that homological analysis should be seen and judged, not as a mistakenly objective, putative 'science', but as a way of illuminating a phenomenon which is capable of producing superior grounds than other approaches for understanding and appreciating that phenomenon, so mobilizing the reader's own experience and imagination, not least in relation to his or her own interests and activities. This result in the reader is more likely to be produced if what is read is a product of the writer's or researcher's operational categories having been adapted to field experience, if terms have been conditioned in their own homological-like (responsive to concrete sense-data inputs) relation to the field of enquiry and its sense/form relations, i.e. through effective ethnographic practice. Ethnographic practice seeks not the empiricist chimera of *direct* knowledge of the real, but a sensuous and theorized relationship to it.

Secondly, I am aware of the imprecision of my formulations in relation to the enormous and vexed, perhaps never to be resolved, question of how to conceptualize or how to approach theorizing, 'the subject'. I am certainly arguing against an assumption of a fully formed, fully creatively armed, independent, humanist subject. Nor do I stipulate a unitary form of subjectivity to be placed on the human side of the sense/form relationships, not least because of the possibly diverse forms of the latter with respect to any one group or individual. A degree of de-centring of the subject is clearly necessary to socio-symbolic analysis, but at the same time it does imply some sort of connected up, at least '*cultural* subject', capable of action. The homological structures formulation may be misleading on the sense side of the equation, because it could imply a mirror image structure within the sensibility of external symbolic form. This is not my purpose so much as a side-effect of settling on a form of words, necessarily imperfectly chosen, to convey a complex 'signified'; this signified is to do with the systematic possibility of the passing and forming of meaning through a human moment, with enduring and reinforcing effect on both form and sense, including the possibility of enabling human action and creativity. Perhaps the 'subject' has to be seen as an indeterminate moving sum – if you like, to borrow from physics, both a wave and a particle – of such and other processes, perpetually reproduced and developed through successive dialectical moments reducible to no one static structure alone.

Perception theory tells us that we have a model of the external world, including our own body and its physical orientations, in our heads. So, too, perhaps we have an internal *cultural* model of our world. In this sense, homological relations may, somehow, be inside us. The cultural self might then be seen, perhaps, not so much as a separate 'model' self (that way lies the insanity of multiple regression) as the totality in movement and relation of these homological forms: the embodiment and moving sum of satisfaction, potential and power arising from them, but brokered always through some relation, and responsive in some way, to a rearrangeable and three-dimensional external world. As the body, perhaps the most crucial aspect of the external world and so far stuck in its own rigid grammar, becomes more rearrangeable or extendable through piercing, body art and modification in the short run and, foreseeably, through prosthetics and cybernetics in the long run, so, too, the possibilities for change in 'the subject' will be extended, perhaps to include post-humanist and possibly 'post-human' cultural selves. But will cyborgs yield their secrets and potentials for change to a linguistic or to a socio-symbolic model of analysis?

Notes

Foreword

1 Herbert Blumer, 'What is wrong with social theory?', *American Sociological Review*, XIX, 1954.
2 C. Geertz, *Local Knowledge: Further Essays in Interpretive Anthropology*, Basic Books, 1983, p. 117.
3 C. Wright Mills, *The Sociological Imagination*, Harmondsworth, Penguin, 1970, p. 12. Now out of print, an interesting book by Paul Atkinson also entitled *The Ethnographic Imagination* (Routledge, 1990) makes a valuable contribution to the literature on ethnographic writing strategies. Taking a complementary but different course from my own, Atkinson provides a detailed, wide ranging and sophisticated analysis of the varieties of writing strategies, including literary and theoretical devices, through which ethnographic writers, often covertly, construct a textual sense of social reality. I intend my book as a conscious identification of that which is productively and clearly brought to observational data, in order to enhance understanding of it, rather than to render it more apparently 'valid', an understanding highlighting artfulness in life rather than, though working through, textual artfulness.
4 The broad case I am arguing and the exemplifications in the book relate to the social majority of differently dominated groups. However, the basic approach is quite applicable to the cultures and cultural practices of dominant social groups. Of course they are

differentiated by much more power in their different kinds of access to different kinds of *form*, and the poignancy of their *social connection* is of a different order, requiring a different specific analysis with respect to the relations of power and social reproduction.

5   Asa Briggs, Fisher Memorial Lecture, University of Adelaide, 1960, quoted in N. Garnham, *Capitalism and Communication*, London, Sage, 1990.
6   P. Willis, *Learning to Labour*, Farnborough, Saxon House, 1977.

Chapter 1   Life as Art

1   See P. Willis, 'Why take the piss?' in D. Holland and J. Lave (eds), *History in Person*, Santa Fe, New Mexico, School for American Research, 2000.
2   It is a diversion from the main argument here, but it may be suggested that although they operate to different sides of what we take to be reality, a cultural form has no less an intrinsic relation to thought than has a dream, or what we think of as the unconscious, and for the same reasons in the extension of the metaphorical functions of language. Cultural forms also operate in their own way, 'unconsciously' to condition and guide the self-conscious thought of their members.
3   The same argument can apply, of course, to the meanings embodied in the texts of visual art – not something usually contested. *A fortiori*, the extra possibilities of real context, movement and the reordering of parts make the moving pictures of sensuous, practical life abundantly expressive.

Chapter 2   Form

1   P. Anderson, *In the Tracks of Historical Materialism: The Welleck Library Lectures*, London, Verso, 1983, p. 54, quoted in A. Milner, *Contemporary Cultural Theory*, London, UCL Press, 1994, p. 90.
2   There is a kind of human freedom in the abstract possibility of exploiting the very arbitrariness of the signifier – but only at the cost of a still more radical reduction of the social. If signifiers are arbitrary, then their differences which produce meaning could mean, or be made to mean, anything or nothing: a private language imagined, enjoyed often as an abundance of nothing, infinite potential proved by all possible but no actual meaning. This is to make of an abstract, secret theoretical space a private reality. But you can break

free from the designated, conventional meaning only once: one person, one style, once.

3   Stuart Hall, *Race, the Floating Signifier*, Northampton, Media Education Foundation video.

4   See, for instance, a recent textbook on Cultural Studies exploring this premise, Chris Barker, *Cultural Studies: Theory and Practice*, London, Sage, 2000.

5   If a code model were relevant at all for understanding cultural forms I would argue that it should be taken from an analogue or iconographic communication paradigm. At least the former maintains some degree of relation between the signifier, signified and referent, and is not bound by rules, or at least not the same rules of grammar. These differences also make it questionable whether digital forms can help to model the internal relations of signifiers in an analogue code, never mind those of the concrete items involved in lived cultural forms.

6   One of a number of points made to me by my colleague Marcus Free, who generously made several constructive criticisms of and suggestions for this chapter.

7   For an interesting and unusual article making a similar point, see V. Nightingale, 'What's "ethnographic" about ethnographic audience research?', *Australian Journal of Communication*, no. 16, 1989.

8   First developed in my *Profane Culture*, London, Routledge & Kegan Paul, 1978; also see the Appendix to this book.

9   See chapter 5, 'Cultural Practices' section for a definition and development of what I mean by *symbolic work*.

10 Of course, there are perhaps insurmountable difficulties in saying, precisely and scientifically, what human creativity might be, but the lack of a theory for things does not stop them from existing. In its own way this book is an attempt at a 'pre-scientific' but beyond 'humanistic' clearing of the brushwood on this matter. Humanistic celebrations of human creativity usually meet with a polite if wearied smile of truism acceptance: good ethnographic writing granted its niche of 'rich description'. Both are disdained in private by *big theory* for their discursive naivety in thinking that their accounts 'report' rather than 'make' the world, and for their lack of theoretical explanation in relation to non-human structures. The theoretical enterprise, its built-in tendency to theoreticism, is, of course, to develop 'anti-creativity theory', to explain human behaviour as being *precisely not* creative, as determined by outside structures of various kinds. The creativity is not the starting point, but the illusion to be explained (away). I am struggling for an account which includes the importance of structures, symbolic and economic, but

which maintains at the centre a theorized notion of agency and human creativity. A proper theory of creativity is the social science equivalent of a unified theory of the laws of physics, but so far we have only the barest clues about our descriptive versions of gravity. In my view we shall find a unifying theory of creativity not in the terms of any one field (language, discourses, genes, the subconscious, social relations etc.) but in some form of the coming together and combusting of all of them, like an internal combustion engine running.

11 Willis, *Profane Culture*.
12 Marcus Free, my colleague, suggested this example and analysis to me.
13 See P. Willis, 'Why take the piss?' in D. Holland and J. Lave (eds), *History in Person*, Santa Fe, New Mexico, School for American Research, 2000.
14 See note 6.
15 Some theoretical manoeuvrings within discourse theory which attempt to represent complexity often show 'the other' of their own signifieds – meaning types and practices not comparable to language. The attachment of psychoanalytic theories to show the 'interior' of 'subject positions' within discourses shows the need for a notion of real concrete, independent subjects producing senses of themselves through cultural practices and dialectical interaction with non-language materials. The increasing focus on the body as the subject and medium of discourses demonstrates the huge absence of the recognition of sensuous and somatic meaningfulness within discursive approaches. The 'sutures', hybridities and articulations of discourses all point to the 'absent presence' of numerous small human sewings of profane materials.

Chapter 3   The Social

1 It is commonplace to understand social process, in a general way, as a historical process, but changing or developing yourself as a social subject is the usually invisible counter-point to wider social change. Taking how and why people change as a concrete focus is a question of social connectedness up as well as down, of two-way flows. I need to clarify this rather than fudge it with general terms. For lack of a clear alternative, I return now to the term penetration for its double sense of *seeing through* something (for instance external ideological accounts) and of *making way*, of entering into or finding new space (for instance in relation to structural conditions and possibilities and

the use of provided materials). It may be that these meanings are irredeemably attached to phallocentrism in our contemporary culture, which is quite different from saying that they are associated only with male practice or that they cannot be rearticulated with changed configurations of gendered meaning in the future.

2 Political Economy and Regulation Theory ask the right questions about capital's reproduction of its own conditions of existence, but they have an impenitently reductive and rationalist view of how it occurs. The maintenance of extended unequal, structured social relationships owes as much to informal cultural production as it does to official and ideological justifications and interventions, not least in mitigating the effects of blatant contradictions in the latter. For instance, ideologies of equality of opportunity (now severely qualified in practice, though the rhetoric remains) and meritocracy for all are full of gaping holes and contradictions, not the least of which is that their success, from which such as 'the lads'' culture delivers them, would produce armies of aspirants for which no social and economic destinations actually exist. Capitalism mutates, struggles with and exploits materials not of its making, accidentally finding unintended consequences and unforeseen conditions of survival. It swims in social-historical seas as a predator, certainly changing, but not commanding the sea.

3 See a previous paper of mine categorizing and theorizing aspects of general processes of cultural reproduction: 'Cultural production and theories of reproduction' in L. Barton and S. Walker (eds), *Class & Education*, London, Croom Helm, 1983.

4 See note 3.

5 P. Bourdieu, *Pascalian Meditations*, Cambridge, Polity Press, 1999, p. 149.

6 See note 3.

7 I have been accused of proclaiming in *Learning to Labour* an all-time fusion between mentalism and the feminine and between manualism and the masculine. This was certainly my case with respect to the formation of 'the lads' and their culture. But my *general* point, throughout this case study, was actually the opposite: to show variability and malleability in how these historically received elements may form and combine, and then durably stick. It is certainly possible to suggest other living permutations. For instance, middle-class males might gain a sense of power and masculinity from a mental control, coordination and direction of the manual powers of others working in production; or working-class females doing manual work might develop their own feminized physical culture or, conversely, dignify menial operations by their association with mental work.

Chapter 4   The Quasi-modo Commodity

1   Statistics taken from P. Willis et al., *Common Culture*, Milton Keynes, Open University Press, 1990. Recent statistics: for TV, 27.18 hours per week per viewer in February 2000, Broadcasters Audience Research Board, *Monthly Viewing Figures*, London <www.barb.co.uk> (accessed 11 April 2000); for radio, 23.6 hours per listener per week for the last quarter of 1999, Radio Joint Audience Research Limited, *Quarterly Summary*, London <www.rajar.co.uk> (accessed 11 April 2000).

2   *Financial Times*, 5 October 1999.

3   Reported in the *Wolverhampton Express & Star*, 21 July 1997.

4   See, for instance, J. McGuigan, *Cultural Populism*, London, Routledge, 1992; N. Garnham, *Capitalism and Communication*, London, Sage, 1990; G. Murdoch and P. Golding, 'Ideology and the mass media: the question of determination' in M. Barrett et al. (eds), *Ideology and Cultural Production*, Croom Helm, 1979; J. Curran et al., *Mass Communication and Society*, London, Arnold, 1977.

5   Nicholas Garnham, cited in the previous note, makes several highly pertinent points about the commodity form and commoditization in relation to communication and communication systems, but mysteriously stops short of analysing fetishism, perhaps the central ideological category for Marx, even though his chosen focus is a Marxist and ideological analysis. In several places Garnham interestingly skirts the issue in his analysis arguing that the 'use values' of cultural commodities are different from those of physical or subsistence commodities. He discusses cultural consumption producing new needs (p. 52) and the role of 'socially posited needs' (p. 47). He refers to 'positional goods' (p. 161) as to do with marking social and individual difference. But nowhere is there any reference to fetishism. There is an oblique reference, perhaps, in his argument that it is difficult to locate the use values of communication commodities, and his related discussion of the variety of institutional ways in which capital approaches the difficulty of realizing value from the exchange of cultural commodities is relevant and very thorough (p. 39ff). Especially important are his arguments concerning the control of distribution channels and the role of informational commodities in delivering audiences to advertisers so that value can be realized from the sale of other kinds of goods. But there is still no discussion of the internalities of form in relation to commodity fetishism and specific types of cultural needs in audiences. Substituting control of distribution and advertising for this missing gap only delays the problem: why do consumers come into the controlled distribution channels to

start with, and how do adverts, a fetishized communication if ever there was one, function themselves at an ideological level? I would argue that, in the case of cultural commodities, for a non-reductive circuit of capital model to work, free of economic involutions, there is an inescapable need to build in a subjective moment of creative consumption and identity construction considered in its own terms. This leads inescapably to questions of form and to the crunch issue of fetishism as a central feature of the commodity and of ideological process in the whole social formation. Only the prejudices among political economists concerning their own fear of 'cultural populism' and disdain for 'soft' methods and analyses, not immediately traceable to economic causation, have prevented them from pursuing the rich qualitative possibilities offered by a consideration of fetishism in relation to cultural commodities.

Coming from almost exactly the opposite direction, Judith Williamson's fascinating book *Consuming Passions* explores crucial aspects of fetishism without ever mentioning the word or considering its specificity to the *cultural* commodity. Drawing on her own cultural and social experience she makes evocative and insightful commentaries on popular textual forms, especially film, but there is no ethnographic or theoretical development of the concept: Judith Williamson, *Consuming Passions*, London, Marion Boyars, 1986.

6 Karl Marx, *Capital*, Moore and Aveling translation, London, Allen & Unwin, 1957, p. 42.

7 If capitalists could really control the internal workings of the cultural commodity, the first order they would give would be for the commodity to turn itself back into money. Since this requirement is so often unfulfilled, we should have our doubts about other social orders. Cultural commodities make for us, all on their own and by their very existence, a practical distinction and separation between the social relations of production and the social relations of consumption. One escape for the capitalist may be to sell the product before it is made – eldorado! This is certainly one of the driving forces behind modern production technology and the sporadic arrival of 'post-Fordism': i.e. advance orders for cars, which are not made except to specification with customers waiting. But cultural commodities must certainly be made before they are sold, and there are enormous dangers that the product 'will stop in the warehouse'. Negative and uncreative responses to this danger include flooding and repetition – producing lots of items almost randomly in order to maximize the odds of producing at least one winner and repeating *ad nauseam* the formulas of the occasional winners, the standardized genres and cliché'd visual imagery that surrounds us. From here flow tendencies

towards the much discussed homogeneity of capitalist culture, towards the restriction of choice and towards the levelling down to lowest common denominators. There are, however, counter-tendencies which rely on the exploitation of informal circuits of symbolic production as discussed in later chapters.

8   There are, of course, rules for the consumption of cultural commodities, not least about having the cash for legal purchase and ownership and conformity with the requirements of copyright law. Compared with the norms and requirements surrounding the consumption of high material cultural items, these are at least explicit, visible and simple – and frequently their own incitement to transgression.

9   The late Freddie Mercury of Queen compared his music to a Bic razor, a disposable consumer commodity fit 'for modern use'. Compare that with this scene. Christmas 1993: an eight-year-old (my daughter) reaches out involuntarily to touch or somehow be nearer to a famous oil painting, Rembrandt's *Andromeda* in the Marithuis in The Hague. She hits the pane in the glass case setting off an alarm, which brings three uniformed attendants to the scene within seconds. She withdraws in confusion and escapes under parental cloaks. The glass cases over the material things of high culture limit, police or even prevent use. They are so valuable that they are in danger of becoming quite useless. The cheap Bic razors of common culture are nothing if not useful. They are used or thrown away, certainly thrown away after use. Compare this with the never used baggage which simply cannot be thrown out of the (subsidized) bulging attics, storerooms and cellars of high material culture.

10   I understand very well that all commodities have inseparable material and symbolic sides. It is the balance or preponderance I am referring to here. Furthermore, it is also in my mind that, while the possibility exists of a notional 'innocent' finding a way to sit on a chair without access to the prior signification of 'sitting', no such possibility exists for their understanding and appreciation of Beethoven.

11   'Hippie capitalism' has long understood the importance of 'imagined community', the most important miscegenation from the counter-cultures of the 1960s. The bible (M. Phillips and S. Rasberry, *Honest Business*, New York, Random House) of 'hippie capitalism' stresses the importance of building and maintaining communities of customers in all possible and sensuous ways: Harley Davidson and the Grateful Dead succeed to the extent of faithful consumers *branding* themselves – tattooing these famous brandnames on their own skins.

12 *The Times*, 21 November 1997.

13 See note 3.

14 Perhaps it is no accident that we had to wait for the current invasion of cultural commoditization on the materials of everyday life to be sensitized to the discovery of the importance of quotidian 'material culture' in every epoch, viz. the rise of new branches of anthropology, historical sociology and social history.

15 Derrida's 'traces' or 'grammes' can be seen as held up or interrupted in their interminable 'delays' and 'deferrals' by *culturalization*. In sensuous relationship to them, *socio symbolic homologies* 'hold' meanings, so also holding up the passage of the 'mystical present'.

Chapter 5   Penetrations in the Postmodern World

1 P. Willis, S. Jones, J. Canaan and G. Hurd, *Common Culture*, Milton Keynes, Open University, 1990.

2 The subject can be seen as a site of forces or tendencies in conflict. We are well supplied with poststructuralist and postmodernist accounts of the processes, systems and discursive effects making for the decentring of the subject. I am rescuing the opposing tendencies. But I accept multiple, complex and contradictory currents in the meaning-making of everyday material life. I am not hanging out for the resurrection of a unified class cultural model of identity, now with more whistles and bells. While 'centripetal' meaning-making may be about contemporary ways of making sense of work, school and neighbourhood, in some way continuous with the older patterns, there is also a more 'centrifugal' meaning-making which reaches out for a cultural significance denied or difficult to sustain in the immediate relations and resources of locating (and enclosing) sites and institutions. Even in the latter case, however, there are always moorings, to the social however unrecognized or wrongly recognized.

3 Think of it in terms of the *langue/parole* distinction in linguistics. From the given commodity universe as a *langue*, informal producers create their own specific *parole*. But over time further circuits of commoditization may turn this *parole* back into a generalized *langue*, thereby debasing its specificity and concrete belongingness for those users. Equally, however, the *langue* they inherited and creatively used was, itself, likely to be in part the product of the corruption of previous non-commodity *paroles*. Nor should we forget, in the ceaselessly shifting sands of the interlinks between capital's formal and informal circuits, that newly created *langues*, whatever

the mess of disillusion they leave behind, create new opportunities for still other and wider groups to develop the creativities of their own *paroles*.

4   There are deep-running questions here concerning the relations of the imaginary to the real. On the one hand, imaginary connections and projections, much aided by the exoticism and imaginary communities of cultural commodities, can be enjoyed for their own sake and for their role in developing the powers of the expressive self, carrying implications for, but not immediately involved in, 'social understanding'. They run parallel to the 'real', reproducing in expanded form appetites for their own experiences. On the other hand, in another way the 'imaginary' can drive a wedge into the 'real', which located symbolic work can amplify and twine into local parameters of meaning-makings relevant to immediate conditions.

5   I do not want to underestimate the continuity and overlap between 'traditional' informal cultures and emergent commodity related ones. All forms of working-class and subordinate culture, as well as the informal female production of femininity, as well as ethnic and anti-racist meanings, as well as the subcultural production of style – all negotiate and make important meanings partly through their own informal symbolic work of adapting to purpose various kinds of inherited and current meanings and symbolic resources. This includes symbolic work on available cultural commodities. But the contemporary commodity-based informal mode is distinct from, or is distinctively tugging on, traditional modes in at least two basic ways.

First, there is a point at which overwhelming quantitative change produces qualitative change: the dominance of commodity relations now producing 'commodity culture' as the norm. The flooding over of commodity and electronic culture has brought a semiotic saturation, bringing contradictory symbolic resources from the four corners of the earth into every nook and cranny of our lives and homes, far beyond the narrow range of reference in older ways of life. Commodity and electronic culture has vastly expanded the semiotic resources which surround us, so that there is now a literally environmental supply of symbols. The throw-away society is a society 'beyond scarcity' at least at the level of symbols. This very multiplicity plus the commodity command to use – no matter what for – has made these environmental, symbolic resources open to guiltless use. There is an absence, suppression or suspension of prescribed norms for their use. Informal creativity can now respond to these possibilities, whereas the shortage of materials, dependence and deference had limited them before. Furthermore the voracity and promiscuity of commodity production brings in quite new materials and meanings – crossing classes, barriers, races, genders, politics – in its endless search for innovation and new sales. This brings cross-cultural polysemy and semiotic 'stickiness' into the heart of cultural processes. It brings clues about other ways of life. It brings codes from other cultures for guiltless hybridization and multiple using, whereas the previous forms all too often enforced only the single using of parochial and in-turned cultural elements.

Secondly, modern informal practices are fairly distinct in that they function in the historical wake of the relative collapse and break up of, at least loss of continuity in, the public traditions and institutions (particularly those of the labour movement) undergirding the older informal cultures. There is a relative scarcity of non-commodity symbolic materials, icons and artefacts in daily life. Young people, especially, are now forced into a modern mode of informal production to make sense of their commodity worlds and much else, because there are fewer and fewer 'passable' materials and practices coming down to them from any other inheritance.

6 For instance, Ulrich Beck in *Risk Society* (London, Sage, 1992): individuals are 'dependent on education, consumption, welfare state regulations and support, traffic planning, consumer supplies, and on possibilities and fashions in medical, psychological and pedagogic counselling and care. This all points to the *institution-dependent control structure* of individual situations. Individualisation becomes the *most advanced* form of societization dependent on the market, law, education and so on' (pp. 130–1, original emphasis); quoted in P. Kelly, 'Wild and tame zones: regulating the transitions of youth at risk', *Journal of Youth Studies*, vol. 2, no. 2, 1999. See also U. Beck, A. Giddens and S. Lash (eds), *Reflexive Modernisatation: Politics, Tradition and Aesthetics in the Modern Social Order*, Cambridge, Polity, 1994.

7 New tribalisms and nationalisms may seem to contradict the arguments for self-consciousness and hybridization advanced here. But the poles of identity – hybridity and tradition – may be less polar than they appear. In post-, late- and modern societies at least, nationalistic identities and cultures cannot relate innocently to an authentic past any more than can hybrid cultural forms – both work through modern fetishism and representation. The signs and symbols of the new tribalisms and nationalisms may relate to older national identities, rather as Doc Martin boots relate to an imagined hardness of traditional working-class culture.

8 It could be argued, for instance, that developments in Asian popular cultural forms have changed attitudes both within and to the Asian community more effectively than have decades of official politics.

The Bhangra phenomenon makes an interesting case study. The new glamour and extroversion, beat and boisterous collectivity of Bhangra is helping to transform the received young, white, working-class image of Asian personality, stereotypically seen as backwardly traditional, passive and individualistic. Within the Asian community, too, have arisen some profound new directions of change. Originally derived from Punjabi wedding music, Bhangra is now often played at British Asian weddings; but single women, instead of sitting quietly for the sake of family pride, now arise collectively to dance to *their* music. Whereas individual family pride had suppressed any possibility of, or recognition of, changes in behaviour judged to be appropriate for women, the collective sweep of the music releases all families simultaneously from the bind of not being the first to loosen control on family daughters. From this there are two developments, uneven of course, and influenced by many other factors and countertendencies (not least the fear of racist attack and abuse in public). First, young Asian women are gaining an independence and an increased ability to move outside their homes. Secondly, our changing representations enable them to gain greater material and symbolic space for themselves.

Chapter 6   Social Reproduction as Social History

1   In the early 1980s the UK was the first industrialized country to experience massive losses of manual industrial work available to the working classes. This trend is now firmly established across the industrialized world. Since 1979 in the UK over four million manufacturing jobs have been lost, with a concomitant and slightly larger reduction in trade union membership. At the same time there has been a virtually epochal restructuration of the kind of work available, essentially from well-paid skilled and semi-skilled manual industrial work to lower-paid service and white-collar work. For instance, taken together, the new call centres around the UK and the hotel and catering industries now employ more than twice the number of workers employed in the old 'smoke stack' industries (cars, shipbuilding, steel, engineering, coal-mining). The whole working class, but young people, older workers and ethnic minorities in particular, have been badly affected by the diminution in both the quality and the quantity of jobs available. During the late 1990s unemployment dropped considerably, and is now about 7 per cent, but this bald figure conceals both a high turnover in part-time, casual, insecure low-paid work and also huge geographical variations, large, predominantly

middle-class areas enjoying virtually full employment and the older industrial areas and inner cities suffering from rates of 20 per cent and more, much higher still for the continuingly vulnerable groups. One in two less skilled men are without work, and one in five households lack access to earned income. See P. Willis et al., *The Youth Review*, Aldershot, Avebury, 1988; P. Gregg and J. Wadsworth (eds), *The State of Working Britain*, Manchester, Manchester University Press, 1999.

2   The Welfare to Work programme is of two years duration and provides three options: work experience, training or voluntary work. For the first time on such schemes, a refusal to participate is not an option, since benefits are withdrawn if a young person does not take one of these programmes. As a result, a large group of at least 100,000 young people who do not wish to participate have become 'invisible' and simply do not register in official figures and contact. A further substantial group, about 15 per cent in the older industrial areas, have registered but have subsequently suffered sanctions. It is too early to determine the overall success of the scheme in terms of final job placement. See *Working Brief* 107, August/September 1999, published by the Unemployment Unit, Poland Street, London.

3   There are real problems with the notion of 'under-class'. If it is really a class then what is wrong with lower working class, or fraction thereof, or lumpen proletariat? New conditions for the working class have certainly emerged, including a worsened economic situation and a changed relationship to a coercive disciplining 'father' state rather than welfare 'mother' state, but the point for me is to understand these things from the point of view of the active and creative responses of those subject to them. There may be important cultural changes in attitudes and values here – though always in some relation to and using what has gone before. The 'under' bit of the term underclass, however, seems to connote the below ground, the pathological, the deviant and disturbing, as if the real issue were the moral turpitude of individuals. Programmes of coercive correction can then seem legitimate in order to straighten out and inculcate self-responsibility in these people. This distracts attention from, even inverts, a focus on the creative and penetrative forms of cultural adaptation and invention which are about lively survival and the maintenance of dignity in imposed conditions. Under-class implies a social theory of the inexplicable collapse of part of the working class into a moral degeneracy, which has somehow *produced* the conditions which weigh them down.

4   Some of the changes in work may complement these processes, even among the manually employed. The speed-up, intensification and

ideological Japanization of work is squeezing, and squeezing out, its informal cells, and so with them their expressive work of combining ideological themes and strands in stable and controlled (even if resistant) ways, again extruding a disgruntled masculinity as a force to be expressed increasingly outside work. Also, the anti-mentalism which is bound up with the manualism and concrete presence may become displaced outside work relations, finding an unjustified domination to be violently opposed in any form of constraint or direction executed through mental, abstract or linguistic form.

5   Chris Woodhead, Chief Inspector of Schools, writing in *The Times*, 14 March 1996, after the publication of School Inspection Reports.

6   I have some difficulty with the notion of a masculine feminism. Are masculine feminists like a slave-owner's club for abolition, their main agenda item being self-immolation (a metaphor I heard Stuart Hall use in a talk)? The question of power has very different consequences for the emancipatory politics of the two genders. Biological foundations give sexual/gender difference, the main category of founding separation, but it is only power that renders this inert difference into social and cultural versions of superior/inferior. Female feminists have no difficulty seeing male power as arising *generally* from patriarchy, and in some real experiential sense it does not matter too much exactly where this power is ultimately lodged because it can be seen as *expressed* through all men. As Muhammad Ali asked long ago with respect to anti-racist whites, why should he be concerned to sort out the odd good one when confronted by a host of rattlesnakes all looking the same? For many women the collective agent of oppression is the same as the source of oppression. But for men, and different kinds of men, the question of power is crucial. Where is it? Some have it; others do not. Is the 'original' base of power in forms of surplus extraction from domestic labour or of surplus extraction from capitalist production, or in the securing of a safe line of inheritance of the proceeds from both. Short of an easy essentialism short circuiting back to biology, just why is it that (some) men are on top?

The notion of 'hegemonic masculinity' is also confusing for me here, since hegemony as power must be socially located and articulated to some source other than mere biological difference. For masculinity studies and masculine feminists, the articulations of which kinds of power, for which groups, where and when, are crucial in a way they are not for female feminists. From this point of view, it is crucial to study and understand the large groups of powerless men, such as single, unemployed working-class men without capital resources of any kind. Can there be 'male dominance' or 'male power' without articulation to separate bases of power?

7   The deep form of this may be understood as a reversal in the orders of human re-creation: what is seen as necessary to re-create the human power to labour. For the dominant mode of production, non-work, or leisure, is simply a time for recuperation, for regaining the power to labour again in the capitalist labour process. Night-time leisure and recreation supply the commodity, labour power, for day-time production. Informal cultural productivity inverts this. So-called leisure is *the* field of real work and real production. It is, in fact, day work (wage labour) which (through the power of the wage over the cultural market) supplies the means and reproduces the possibility of applying sensuous and non-alienated labour power to informal cultural production at night. Wage labour provides the only access to cultural commodities. The availability of cultural commodities for productive consumption is the *sine qua non* of informal symbolic work, just as the availability of fresh labour power is the *sine qua non* of the capitalist labour process. The re-creations necessary, the factors of production required, for each type of production are opposite complements, not hierarchies of oppression. The orders of signification are contrary and overlap the same external items, but produce different interpretations of them. Maybe the looking-glass world has finally arrived – not in the phantasms of postmodern theorists in their purely discursive worlds, but in the material lack of opposing kinds of production, as they are sensuously perceived, experienced and lived. It is a question for ethnographic research, how far this theoretical schema is useful only for understanding exploited youth labour and for those involved, perhaps, in more formal craft, design and artistic production in their own time, rather than for (or setting up contradictions for) the generality of adult labour. In the latter case financial burdens, parental responsibilities and critical concerns about the cultural practices of dependents may all shift the balance.

8   P. Willis et al., *Common Culture*, Milton Keynes, Open University Press, 1990.

9   In her book *Consuming Passions*, Judith Williamson makes a similar point without theoretical elaboration or any consideration of what I call *symbolic work*:

> Marx talks of the commodity as 'congealed labour', the frozen form of a past activity; to the consumer it is also congealed longing, the final form of an active wish. And the shape in which fulfilment is offered seems to become the shape of the wish itself. The need for change, the sense that there must be something else, something different from the way things are,

becomes the need for a new purchase, a new hairstyle, a new coat of paint. Consuming products does give a thrill, a sense of both belonging and being different... Our emotions are wound into these forms, only to spring back at us with an apparent life of their own. Movies seem to *contain* feelings, two-dimensional photographs seem to *contain* truths. The world itself seems filled with obviousness, full of natural meanings which these media merely reflect. But *we* invest the world with its significance. It doesn't have to be the way it is, or to mean what it does. (Pages 12, 13 and 14 original emphasis.)

Within developing forms of commercial provision are practical recognitions of 'consumers' symbolic work, packaged of course as something belonging to the expanding and new 'service' element of the product or brand rather than as anything arising in interaction with the consumer. The latest development is to sell packaged 'experiences' in, for instance, The Forum in Las Vegas, a shopping mall that attempts to recreate an ancient Roman market place, or the Third Street Promenade in Santa Monica replicating the feel of a European street, or in the provision of packaged whole birthday parties for children. In their book *The Experience Economy*, B. Joseph Pine and James Gilmore tell us that the next horizon is to find a way to wrap 'an experience' around every product or service. The accelerating rise of the whole service economy, the customizing of products, narrow banding to consumers in broadcasting: these are all profound sources of change displacing traditional patterns of anonymous production for the general market. They are contradictory attempts, from the side of exchange, to maximize the possibility of locally imagined use values. Whether the associated patterns of increased local symbolic work can be held forever in thrall to new kinds of fetishism must be an open question.

Judith Williamson, *Consuming Passions*, London, Marion Boyars, 1986; B. Joseph Pine and James Gilmore, *The Experience Economy*, HBS Press, 2000.

10 Marx's original discussion of commodity fetishism was crucial to his whole system of thought, not least in explaining the ideological and subjective inhabitation of labour power in relation to its actual exploitative use in capitalist labour processes. In the Marxist system, of course, labour power is the only source of profit. This was the essence of Marx's advance over classical theorists, who had seen profit arising from the simple ownership of capital or land. Labour is the source of profit because it is unique, in that you can get more out of it than it costs you to buy it. You can also get more out of it through intensification and squeezing its pores of inactivity. Through the application of science and technology it can be made

more productive, more or less without limit. Labour power is, therefore, a living thing capable of recouping its costs many times over, depending on the type of productive relation it enters. It is a supremely elastic and variable thing. Crucially, however, labour power is bought and sold not as a variable capacity but as a fixed capacity. It is bought as a dead thing like any other commodity on the market. Once it is sold like a can of beans, it is up to the new owner to decide what to do with it – within work hours. If the new owner can get the labourer to produce a hundred times more than what the labourer costs, then so much the better for the owner. Commodity fetishism, now applied by labourers to the commodity of their own labour power as well as to all other commodities, ensures that they ask no questions about this. They have received a fair day's pay – the price duly paid for the only commodity a worker has to sell, labour power – and it is no business of theirs to criticize the way the employer has gone about extracting a fair day's work, or to question the kind of intensified production into which their labour power has been inserted. There are many qualifications and adjustments to be made to this classical model to make it stand up to scrutiny, but the essential point concerns the way in which labour power is bought and sold as a commodity and is subject therefore to the same fetishizing process as any other commodity.

11 Ironically, of course, in so far as labour power in paid work is continuingly fetishized, this is a further misrecognition which aids the experiential separation of the two labours. All ways round, we see the fundamental problem: the widespread inability under the dominance of the regime of fetishism to understand sensuous human labour to be the starting point for all social processes, no matter how different their forms. Labour has become invisible even as there has never been more of it! As a procedural starting point for all forms of analysis, even of the esoteric postmodern cultural forms around us, I recommend that we 'think of it as labour'.

Chapter 7 The Ethnographic Imagination and 'Whole Ways of Life'

1 See the article of the same name by Williams, first published in N. McKenzie (ed.), *Convictions*, London, MacGibbon & Kee, 1958, and reprinted in R. Williams, *Resources of Hope*, Verso, 1989.
2 R. Williams, *The Long Revolution*, London, Pelican, 1965, p. 63.
3 It is true that the debate about the 'under-class' and its state management echoes themes of containing and civilizing the 'dangerous

classes' (see the previous chapter). But the dominant emphasis is on regulation and bringing individuals into low-wage labour and into economic 'self-responsibility' rather than on the 'lifting' of their collective cultures in the image of 'the best that has been thought and said'. Nor are there yet clear internal organizational forms (such as trade unionism for the original working class) or external analyses that *positively* investigate and promote emergent cultural forms, within what I would still prefer to call the lower or most threatened strata of the working class. Either way, the original passion, ambition and, in its way, nobility of the arguments over culture have either disappeared or become wholly debased.

4 Williams, *The Long Revolution*, p. 63.
5 For me this is a problem for the whole genre of 'audience studies'. Watching TV is certainly an important element, but where is the relation to other elements? You cannot take simple verbal decodings recorded at the site of consumption as evidence of social resistance or reproduction. That would require reciprocal understandings of the implications of symbolic work at consumption sites *and* at other main sites.
6 Social mobility rates have remained more or less constant in the UK since the beginning of the century. The chances that a child from a working-class (manual) background will move into the 'salariat' are five to six times less than those for a similar child from a non-manual background. The chances of death for individuals of the same age in a given year are almost twice as high for manual workers. G. Marshall, *Repositioning Class*, London, Sage, 1997; A. Swift and G. Marshall, 'Meritocratic equality of opportunity', *Policy Studies*, vol. 18, 1997; M. Bartley et al., 'Measuring inequalities in health', *Sociology of Health and Illness*, vol. 4, 1996.
7 See my 'Notes on method' in S. Hall et al. (eds), *Culture, Media, Language*, London, Hutchinson, 1980, first published as 'Man in the iron cage', *Working Papers in Cultural Studies*, no. 9, Birmingham University, Centre for Contemporary Cultural Studies, 1976.
8 For a fuller discussion, see my 'TIES: theoretically informed ethnographic study' in S. Nugent and C. Shore (eds), *Anthropology and Cultural Studies*, Pluto Press, 1977.
9 See previous two notes.
10 Many of the theoretical resources, especially relating to the social 'element' of an ethnographic focus, have in the first instance to be taken on trust from elsewhere, increasing methodological and epistemological dangers, but the process outlined here of refining and developing them in relation to a concrete empirical site can turn them into their own new thing, not simply taken and transplanted

from the outside – capable also of regenerating or redirecting the theoretical resources whence they came. For an example of taking a piece of Marxist theory, for its honing in the field, and for the difficulties and illuminations encountered when subjects disagree with the interpretation, see my paper 'Why take the piss' in D. Holland and J. Lave (eds), *History in Person*, Santa Fe, New Mexico, School for American Research, 2000.

11 For a fuller outline see the Appendix to my *Profane Culture*, London, Routledge and Kegan Paul, 1978.

12 Richard Sennett notes in his book *Authority* (1980) p. 133, 'Any sequence which gives consciousness a structure is, as William James remarked, a "catalyst": thinking about x permits me to think more openly about y. In technical terms, there is a necessary "evolutionary ontology" in performing interpretive tasks.' One of the aims of this book is to argue not only for the general importance of reflexivity (often ill-defined) in research practices but also for the importance of respect for, and the responsible provision of possible materials towards, the reflexivity of social agents themselves. Crucial here and missed from most accounts is the importance of reflexivity to agents' reflexivity to social structures and their ideological/linguistic repertoires and effects. A perspective on the understanding of social reality which builds in, methodologically and theoretically, a role for the cultural production of human agents in producing it also indicates alternatives, sensitive cultural levers and unintended consequences within those practices that are of, at least potential, interest to those who execute them.

13 P. Willis, 'Notes on common culture: towards a cultural policy for grounded aesthetics', *Cultural Policy*, vol. 4, no. 2, 1998; P. Willis, *Moving Culture*, London, Gulbenkian Foundation, 1990.

Appendix: Homology

1 Dick Hebdige, *Subculture: The Meaning of Style*, London, Methuen, 1979.

Index

Use Your Head

Tony Buzan

Tony Buzan is the originator of Mind Maps, the SEM³ (Self-Enhancing Master Memory Matrix), the Group/Family/Work/Study Technique, and new concepts in brain functioning relating to the process of Change and Metapositive Thinking. He is also the Founder of the International Brain Clubs and Buzan Centres.

Born in London in 1942, he emigrated to Vancouver in 1954 and graduated from the University of British Columbia in 1964, achieving double Honours in Psychology, English, Mathematics and the General Sciences. Returning to England in 1966, he worked on Fleet Street, also editing the *International Journal of MENSA* (the high IQ Society). Since then he has published 10 books (nine on the brain and learning and one volume of poetry). His books have been published in 50 countries and translated into 20 languages. His best-seller *Use your Head* has achieved worldwide sales of more than a million and is a standard introductory text for the Open University.

Tony Buzan has featured in, presented and co-produced many television, video and radio programmes, including the record-breaking *Use Your Head* series (BBC TV), the *Open Mind* series (ITV) and *The Enchanted Loom* (Thames). He is adviser to royalty, governments and multi-national organisations, and is a regular lecturer at the leading international universities and schools.

He is a Fellow of the Institute of Training and Development, the Jamaican Institute of Management and the Swedish Management Group, and is an elected member of the International Faculty of the Young Presidents' Organisation and the International Council of Psychologists. A Member of the Institute of Directors, and a Freeman of the City of London, he is also adviser to the British Olympic Rowing Squad.

ALSO BY TONY BUZAN

Books

Use Your Memory
Speed (and Range) Reading
Master Your Memory
Memory Visions (workbook for *Master Your Memory*)
The Brain User's Guide
Make the Most of Your Mind
Harnessing the ParaBrain
   (Business version of *Make the Most of Your Mind*)
Spore One (poetry – limited edition)

Videotapes

Use Your Head
The Enchanted Loom
Buzan Business Training
Family Genius Training

Audiotapes

Learning and Memory
The Intelligence Revolution
Make the Most of Your Mind
Supercreativity and Mind Mapping

Other Works

The Universal Personal Organiser
'Body and Soul' (Master Mind Map poster)
The Mind Map Kit
Master Your Memory Matrix (SEM^3) 0–10,000
The Brain Club Manifesto
The Brain Club Magazine

see *Appendix* for more information, including how to order these items

use your HeAD

TONY BUZAN

BBC BOOKS

DEDICATED TO YOU

**and to my beloved Mum and Dad,
Jean and Gordon Buzan**

External Editor-in-chief: Vanda North

With thanks to all those whose effort and
co-operation enabled me to write this book:

Zita Albes; Jennie Allen; Astrid Andersen;
Jeannie Beattie; Nick Beytes; Mark Brown; Joy Buttery;
my brother, Barry Buzan; Bernard Chibnall;
Carol Coaker; Steve and Fanny Colling; Charlotte Crace,
Susan Crockford; Tricia Date; Janet Dominey;
Charles Elton; Lorraine Gill; Bill Harris;
Brian Helweg-Larsen; Thomas Jarlov; Trish Lillis;
Hermione Lovell; Annette McGee; Joe McMahon;
Vanda North; Khalid Ranjah; Pep Reiff; Auriol Roberts;
Ian Rosenbloom; Caitrina Ni Shuilleabhain;
Robert Millard Smith; Sarah Spalding;
Chris and Pat Stevens; Jan Streit; Christopher Tatham;
Lee Taylor; Nancy Thomas; Sue Vaudin; Jim Ward;
Bill Watts; Gillian Watts; Phyllida Wilson.

First published 1974
Revised and extended edition first published 1982
Reprinted 1983 (twice), 1984, 1985 (twice), 1986, 1987 (twice)
Hardback edition first published 1984
This revised edition published 1989
Reprinted 1989
Reprinted 1990, 1991 (twice), 1992
Reprinted 1993

Published by BBC Books
a division of BBC Enterprises Ltd
Woodlands, 80 Wood Lane, London W12 0TT

Set in Univers 9/11 by Phoenix Photosetting
Printed and bound in Great Britain by
Redwood Press Ltd, Melksham, Wiltshire

ISBN 0 563 20811 2 (paperback)
ISBN 0 563 20812 0 (hardback)

Contents

HAMLET: Prince of Denmark

Act IV, Scene IV
A plain in Denmark

Hamlet:

> *What is a man,*
> *If his chief good and market of his time*
> *Be but to sleep and feed? a beast, no more.*
> *Sure, he that made us with such large discourse,*
> *Looking before and after, gave us not*
> *That capability and god-like reason*
> *To fust in us unused.*

Introduction

Use Your Head is written to help you do just that. By the time you have finished the book you should understand much more about how your mind works and how to use it to the best advantage, be able to read faster and more efficiently, to study more effectively, to solve problems more readily and to increase the power of your memory.

This introductory section gives general guide lines about the book's contents, and the way in which these contents are best approached.

THE CHAPTERS

Each chapter deals with a different aspect of your brain's functioning. First the book outlines the most up-to-date information about the brain and then applies this information to the way in which your vision can be best used.

The fifth chapter explains how you can improve memory both during and after learning. In addition a special system is introduced for the perfect memorisation of listed items.

The middle chapters explore your mind's internal 'maps'. This information about how you think is applied to the way in which you can use language, words and imagery for recording, organising, remembering, creative thinking and problem solving.

The ninth chapter deals with the new Mind Map Organic Study Technique which will enable you to study any subject ranging from English to Higher Mathematics, Philosophy to Languages.

The final chapter summarises the gigantic leaps made in the last fifteen years, gives a new perspective on the ageing brain and leads you into new directions for the future.

In the colour section you will find Mind Maps which you are advised to look at before and after reading each relevant chapter – they serve as a preview/review summary.

In certain of the chapters, important key concepts are printed in bold type to enable your easy reference in previewing and reviewing.

YOUR EFFORT

It is essential that you practise if you wish to be able to use effectively the methods and information outlined. At various stages in the book there are exercises and suggestions for further activity. In addition you should work out your own practice and study schedule, keeping to it as firmly as possible.

PERSONAL NOTES

At the end of each chapter and at the end of the book you will find pages for 'Personal notes and applications'. These are for any jottings you might wish to make during reading and can also be used when you discover further information and applications after you have 'finished' the book.

BIBLIOGRAPHY

On page 151 you will find a special list of books. These are not just books of academic reference, but include books which will help you develop your general knowledge as well as giving you more specialised information concerning some of the areas covered in *Use Your Head*.

YOU AND YOURSELF

It is hoped that *Use Your Head* will help you to expand as an individual, and that through an increasing awareness of yourself you will be able to develop your own ways of thinking.

Each person using information from this book starts with different levels of learning ability, and will progress at the pace best suited to him. It is important therefore to measure improvement in relation to yourself and not to others.

Although much of the information has been presented in connection with reading, formal noting and studying, the complete application is much wider. When you have finished and reviewed the book, browse through it again to see in which other areas of your life the information can be helpfully applied.

1 A Use Your Head tale: an impossible dream – the Edward Hughes story

THE BEGINNING

After *Use Your Head* was first published in 1974, a 'fairly average student, middle of the form, not doing particularly well in any subject' took, in 1982, at the age of 15, his 'O' level examinations.

His results, as expected, and as they had always been, were C's and B's. He was disappointed with the results because he had set his heart on going to Cambridge University and realised that if he carried on academically the way he was, then he didn't stand a chance.

The student's name was Edward Hughes.

A little while later Edward's father, George, introduced him to *Use Your Head*, and armed with new information about himself, and about how to Mind Map, learn and study, Edward went back to school revitalised and motivated. He announced that he was going for A's in all his subjects, and that he definitely wanted to be put forward for Cambridge.

The reaction of his teachers was understandably bemused and varied. 'You can't be serious: come on, you've got no chance – your academic results have never been anywhere *near* the standard which Cambridge requires,' said one.

'Don't be daft! You could possibly get a B, but you'll probably get a C,' said the second. When Edward said he wished to take not only the standard exam, but also to write the Scholarship paper, the master said flatly, 'No, it's a waste of the school's money and your time entering for that exam. We don't think you'll pass, for the exams are very, *very* difficult – we don't even get many passes from our best candidates.' After Edward persisted, the school was willing to put him forward, but he had to pay his own £20 entrance fee in order not to 'waste the school's money'.

The third teacher said that he had been teaching the same subject for the last twelve years, that he was the expert in the area, and that he knew what he was talking about when he said that Hughes would only get a B or a C. The teacher named 'another chap' who was a much better student than Edward, and said that Edward would never be as good as the other. As Edward said at the time, 'I disagreed with his reading of the situation!'

The fourth teacher chuckled, said he obviously admired Edward's ambition, said that Edward's dream was possible but unlikely, said that even if he worked hard he'd only get a B, but wished him luck and said that he always liked someone who showed a bit of initiative.

'I WILL GET AN A'

To each of the teachers, and to anyone who questioned his goals, Edward's final response was always simply: 'I will get an A.'

The school initially did not want to put Edward's name forward for Cambridge, but after a while agreed to do so, letting the colleges at Cambridge know that they didn't really think that this particular student was likely to get the place for which he applied.

The next and immediate stage was the college interviews. At these, the Cambridge dons informed Edward of the school's opinion of him, agreed with the school that his probability of success was very low, admired his initiative, told him that he'd need at least two B's and an A, but more probably two A's and a B, or three A's, and wished him luck.

Still undaunted, Edward pursued a plan of Use Your Head and physical training. In his own words: 'I was getting nearer the exams. I summarised my last two years of school notes neatly into Mind Maps. I then coloured them, highlighted them, and produced giant Master Mind Maps for each of the courses, and in some instances for each major section of each course. In this way I could see where and how the more detailed elements fitted together, and in addition get a good overview, thus enabling me to be able to "just flick through" giant sections of the course with completely accurate recall.

'I kept reviewing these Mind Maps once a week, and as it got nearer to the exams, even more regularly. I practised my Recall Mind Maps, not looking at my books or other notes, simply drawing from my memory what knowledge and understanding of the subjects I had, and then comparing these Mind Maps with my Master Mind Maps, checking the differences.

'I also made sure that I had read all the main key books, and then sorted these down to a few, read them in depth, and Mind Mapped them so that my understanding and memory were maximised. In addition I studied good essay form and style, and used my own Mind Maps as a basis for practising essay and examination writing.

'I accompanied this by getting fitter, by running two to three miles, two to three times per week, getting lots of fresh air, doing lots of press-ups and sit-ups, and working out in a gym. I became better physically, which I found helped my concentration enormously. As they say, healthy body, healthy mind; healthy mind, healthy body. I felt better about myself and I felt better about my work.'

THE EXAMINATIONS – THE RESULTS

Eventually Edward sat four examinations: Geography, the Geography Scholarship paper, Business Studies and Mediaeval History.
His results were as follows:

Subject	Mark	Rank
Geography	A	Top student
Geography Scholarship	Distinction	Top student
Mediaeval History	A	Top student
Business Studies	A and 2 Distinctions	Top student ever

Within a day of the publication of the results, Edward's first-choice college at Cambridge had confirmed his place, and accepted his request for a 'year off' to see a bit of the world before he started his University career. During his year's 'sabbatical' he worked in Singapore, as a cowboy in Australia and also had a holiday in Fiji and Hawaii. He then flew across to California where he worked in embryo transfer units and on cattle ranges. He worked his way across America on farms, and then returned to England.

Before going to Cambridge, Edward decided that, in addition to academic success throughout his time at University, he would set himself the goals of creating a new student society, playing lots of sports for the college, making many new friends, and basically having 'a tremendous time!'

AT CAMBRIDGE

In sports he was immediately successful, playing in the college soccer, tennis and squash teams. And in the area of student societies he might even be termed an over-achiever. For in addition to founding the Young Entrepreneurs Society, the largest of its kind in Europe, he was asked to preside over the Very Nice Society, a charitable society of 3,600 members, which grew to 4,500 under his presidency – the largest society in the history of the University. In view of his work for these two societies, the other society presidents asked Edward to form and preside over a society for presidents. This he did and became the President of the Presidents Club!

Academically he first studied the habits of the 'average student' and reported: 'They spent about 12–13 hours reading for each essay, linearly noting all the information they could, reading all possible books, after which they'd spend 3–4 hours writing the essay itself (some students would actually rewrite their essays, occasionally spending an entire week on one essay).'

In view of his experience with the 'O' level preparation and examinations, Edward decided to allocate himself 2–3 hours a day, 5 days a week, to study. 'During those three hours I went to a key lecture, summarising all the relevant information in Mind Map form. I set myself the goal that as soon as any essays were set, I'd go away and do a Mind Map on what I knew about the subject or what I thought was relevant. And then leave it for a couple of days, think about it, turn it over in my mind, and then speed and range read the relevant books, Mind Mapping the relevant information from them. I'd then take a break or do some exercise, and then come back and do a Mind Map on the essay itself. Having completed my essay plan, I'd take another break, and then sit down and complete the essay *always* within 45 minutes. With this technique I regularly achieved high marks.'

Before the final Cambridge examinations, Edward worked to a schedule virtually identical to that with which he prepared his 'A' levels, and took six final examinations.

The results?

THE RESULTS

In the first, he was given a pass, normally considered fair but here excellent because 50% of those taking the examination failed it, and no firsts were given; in the second, third and fourth, three 2.1's; and in the final exams two first classes – not only first classes, but *Star Firsts*, the highest marks in the University for that subject.

Immediately after graduation, Edward was offered employment as a Strategic Thinker for a multi-national entrepreneurial company, a job described by the University as 'one of the best ever' for a Cambridge undergraduate. As Edward summarised: 'Cambridge was fantastic. I was fortunate enough to get a lot out of it – a lot of friends, a lot of experience, a lot of physical activity, a lot of enthusiasm for and success in academia, and three years of absolutely great enjoyment. The major difference between myself and the others was simply that I knew how to think – how to use my head. I was a C and B student before I knew how to "get an A". I did it. Anyone can.'

(Reader: do *you* have a Use Your Head tale? If you do, please send it to Tony Buzan c/o address on page 149.)

2 Your mind is better than you think

MAN'S UNDERSTANDING OF HIS OWN MIND

Since I wrote the introductory chapter on the brain for the first edition of *Use Your Head* in 1974, research in that area has been exploding with new and exciting discoveries. Rather than stating, as I did then, that 'only in the last 150 years' has the bulk of progress been made in this area, I can now state that only in the last *fifteen* years has the bulk of our knowledge been accumulated. This seems extraordinarily late when you consider that life appeared on earth 3,500,000 years ago. Bear in mind, however, that mankind has only known the *location* of its brain for the last 500 years. In some ways this is not surprising. Consider for a moment that you have no idea where your brain is to be found, and a friend asks: 'Where is the centre of your feelings, emotions, thoughts, memories, drives and desires located?'. You, like most others (including Aristotle!) might quite rationally decide that your brain was located in the heart and stomach area, because that is where you experience the direct physical manifestation of mental activity most regularly and dramatically.

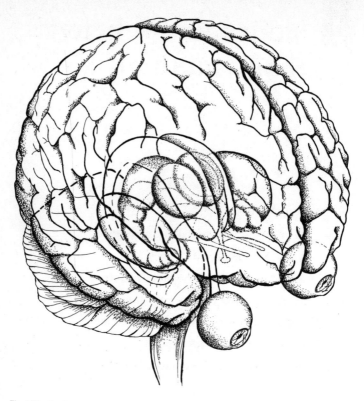

Fig 1 The brain
Source: SCIENTIFIC AMERICAN (see page 150 for details)

If, even now, as we pursue with computers and electron micro-scopes what must be the most elusive quarry man has ever chased, we must still admit that the sum total of the knowledge we have acquired today is probably less than 1% of what there is to know. Just when tests seem to prove that the mind works in a given way, along comes another test which shows another picture, or along comes another human being with a brain who manages to make us need to rework the whole frame.

What we are gathering from our efforts at the moment is a knowledge that the mind is infinitely more subtle than we had previously thought, and that everyone who has what is ironically called a 'normal' mind has a much larger ability and potential than was previously believed.

A few examples will help to make this clear.
Most of the more scientific disciplines, despite their apparent

differences of direction, are all being drawn into a whirlpool, the centre of which is the mind. Chemists are now involved with the intricate chemical structures that exist and interact inside our heads; biologists are uncovering the brain's biological functions; physicists are finding parallels with their investigations into the farthest reaches of space; psychologists are trying to pin the mind down and are finding the experience frustratingly like trying to place a finger on a little globule of mercury; and mathematicians who have constructed models for complex computers and even for the Universe itself, still can't come up with a formula for the operations that go on regularly inside each of our heads every day of our lives.

MORE THAN ONE BRAIN

What we *have* discovered during the last fifteen years is that you have two upper brains rather than one, and that they operate in different degrees in the different mental areas; that the potential patterns your brain can make is even greater than was thought at the end of the 1960s, and that your brain requires very different kinds of food if it is to survive, *see fig 2*.

In Californian laboratories in the late 1960s and early 1970s, research was begun which was to change the history of our appreciation of the human brain, and which was eventually to win Roger Sperry of the California Institute of Technology a Nobel Prize and Robert Ornstein worldwide fame for his work on brain waves and specialisation of function, carried on through the 1980s by Professor Eran Zaidel.

In summary, what Sperry and Ornstein discovered was that the two sides of your brain, or your two cortices, which are linked by a fantastically complex network of nerve fibres called the Corpus Callosum, deal dominantly with different types of mental activity.

In most people the left cortex deals with logic, words, reasoning, number, linearity, and analysis etc, the so-called 'academic' activities. While the left cortex is engaged in these activities, the right cortex is more in the 'alpha wave' or resting state. The right cortex deals with rhythm, images and imagination, colour, day-dreaming, face recognition, and pattern or map recognition.

Subsequent researches showed that when people were encouraged to develop a mental area they had previously considered weak, this development, rather than detracting from other areas, seemed to produce a synergetic effect in which all areas of mental performance improved.

Professor Zaidel continued Sperry's work at the University of California with some startling results. He discovered that each hemis-

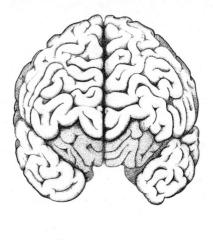

R	L
rhythm	words
spatial awareness	logic
Gestalt (whole picture)	numbers
imagination	sequence
daydreaming	linearity
colour	analysis
dimension	lists

Fig 2 Front view of the two sides of your cortex and their dominant processes

phere contains many more of the 'other side's' abilities than had been previously thought, and that each hemisphere also is capable of a much wider and much more subtle range of mental activities.

At first glance history seemed to deny this finding however, for most of the 'Great Brains' appeared very lopsided in mental terms: Einstein and other great scientists seemed to be predominantly 'left-cortex' dominant, while Picasso, Cézanne and other great artists and musicians appeared to be 'right-cortex' dominant.

A more thorough investigation unearthed some fascinating truths: Einstein failed French at school and numbered among his activities violin playing, art, sailing, and imagination games!

To his imagination games Einstein gave credit for many of his more significant scientific insights. While daydreaming on a hill one summer day, he imagined riding sunbeams to the far extremities of the Universe, and upon finding himself returned, 'illogically', to the surface of the sun, he realised that the Universe must indeed be curved, and that his previous 'logical' training was incomplete. The numbers, equations and words he wrapped around this new image gave us the Theory of Relativity – a left *and* right cortex synthesis.

Similarly the great artists turned out to be 'whole-brained'. Rather than note books filled with stories of drunken parties, and paint slapped haphazardly to produce masterpieces, entries similar to the following were found:

'Up at 6 am. Spent seventeenth day on painting number six of the latest series. Mixed four parts orange with two parts yellow to produce a colour combination which I placed in upper left-hand corner of canvas, to act in visual opposition to spiral structures in lower right-hand corner, producing desired balance in eye of perceiver.' – Telling examples of just how much left-cortex activity goes into what we normally consider right-cortex pursuits.

In addition to the researches of Sperry and Ornstein, the experimental evidence of increased overall performance, and the confirming historical fact that many of the 'Great Brains' were indeed using both ranges of their capacity, one man in the last thousand years stands out as a supreme example of what a single human being can do if both sides of the brain are developed simultaneously: Leonardo da Vinci. In his time he was arguably the most accomplished man in *each* of the following disciplines: art, sculpture, physiology, general science, architecture, mechanics, anatomy, physics, invention, meteorology, geology, engineering and aviation. He could also play, compose and sing spontaneous ballads when thrown any stringed instrument in the courts of Europe. Rather than separating these different areas of his latent ability, he *combined* them. Leonardo's scientific note books are filled with 3-dimensional drawings and images; and equally as interesting, the final plans for his great painting masterpieces often look like architectural plans: straight lines, angles, curves and numbers incorporating mathematical, logical and precise measurements.

It seems, then, that when we describe ourselves as talented in certain areas and not talented in others, what we are *really* describing is those areas of our potential that we have successfully developed, and those areas of our potential that still lie dormant, which in reality could, with the right nurturing, flourish.

The right and left cortex findings give added support to the work you will be doing on memory systems, on note taking and communication, and on advanced Mind Mapping, for in each of these areas it is essential to use *both* sides of your upper brain.

INTERCONNECTIONS OF THE BRAIN'S NEURONS

It is also interesting to note that Dr David Samuels of the Weizmann Institute estimated that underlying the brain's basic range of activities, there are between 100,000 and 1,000,000 different chemical reactions taking place every minute!

In your brain there are a minimum of 1,000,000,000,000 individual neurons or nerve cells. This figure becomes even more astounding when it is realised that each of your neurons can interact with from 1 to 100,000 other neurons in many ways. At the time I was writing the first edition of *Use Your Head* in 1974, it had been recently estimated that the number of permutations might be as many as 1 followed by eight hundred noughts. To realise just how enormous this number is, compare it with a mathematical fact about the Universe: one of the smallest items in the Universe is the atom. The biggest thing we know is the Universe itself. The number of atoms in the known Universe is predictably enormous: 10 with one hundred noughts after it. The number of possible thought-maps in *one* brain makes even this number seem tiny. *See figs 3 and 4.*

Shortly after the first edition of *Use Your Head* was published, Dr Pyotr Anokhin of Moscow University, who had spent the last few years of his life studying the information processing capabilities of the brain, stated that the number one followed by 800 noughts was a gross under-estimation. The new number he had calculated was conservative due to the relative clumsiness of our current measuring instruments in comparison to the incredible delicacy of the brain. The number was not one, followed by 800 noughts. The pattern-making capability of the brain, or 'degrees of freedom' throughout the brain is

'so great that writing it would take a line of figures, in normal manuscript characters, more than 10.5 million kilometres in length! With such a number of possibilities, the brain is a keyboard on which hundreds of millions of different melodies – acts of behaviour or intelligence – can be played. No man yet exists or has existed who has even approached using his full brain. We accept no limitations on the power of the brain – it is limitless.'

Use Your Head is written to help you play your virtually infinite mental keyboard.

Other examples of the mind's abilities abound – examples of extraordinary memory feats, feats of super-strength, and unusual control of body functions defying the 'laws of science', are becoming more widespread. They are now fortunately more documented, generally recognised and usefully applied. .

10,000,000,000,000,000,000,000,000,000,000,000,000,
000,000,000,000,000,000,000,000,000,000,000,000,000
000,000,000,000,000,000,000

Fig 3 The number of atoms (one of the smallest particles we know of) in the known Universe (the largest thing we know of). *See text on facing page.*

10,000,000,000,000,000,000,000,000,000,000,000,000,
000,000,000,000,000,000,000,000,000,000,000,000,000,
000,000,000,000,000,000,000,000,000,000,000,000,000,
000,000,000,000,000,000,000,000,000,000,000,000,000,
000,000,000,000,000,000,000,000,000,000,000,000,000,
000,000,000,000,000,000,000,000,000,000,000,000,000,
000,000,000,000,000,000,000,000,000,000,000,000,000,
000,000,000,000,000,000,000,000,000,000,000,000,000,
000,000,000,000,000,000,000,000,000,000,000,000,000,
000,000,000,000,000,000,000,000,000,000,000,000,000,
000,000,000,000,000,000,000,000,000,000,000,000,000,
000,000,000,000,000,000,000,000,000,000,000,000,000,
000,000,000,000,000,000,000,000,000,000,000,000,000,
000,000,000,000,000,000,000,000,000,000,000,000,000,
000,000,000,000,000,000,000,000,000,000,000,000,000,
000,000,000,000,000,000,000,000,000,000,000,000,000,
000,000,000,000,000,000,000,000,000,000,000,000,000,
000,000,000,000,000,000,000,000,000,000,000,000,000,
000,000,000,000,000,000,000,000,000,000,000,000,000,
000,000

Fig 4 In the late 1960s it was calculated that the number of different patterns the 1,000,000,000,000 individual nerve cells of the brain could make was 1 followed by 800 noughts. Recent estimates have shown that even this number is too small! *See text on facing page.*

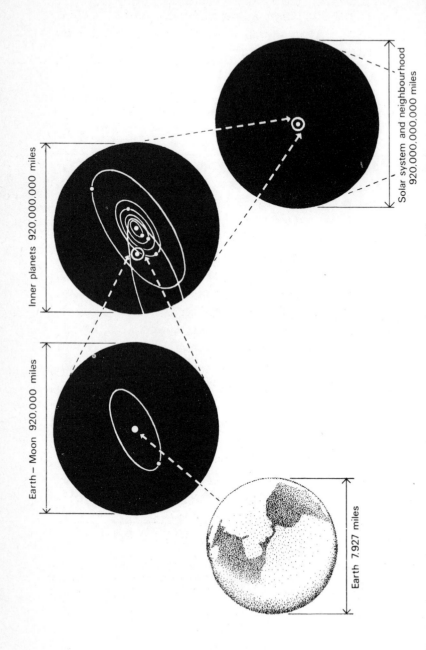

Solar system and neighbourhood 920,000,000,000 miles

Inner planets 920,000,000 miles

Earth – Moon 920,000 miles

Earth 7,927 miles

22

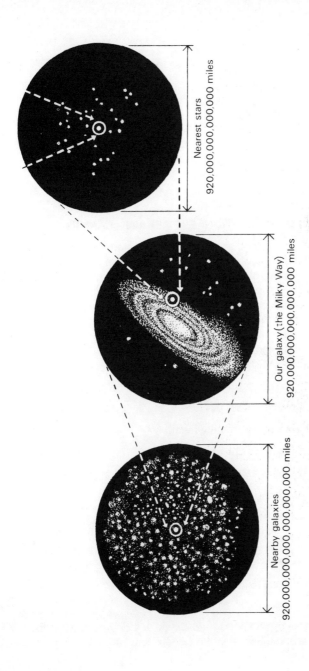

Fig 5 The enormous size of the known Universe. Each successive black sphere is a thousand million times (1,000,000,000) as big as the one before it. *See text on page 20.*

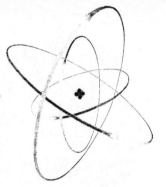

Fig 6 The atom – one of the tiniest entities known. In the tip of a person's finger there are many billions of atoms, and in the entire Universe a number equal to 10 with 100 noughts after it.
For the relationship between these facts and the brain's interconnecting networks, see figs 3 and 4 and text on page 20.

MODELS OF PERCEPTION: EYE – BRAIN – CAMERA

First let us consider the eye/brain/mind system: as recently as the 1950s the camera provided the model for our perception and mental imaging: the lens of the camera corresponded to the lens of the eye, and the photographic plate to the brain itself. *See fig 7.* This conception was held for some time but was very inadequate. You can confirm this inadequacy by doing the following exercises: in the way that one normally does when drowsily day-dreaming, close your eyes and imagine your favourite object. Having clearly registered the image on your inner eye, perform the following activities.

Rotate it in front of you

Look at it from the top

Look at it from underneath

Change its colour at least three times

Move it away as if it were seen from a long distance

Bring it close again

Make it gigantic

Make it tiny

Totally change the shape of it

Make it disappear

Bring it back

These feats can be performed by you without much difficulty; the apparatus and machinery of a camera could not even begin to perform them.

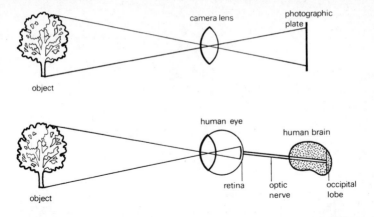

Fig 7 Contrary to earlier thought the brain operates in a much more complex manner than the camera. *See text on page 24.*

THE HOLOGRAM AS A MODEL FOR THE BRAIN

Recent developments in more refined technology have fortunately given us a much better analogy: the hologram.

In this technique, an especially concentrated light or laser beam is split into two. One half of the ray is directed to the plate, while the other half is bounced off the image and then directed back to the other half of the ray. The special holographic plate records the millions of fragments into which the rays shatter when they collide. When this plate is held up in front of the laser beams directed at special angles towards it, the original image is recreated. Amazingly, it is not recreated as a flat picture on the plate, but is perfectly duplicated as a three-dimensional ghost object that hangs in space. If the object is looked at from above, below or the side, it is seen in exactly the same way as the original object would be seen.

Even more amazingly, if the original holographic plate is rotated through 90 degrees, as many as 90 images can be recorded on the same plate with no interference.

And to add still further to the extraordinary nature of this new development, if the plate is taken and smashed to smithereens with a hammer, each particle of the shattered plate will, when it is placed in front of the specially directed lasers, still produce the complete three-dimensional ghost.

The holograph thus becomes a far more reasonable model than the camera for the way in which your brain works, and begins to give us some idea of just how complex an organ it is that we carry about with us.

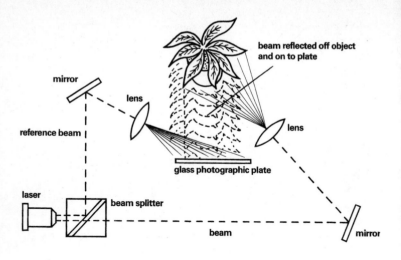

Fig 8 The holograph – a more appropriate model for your multi-faceted brain.

But even this extremely refined piece of technology falls far short of the unique capabilities of the brain. The holograph certainly approximates more closely the three-dimensional nature of our imaginations, but its storage capacity is puny compared to the millions of images that our brains can call up at an instant's notice, and randomly. The holograph is also static. It cannot perform any of the directional exercises of the kind described on page 24 which the brain finds so easy and yet which must involve the most unimaginably intricate machinery. And even if the holograph were able to accomplish all this, it would not be able to do what our minds can: to see its own self, with eyes closed, performing the operations!

IQ AND OUR BRILLIANCE

They say that IQ tests measure our 'absolute intelligence' so therefore *they* must be right. Apart from the fact that an IQ score can be significantly changed by even a small amount of well-directed practice, there are other arguments against these tests.

First, the Berkeley Study on Creativity showed that a person whose IQ assessment was high was not necessarily: independent in thought; independent in action; either possessed of or able to value a good sense of humour; appreciative of beauty; reasonable; relativistic; able to enjoy complexity and novelty; original;

comprehensively knowledgeable; fluent; flexible; or astute.

Secondly, those who argue that IQ does measure a wide and absolute range of human abilities have failed to consider that the test should be concerned with three major areas: 1) the brain being tested; 2) the test itself; 3) the results. Unfortunately the IQ protagonists have become too obsessed with the test and the results and have neglected the real nature of the brain being tested.

They have failed to realise that their tests do not test basic human ability, but measure untrained and undeveloped human performance. Their claims are much like those of an imaginary surveyor of women's feet sizes in the Orient at the time when their feet were restricted to make them small. From the crib the foot was placed in bandages until the woman was nearly full grown. This was done to stunt the growth and to produce 'dainty' feet.

To assume, however, as the surveyor might have done, that these measurements represent natural and fully developed bodily dimensions is as absurd as it is to assume that intelligence tests measure the natural dimensions of our minds. Our minds, like the women's feet, have been 'bound' by the way we have misjudged and mistrained them, and are therefore not naturally developed.

In defence of IQ tests, it is interesting to note their history. They were *not* developed as a method, so often assumed, of 'suppressing the masses'. On the contrary, the French psychologist Binet observed that those children getting higher education were almost exclusively from the upper classes. He considered this unfair, and devised the first IQ tests in order to allow *any* child with developed mental abilities to qualify for ongoing studies. The tests gave unparalleled opportunities for children who would otherwise have been deprived.

If IQ tests are considered as games, or 'markers' of a current stage of mental development in a few specified areas, they can be used both to gauge present developments in those areas, and as a basis from which those skills can be improved and developed, and the IQ score raised appropriately.

THE HUMAN BABY – A MODEL OF EXCELLENCE

Another most convincing case for the excellence of the human brain is the functioning and development of the human baby. Far from being the 'helpless and incapable little thing' that many people assume it to be, it is the most extraordinary learning, remembering and intellectually advanced being – even in its most early stages it surpasses the performance of the most sophisticated computers.

With very few exceptions, all babies learn to speak by the time they are two, and many even earlier. Because this is so universal it is taken for granted, but if the process is examined more closely it is seen to be extremely complex.

Try listening to someone speaking while pretending that you have no knowledge of language and very little knowledge of the objects and ideas the language discusses. Not only will this task be difficult, but because of the way sounds run into each other the distinction between different words will often be totally unclear. Every baby who has learned to talk has overcome not only these difficulties but also the difficulties of sorting out what makes sense and what doesn't. When he is confronted with sounds like 'koooochiekooo-chiekoooooooooaahhhhisn'tealovelelyli'ldarling!' one wonders how he ever manages to make sense of us at all!

The young child's ability to learn language involves him in processes which include a subtle control of, and an inherent understanding of, rhythm, mathematics, music, physics, linguistics, spatial relations, memory; integration, creativity, logical reasoning and thinking – left and right cortex working from the word go.

You who still doubt your own abilities have yourself learned to talk and to read. You should therefore find it difficult to attack a position of which you yourself are evidence for the defence.

There really is no doubt that your brain is capable of infinitely more complex tasks than has been thought. The remainder of *Use Your Head* will shed light on a number of the areas in which performance and self-realisation can be achieved.

Personal notes and applications

3 How the human brain has been reined in

OVERVIEW

▶ **Why performance does not match potential**

▶ **'Only human'**

▶ **The operations manual for the brain**

WHY PERFORMANCE DOES NOT MATCH POTENTIAL

Even with the mounting evidence, a number of people still remain sceptical about the potential of the human brain, pointing to the performance of most of us as a contradiction of that evidence. In response to this objection a questionnaire was given to people from all areas of life to determine why this amazing organ is so under-used. The questions are noted below, and underneath each question is noted the reply given by at least 95 per cent. As you read ask yourself the questions.

▶ In school were you taught anything about your brain and how understanding its functions could help you learn, memorise, think, etc?
No.

▶ Were you taught anything about how your memory functions?
No.

▶ Were you taught anything about special and advanced memory techniques?
No.

▶ Anything about how your eye functions when you are learning and about how you can use this knowledge to your advantage?
No.

▶ Anything about the ranges of study techniques and how they can be applied to different disciplines?
No.

▶ Anything about the nature of concentration and how to maintain it when necessary?
No.

▶ Anything about motivation, how it affects your abilities, and how you can use it to your advantage?
No.

▶ Anything about the nature of key words and key concepts and how they relate to note taking and imagination etc?
No.

▶ Anything about thinking?
No.

▶ Anything about creativity?
No.

By now the answer to the original objection should be clear: the reasons why our performances do not match even our minimum potentials is that we are given no information about what we are, or about how we can best utilise our inherent capacities.

'ONLY HUMAN'!

Another survey I have carried out over the last thirty years, and in fifty different countries, is to ask people to imagine themselves in the following situation:

They have 'completed' an assignment, and the results are totally and utterly disastrous. They attempt to avoid taking responsibility, by giving such standard excuses for failure as 'so and so didn't send me the fax on time', 'I had to go to the doctor *just* at the crucial time in the project', 'It was *their* fault – if the communications systems in this company had been better, everything would have been all right', 'My boss wouldn't let me do it in the way I suggested', and so on.

They are next asked to imagine that despite all their brilliant excuse-making, they are finally 'cornered' and have to admit that the whole catastrophe was indeed their responsibility.

Finally, they are asked to complete the 'admission of guilt' sentence that people commonly use: 'All *right*, all *right*, it was my fault, but what do you expect, I'm . . . . !'

In every group surveyed, in every country, and in every language, the unanimous phrase to complete the sentence was: 'only human!'

Humorous though this may initially seem, it reflects a worldwide and seriously misguided myth that the human being is somehow fundamentally inadequate and flawed, and that it is *this* that is responsible for the mounting catalogue of human 'mistakes' and 'failures'.

To gain another perspective on the scenario described above, consider these opposites: you have done an astounding job, and people are beginning to call you 'extraordinary, wonderful, amazing, a genius, brilliant', and they are describing your work as 'astounding, the best they have ever seen, unbelievable, and unparalleled in its excellence'. For a little while you go through the standard routines of denial, but in the end have to admit to your excellence. How many times have you yourself or have you seen other people stand up proudly and pronounce 'Yes! I am brilliant, I am a genius, and the job I have done is indeed amazing – so amazing it amazed even me! and the reason is because *I'm human*!'

Probably never . . .

And yet it is this second scenario that is the more natural and indeed appropriate of the two. For the human being, you, as has been described in chapter 2, is indeed an extraordinary, and many would say miraculous creation.

The reason for our 'mistakes' and 'failures' is not that we are 'only human' but that at this very early stage in our evolution we are still taking our first, babyish and tentative steps towards an understanding of the astounding bio-computer we each possess.

The reason that in our worldwide educational systems we have spent so little time learning about how to learn is that we as a race have not known the fundamental principles of the operation of that bio-computer.

To use a modern computer metaphor, we have not known about the software for the hardware of the brain.

THE OPERATIONS MANUAL FOR THE BRAIN

Use Your Head is the first 'Operations Manual' designed to help you unleash the natural and extraordinary range of mental skills you possess.

4 Reading faster and more efficiently

OVERVIEW

▶ **Reading problems**

▶ **Reading defined**

▶ **Why reading problems exist**

▶ **Reading eye movements**

▶ **Advantages of faster reading**

▶ **Myths about reading**

▶ **Advanced reading techniques**

▶ **Motivational practice**

▶ **Metronome training**

READING PROBLEMS

In the space below and over the page note *all* the problems you have with reading and learning. Be strict with yourself. The more you are able to define, the more completely you will be able to improve.

Note your own definition of the word *Reading*.

Reading teachers have noted over the past fifteen years that in each of their classes, the same general problems arise. Below is the list of those most commonly experienced. The reader is advised to check his own against these, adding to his own list any others that apply — there will probably be quite a few.

vision	fatigue	recall
speed	laziness	impatience
comprehension	boredom	vocabulary
time	interest	subvocalisation
amount	analysis	typography
surroundings	criticism	literary style
noting	motivation	selection
retention	appreciation	rejection
age	organisation	concentration
fear	regression	back-skipping

Each of the problems in the table above is serious, and can by itself disrupt reading and learning. This book is devoted to solving these problems, the current chapter being concerned primarily with vision, speed, comprehension, and the learning environment.

Before getting down to the more physical aspects of reading I shall first define the term, then in the light of this definition shall explain why the wide range of problems that exist is so universally experienced.

READING DEFINED

Reading, which is often defined as 'getting from the book what the author intended' or 'assimilating the written word' deserves a far more complete definition. It can be defined as follows: *Reading is the individual's total interrelationship with symbolic information. It is usually the visual aspect of learning, and contains the following seven steps*:

1 recognition
The reader's knowledge of the alphabetic symbols. This step takes place almost before the physical aspect of reading begins.

2 assimilation
The physical process by which light is reflected from the word and is received by the eye, then transmitted via the optic nerve to the brain. *See fig 7.*

3 intra-integration
The equivalent to basic comprehension and refers to the linking of all parts of the information being read with all other appropriate parts.

4 extra-integration

This includes analysis, criticism, appreciation, selection and rejection. The process in which the reader brings the whole body of his previous knowledge to the new knowledge he is reading, making the appropriate connections.

5 retention

The basic storage of information. Storage can itself become a problem. Most readers will have experienced entering an examination room and storing most of their information during the two hour exam period! Storage, then, is not enough in itself, and must be accompanied by recall.

6 recall

The ability to get back out of storage that which is needed, preferably *when* it is needed.

7 communication

The use to which the information is immediately or eventually put; includes the very important subdivision: thinking.

The definition includes consideration of many of the problems listed on page 37. The only problems not included are those which are, in a sense, 'outside' the reading process, such as the influence of our reaction to our surroundings, time of day, energy level, interest, motivation, age and wellness.

WHY READING PROBLEMS EXIST

You may justifiably ask at this point why so many people experience the problems noted.

The answer, in addition to our previous lack of knowledge about the brain, lies in our approach to the initial teaching of reading. Most of you reading this book who are over twenty-five will probably have been taught by the Phonic or Alphabet Method. Others will probably have been taught by either this or by the Look and Say Method.

The most simplified Phonic Method teaches the child first the alphabet, then the different sounds for each of the letters in the alphabet, then the blending of sounds in syllables, and finally the blending of sounds forming words. From this point on he is given progressively more difficult books, usually in the form of series graded 1 to 10, through which he progresses at his own speed. He becomes a 'silent' reader during the process.

The Look and Say Methods teach children by presenting them with cards on which there are pictures. The names of the objects shown are clearly printed underneath them. Once a child has become familiar with the pictures and the names associated with them, the pictures are removed leaving only the words. When the child has built up enough basic vocabulary he progresses through a series of graded books similar to those for the child taught by the Phonic Method, and also becomes a 'silent' reader.

The outlines given of the two methods are necessarily brief, and there are at least fifty other methods similar to these presently being taught in England and in other English-speaking countries. Similar problems exist all over the world.

The point about these methods, however, is not that they are inadequate for achieving their aim, but that they are inadequate for teaching any child to read in the complete sense of the word.

Referring to the definition of Reading, it can be seen that these methods are designed to cover only the stage of recognition in the process, with some attempt at assimilation and intra-integration. The methods do not touch on the problems of speed, time, amount, retention, recall, selection, rejection, note-taking, concentration, appreciation, criticism, analyses, organisation, motivation, interest, boredom, surroundings, fatigue or typographic style, etc.

It can thus be seen that there is justification for the problems so widely experienced.

Recognition, it is important to note, is hardly ever mentioned as a problem, because it has been taught separately in the early years of school. All the other problems are mentioned because they have *not* been dealt with during the educational process.

Later chapters deal with the majority of these problems. The remainder of this chapter is devoted to eye movement, comprehension and the speed of your reading.

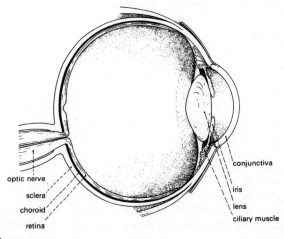

optic nerve
sclera
choroid
retina

conjunctiva
iris
lens
ciliary muscle

Fig 9 Your eye.

READING EYE MOVEMENTS

When asked to show with their forefingers the movement and speed of their eyes as they read most people move their fingers along in smooth lines from left to right, with a quick jump from the end of one line back to the beginning of the next. They normally take between a quarter to one second for each line.

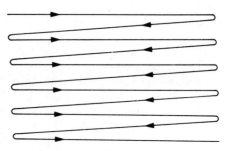

Fig 10 Assumed reading eye movement as shown by people with no knowledge of eye movements. Each line is thought to be covered in less than one second. *See text this page*.

Two major errors are being made.

Speed
Even if the eye moved as slowly as one line per second, words would be covered at the rate of 600–700 words per minute (wpm). As the average reading speed on even light material is 240 wpm, it can be seen that even those estimating slower speeds assume that they cover words much more rapidly than they really do.

Movement
If eyes moved over print in the smooth manner shown above they would be able to take in nothing, because the eye can see things clearly only when it can 'hold them still'. If an object is still, the eye must be still in order to see it, and if an object is moving, the eye must move with the object in order to see it. A simple experiment either by yourself or with a friend will confirm this: hold a forefinger motionless in front of the eyes and either feel your own eyes or watch your friend's eyes as they look at the object. They will remain still. Next move the finger up, down, sideways and around, follow-ing it with the eyes. And finally move the finger up, down and around, holding the eyes still, or cross both hands in front of your face, at the same time looking at them both simultaneously. (If you can accomplish this last feat write to me immediately!) When objects move, eyes move with them if they are to be seen clearly.

Relating all this to reading, it is obvious that if the eyes are going to take in words, and if the words are still, the eyes will have to pause on each word before moving on. Rather than moving in smooth lines as shown in fig 10, the eyes in fact move in a series of stops and quick jumps.

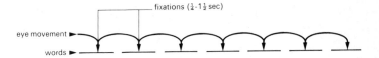

Fig 11 Diagram representing the stop-and-start movement of the eyes during the reading process. *See text this page.*

The jumps themselves are so quick as to take almost no time, but the fixations can take anywhere from ¼ to 1½ seconds. A person who normally reads one word at a time – and who skips back over words and letters is forced, by the simple mathematics of his eye movements, into reading speeds which are often well below 100 wpm, and which mean that he will not be able to understand much of what he reads, nor be able to read much.

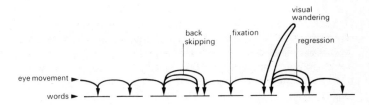

Fig 12 Diagram showing poor reading habits of slow reader: one word read at a time, with unconscious back-skipping, visual wandering, and conscious regressions. *See text this page.*

It might seem at first glance that the slow reader is doomed, but the problem can be solved, and in more than one way.

Speeding up

1 Skipping back over words can be eliminated, as 90 per cent of back-skipping and regression is based on apprehension and is unnecessary for understanding. The 10 per cent of words that do

need to be reconsidered can be noted in Mind Map form as outlined in Chapters 7 and 8 or can be intelligently guessed, marked
and looked up later.

2 The time for each fixation can be reduced to approach the ¼
second minimum – the reader need not fear that this is too short a
time, for his eye is able to register as many as five words in one
one-hundredth of a second.

3 The size of the fixation can be expanded to take in as many as
three to five words at a time.

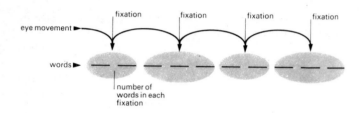

Fig 13 Diagram showing eye movements of a better and more efficient reader.
More words are taken in at each fixation, and back-skipping, regression and
visual wandering are reduced.

This solution might at first seem impossible if it is true that the mind
deals with one word at a time. In fact it can equally well fixate in
groups of words, which is better in nearly all ways: When we read a
sentence we do not read it for the individual meaning of each word,
but for the meaning of the phrases in which the words are contained.
Reading for example, the   cat
                          sat   on   the
road is more difficult than reading the cat sat   on the road.
The slower reader has to do more mental work than the faster,
smoother reader because he has to add the meaning of each word
to the meaning of each following word. In the above example this
amounts to five or six additions. The more efficient reader, absorbing in meaningful units, has only one simple addition.

ADVANTAGES OF FASTER READING

An advantage for the faster reader is that his eyes will be doing less
physical work on each page. Rather than having as many as 500
fixations tightly focused per page as does the slow reader, he will

have as few as 100 fixations per page, each one of which is less muscularly fatiguing.

Another advantage is that the rhythm and flow of the faster reader will carry him comfortably through the meaning, whereas the slow reader, because of his stopping and starting, jerky approach, will be far more likely to become bored, to lose concentration, to mentally drift away and to lose the meaning of what he is reading.

MYTHS ABOUT READING

It can be seen from this that a number of commonly held beliefs about faster readers are false:

Words must be read one at a time:
Wrong. Because of our ability to fixate and because we read for meaning rather than for single words.

Reading faster than 500 wpm is impossible:
Wrong. Because the fact that we can take in as many as six words per fixation and the fact that we can make four fixations a second means that speeds of 1,000 wpm are perfectly feasible.

The faster reader is not able to appreciate:
Wrong. Because the faster reader will be understanding more of the meaning of what he reads, will be concentrating on the material more, and will have considerably more time to go back over areas of special interest and importance to him.

Higher speeds give lower concentration:
Wrong. Because the faster we go the more impetus we gather and the more we concentrate.

Average reading speeds are natural and therefore the best:
Wrong. Because average reading speeds are not natural. They are speeds produced by an incomplete initial training in reading, combined with an inadequate knowledge of how the eye and brain work at the various speeds possible.

ADVANCED READING TECHNIQUES – FASTER AND FASTER

Apart from the general advice given above, some readers may be able to benefit from the following information which is usually prac-tised in conjunction with a qualified instructor:

Visual aid techniques:
When children learn how to read they often point with their finger to the words they are reading. We have traditionally regarded this as a fault and have told them to take their fingers off the page. It is now

realised that it is we and not the children who are at fault. Instead of insisting that they remove their fingers we should ask them to move their fingers faster. It is obvious that the hand does not slow down the eye, and the added values that the aid gives in establishing a smooth rhythmical habit are immeasurable.

To observe the difference between unaided and aided eye movement, ask a friend to imagine a large circle about one foot in front of him, and then ask him to look slowly and carefully around the circumference. Rather than moving in a perfect circle, his eyes will follow a pattern more resembling an arthritic rectangle.

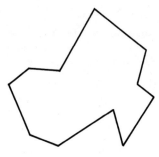

Fig 14 Pattern showing unaided eye movement attempting to move around the circumference of a circle. *See text this page.*

Next trace a circle in the air with your finger asking your friend to follow the tip of your finger as you move smoothly around the circumference. You will observe that the eyes will follow almost perfectly and will trace a circle similar to that shown below.

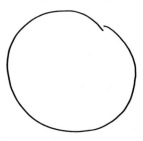

Fig 15 Pattern showing aided eye movement around the circumference of a circle. *See text this page.*

This simple experiment also indicates what an enormous improvement in performance there can be if a person is given the basic information about the physical function of the eye and brain. In many instances no long training or arduous practising is necessary. The results, as in this case, are immediate.

The reader is not restricted to the use of his forefinger as a visual aid, and can use to advantage a pen or a pencil, as many naturally efficient readers do. At first the visual aid will make the reading speed look slow. This is because, as mentioned earlier, we all imagine that we read a lot faster than we actually do. But the aided reading speed will actually be faster.

Expanded focus
In conjunction with visual aid techniques, the reader can practise taking in more than one line at a time. This is certainly not physically impossible and is especially useful on light material or for overviewing and previewing. It will also improve normal reading speeds. It is very important always to use a visual guide during this kind of reading, as without it the eye will tend to wander with comparatively little direction over the page. Various patterns of visual aiding should be experimented with, including diagonal, curving, and straight-down-the-page movements.

High speed perception
This exercise involves turning pages as fast as possible, attempting to see as many words per page as possible. This form of training will increase the ability to take in large groups of words per fixation, will be applicable to overviewing and previewing techniques, and will condition the mind to much more rapid and efficient general reading practices. This high speed conditioning can be compared to driving along a motorway at 90 miles an hour for one hour. Imagine you had been driving at this speed, and you suddenly came to a road sign saying 'slow to 30'. To what speed would you slow down if somebody covered your speedometer and said 'go on, tell me when you reach 30'. The answer of course would be 50 to 60 mph.

The reason for this is that the mind has become conditioned to a much higher speed, which becomes 'normal'. Previous 'normals' are more or less forgotten in the presence of the new ones. The same applies to reading, and after a high speed practice you will often find yourself reading at twice the speed without even feeling the difference. *See fig 16.*

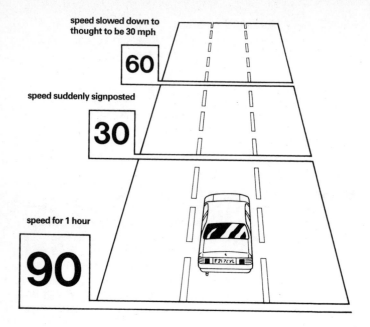

speed slowed down to
thought to be 30 mph

60

speed suddenly signposted

30

speed for 1 hour

90

Fig 16 Illustrations showing how the mind 'gets used to' speed and motion. The same kind of relativistic 'misjudgments' can be used to advantage to help us learn to learn more adequately. *See text on page 45.*

MOTIVATIONAL PRACTICE

Most reading is done at a relaxed and almost lackadaisical pace, a fact of which many speed reading courses have taken advantage. Students are given various exercises and tasks, and it is suggested to them that after each exercise their speed will increase by 10–20 wpm. And so it does, often by as much as 100 per cent over the duration of the lessons. The increase, however, is often due not to the exercises, but to the fact that the student's motivation has been eked out bit by bit during the course.

The same significant increases could be produced by guaranteeing each student, at the beginning of the course, the fulfilment of any wish he desired. Performance would immediately equal those normally achieved at the end of such courses – similar to the un-athletic fellow who runs 100 metres in 10 seconds flat and jumps a 6-foot fence when being chased by a bull. In these cases motivation is the major factor, and the reader will benefit enormously by consciously applying it to each learning experience. If a deep-rooted decision is made to do better, then poor performance will automatically improve.

METRONOME TRAINING

A metronome, which is usually used for keeping musical rhythm, can be most useful for both reading and high speed reading practices. If you set it at a reasonable pace, each beat can indicate a single sweep for your visual aid. In this way a steady and smooth rhythm can be maintained and the usual slowdown that occurs after a little while can be avoided. Once the most comfortable rhythm has been found, your reading speed can be improved by occasionally adding an extra beat per minute.

The metronome can also be used to pace the high speed perception exercises, starting at slower rates and accelerating to exceptionally fast rates, 'looking' at one page per beat.

The information on eye movements, visual aids and advanced reading techniques should be applied by the reader to each of his reading situations. It will be found that these techniques and items of advice will become more useful when applied together with information and techniques from other chapters.

For those especially interested in pursuing the full range of speed and range reading skills, refer to my book *Speed (and Range) Reading* (see page 151).

The graph on the following page is provided for readers wishing to chart their speed reading progress. To calculate your speed in words per minute, take the following steps:

1 Read for one minute – note start and stopping points.

2 Count the number of words on three lines.

3 Divide that number by three to give you the average number of words per line.

4 Count the total number of lines read (balancing short lines out).

5 Multiply the average number of words per line by the number of lines you read, which will equal your reading speed in words per minute (wpm).

NB The formula for working out speed in wpm is:

$$\text{wpm (speed)} = \frac{\text{number of pages read} \times \text{number of words per average page}}{\text{number of minutes spent reading}}$$

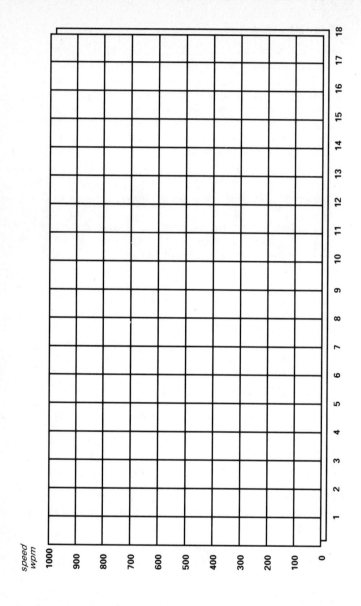

See text on page 47.

Personal notes and applications

5 Memory

QUESTIONS ON MEMORY

Test 1 Recall *during* learning
On the next page is a list of words. Read each word on this list once, quickly, in order, and then turn to page 56 and fill in as many of the words as you can. You may not be able to remember all of them, so simply try for as many as possible. Read the complete list, one after the other. To ensure you do this properly use a small card, covering each word as you read it.

start now

went
the
book
work
and
good
and
start
of
the
late
white
and
paper
Mohammed Ali
light
of
skill
the
own
stair
note
and
rode
will
time
home

Now turn to page 56 and answer questions 1–6.

Test 2 Recall *during* learning

On page 58 you will find a blank graph. Fill it in with a line which represents the amount you think your memory recalls **during** a learning period. The vertical left-hand line marks the **starting point** for the learning; the vertical right-hand line marks the point when **learning stops**; the bottom line represents no recall at all (complete forgetting); and the top line represents perfect recall.

On pages 53 and 54 are examples of graphs filled in by three people, representing the amount they felt their memories recalled **during** a learning period. These graphs start at 75% because it is assumed that most standard learning does not produce 100% understanding or recall. There are, of course, many other alternatives, so when you have looked at these, turn to page 58 and complete the graph for the way you think *your* recall works.

Fig 17 Three example of graphs filled in to indicate recall during a learning period.

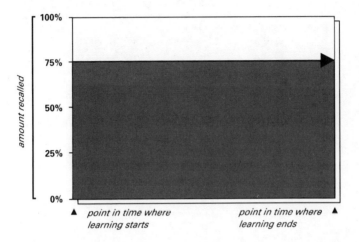

A who thought his recall of the new information he was understanding stayed constant during his learning.

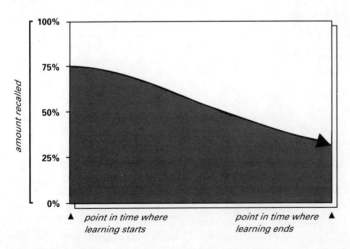

B who thought he remembered more from the beginning of a learning period and less from the end.

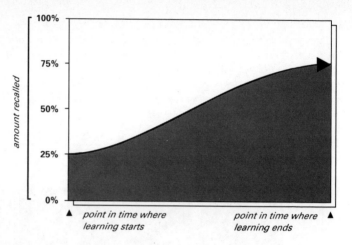

C who thought he remembered less from the start and more from the end.

Test 3 Recall *after* learning

On page 58 is a blank graph to show the way your memory behaves *after* a learning period has been completed. The vertical left-hand line marks the end point of your learning; there is no right-hand vertical line because it is assumed that the 'afterwards' would be for a few years!; the bottom line represents no recall at all; and the top line represents perfect recall. These graphs show three people's assessment of their recall after learning.

Fig 18 Three examples of graphs filled in to show recall after a learning period has been completed.

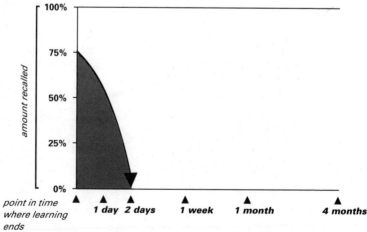

A who thought he forgot nearly everything in a very short period of time.

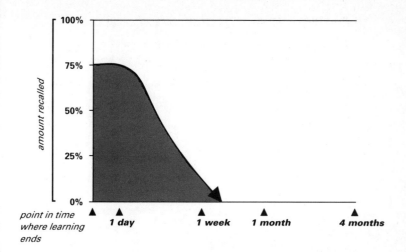

B who thought his recall was constant for a little while and then dropped off fairly steeply.

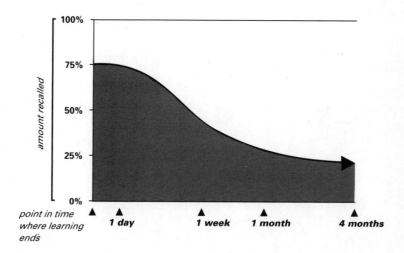

C who thought his memory stayed constant for a while and then dropped off more slowly, levelling out at a certain point.

As with Test 2 there are many alternatives, so now turn to page 58 and complete the graph in the way which most closely represents what you feel to be your normal pattern of forgetting. For the purpose of the exercise you can assume that nothing happens after your learning period to remind you of the information you learned.

TEST RESPONSES AND FURTHER QUESTIONS

Test 1: responses   Recall *during* learning
When answering the questions, do not refer to the original list

1 Fill in as many of the words, in order, as you can.

2 How many of the words from the beginning of the list did you remember before making the first error?

3 Can you recall any words which appeared more than once in the list? If so note them.

4 How many of the words within the last five did you remember?

5 Do you remember any item from the list which was outstandingly different from the rest?

6 How many words from the middle of the list can you remember which you have not already noted in answers to previous questions?

Test 2: responses   Recall *during* learning

Fill in, as demonstrated in the examples of *fig 17 pages 53 and 54*, the line which represents the way your memory recalls **during** a learning period.

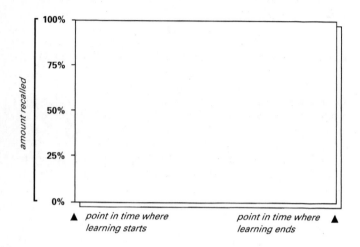

Test 3: responses   Recall *after* learning

Fill in the graph below in the way you think your recall behaves **after** a learning period has been completed. *See examples fig 18 pages 54 and 55.*

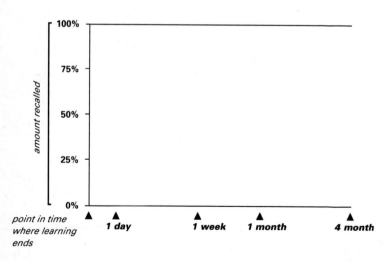

Recall *during* learning – discussion of Tests 1 and 2

Test 1 showed how recall functions **during** a period of learning, as long as understanding remains fairly constant (the words in the list were not 'difficult').

In this test virtually everyone has the following results: anywhere between 2 and 8 of the words at the beginning of the list are recalled; most of the words which appear more than once are recalled (in this case 'the', 'and', 'of'); one or two of the last five words are recalled; and the outstanding word or phrase is recalled (in this case Mohammed Ali); very few of the words from the middle are recalled.

This is a pattern of test scores which shows very dramatically that **memory** and **understanding** do not work in exactly the same way as time progresses – all the words were understood, but only some were recalled. The differences between the way in which memory and understanding function help explain why so many people find they don't recall very much after hours of learning and understanding. The reason is that recall tends to get progressively worse as time goes on unless the mind is given brief rests. *See fig 19.*

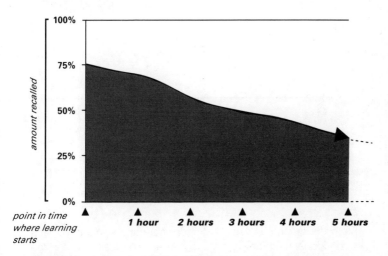

Fig 19 As time goes on, recall of material being learned tends to get progressively worse unless the mind is given proper rests. *See text this page.*

Thus the graph requested in Test 2 will be more complex than the simple examples given. It will probably also be more complex than the graph you have traced for your own recall behaviour during learning. Average scores from Test 1 produce a graph similar to fig 20.

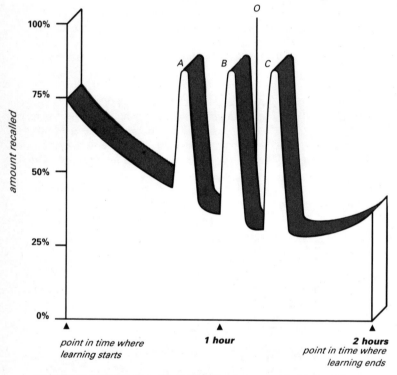

Fig 20 Recall **during** learning. Graph indicating that we recall more from the beginning and ends of a learning period. We also recall more when things are associated or linked (A, B and C) and more when things are outstanding or unique (O). *See text pages 59, 60 and 61.*

From the graph it is clear that under normal circumstances and with understanding fairly constant, we tend to recall: more at the beginning and ends of learning periods; more of items which are associated by repetition, sense, rhyming etc.; more of things which are outstanding or unique (the psychologist who discovered this characteristic was Von Restorff, and such a memorisation event is known as the Von Restorff effect); and considerably *less* of things from the middle of learning periods.

If recall is going to be kept at a reasonable level, it is necessary to find the point at which recall and understanding work in greatest harmony. For normal purposes this point occurs in a time period of between 20 to 50 minutes. A shorter period does not give the mind enough time to appreciate the rhythm and organisation of the material, and a longer period results in the continuing decline of the amount recalled (*as graphed in fig 19*).

If a period of learning from a lecture, a book or the mass media is to take two hours, it is far better to arrange for brief breaks during these two hours. In this way the recall curve can be kept high, and can be prevented from dropping during the later stages of learning. The small breaks will guarantee eight relatively high points of recall, with four small drops in the middle. Each of the drops will be less than the main drop would have been were there no breaks. *See fig 21.*

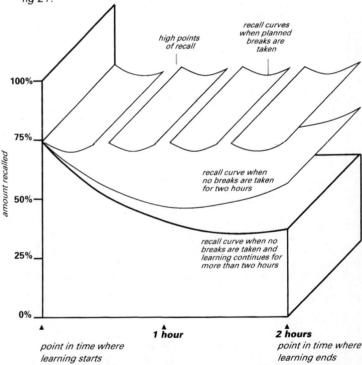

Fig 21 Recall **during** learning – with and without breaks. A learning period of between 20–50 minutes produces the best relationship between understanding and recall. *See text this page.*

Breaks are additionally useful as relaxation points. They get rid of the muscular and mental tension which inevitably builds up during periods of concentration.

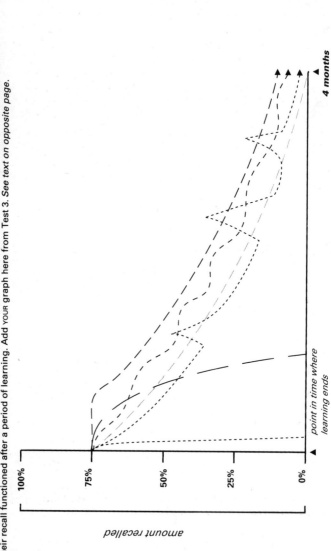

Fig 22 Recall *after* a learning period – people's estimates. Graph showing the different kinds of answers people gave when asked to show how their recall functioned after a period of learning. Add YOUR graph here from Test 3. *See text on opposite page.*

Recall *after* a learning period – discussion of Test 3 and answers

In Test 3 you were asked to fill in a graph indicating the way you thought your recall functioned after a period of learning had been completed. The examples on pages 54 and 55 were answers many people have given when asked this question, although a much wider variety of responses overall was registered.

Apart from those graphed on pages 54 and 55, other answers included: straight lines plunging almost immediately to nothing: variations on the more rapid drop, some falling to 0%, others always maintaining some per cent, however small; variations on the slower fall-off, also with some falling to 0% and others maintaining; and variations on these themes, showing rises and falls of varying degree. *See fig 22 opposite.*

The surprising truth of the matter is that none of the examples shown earlier, and none of the estimates shown, is correct. They have all neglected a particularly significant factor: recall after a learning period initially *rises*, and only then declines, following a steeply falling concave curve that levels off. *See fig 23.*

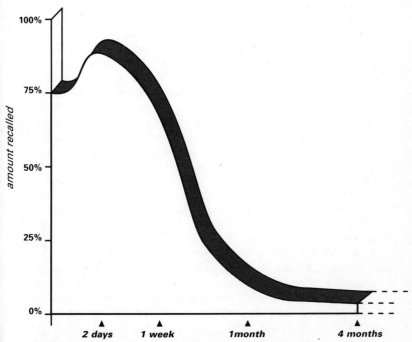

Fig 23 Graph showing how human recall rises for a short while after learning, and then falls steeply (80% of detail forgotten within 24 hours). *See text pages 63 and 64.*

Once it is realised that the brief rise does take place, the reason for it can be understood: at the very moment when a learning period is finished, the brain has not had enough time to integrate the new information it has assimilated, especially the last items. It needs a few minutes to complete and link firmly all the interconnections within the new material – to let it 'sink in'.

The decline that takes place after the small rise is a steep one – within 24 hours of a one-hour learning period at least 80 per cent of detailed information is lost. This enormous drop must be prevented, and can be by proper techniques of review.

MEMORY – REVIEW TECHNIQUES AND THEORY

If review is organised properly, the graph shown in fig 23 can be changed to keep recall at the high point reached shortly after learning has been completed. In order to accomplish this, a programmed pattern of review must take place, each review being done at the time just before recall is about to drop. For example, the first review should take place about 10 minutes after a one-hour learning period and should itself take 10 minutes. This will keep the recall high for approximately one day, when the next review should take place, this time for a period of 2 to 4 minutes. After this, recall will probably be retained for approximately a week, when another 2 minutes review can be completed followed by a further review after about one month. After this time the knowledge will be lodged in Long Term Memory. This means it will be familiar in the way a personal telephone number is familiar, needing only the most occasional nudge to maintain it. *See fig 24 opposite.*

The first review, especially if notes have been taken, should be a fairly complete note revision which may mean scrapping original notes and substituting for them revised and final copy. The second, third and fourth etc. review sessions should take the following form: without referring to final notes, jot down on a piece of paper everything that can be recalled. This should then be checked against the final notes and any corrections or additions to what has been recalled should be made. Both notes and jottings should be in the form of Mind Maps, as explained on pages 93–101.

One of the most significant aspects of proper review is the accumulative effect it has on all aspects of learning, thinking and remembering. The person who does not review is continually wasting the effort he does put in to any learning task, and putting himself at a serious disadvantage.

Fig 24 opposite Graph showing how properly spaced review can keep recall constantly high. *See text above.*

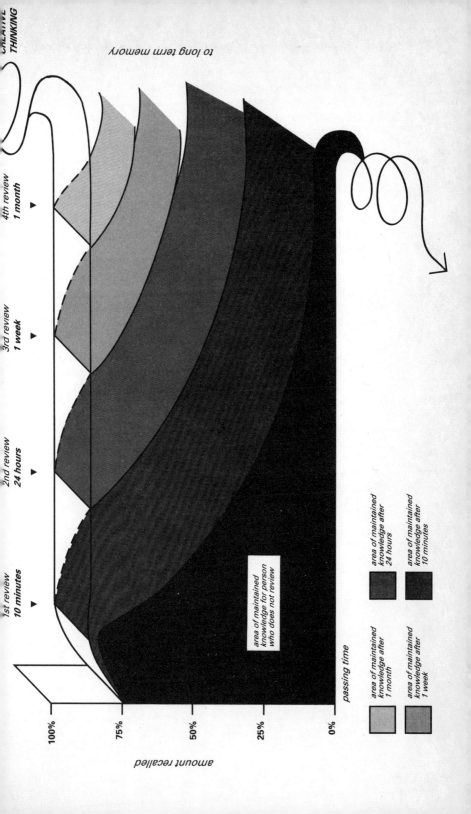

Each time he approaches a new learning situation his recall of previous knowledge gained will be at a very low ebb, and the connections which should be made automatically will be dismissed. This will mean that his understanding of the new material will not be as complete as it could be, and that his efficiency and speed through the new material will also be less. This continuingly negative process results in a downward spiral that ends in a general despair of ever being able to learn anything – each time new material is learned it is forgotten, and each time new material is approached it seems to become more oppressive. The result is that many people, after having finished their formal exams, seldom, if ever, approach text books again.

Failure to review is equally as bad for general memory. If each new piece of information is neglected, it will not remain at a conscious level, and will not be available to form new memory connections. As memory is a process which is based on linking and association, the fewer items there are in the 'recall store', the less will be the possibility for new items to be registered and connected.

On the opposite side of this coin, the advantages of reviewing are enormous. The more you maintain your current body of knowledge, the more you will be able to absorb and handle. When you study, the expanding amount of knowledge at your command will enable you to digest new knowledge far more easily, each new piece of information being absorbed in the context of your existing store of relevant information, see fig 24. The process is much more like that of the traditional snowball rolling, where the snowball gets rapidly bigger the more it rolls and eventually continues rolling under its own momentum.

SPECIAL MEMORY SYSTEMS AND MNEMONICS

Test 4 Memory Systems

Here is a list of words next to numbers. As with Test 1 read each item once, covering the ones read with a card as you progress down the list. The purpose of this is to remember which words went with which number:

4 leaf
9 shirt
1 table
6 orange
10 poker
5 student
8 pencil
3 cat
7 car
2 feather

Now turn over and fill in the answers in the order requested.

Test 4: responses   Memory Systems
Here are the numbers 1 to 10. Fill in next to each number the word which originally appeared next to it. The numbers are not listed in the same order as before. Do not refer back until you have filled in as many as you can.

1	7
5	4
3	6
8	10
9	2

Score _____

The Systems

Since the time of the Greeks certain individuals have impressed their fellow men with the most amazing feats of memory. They have been able to remember hundreds of items backwards and forwards and in any order; dates and numbers; names and faces; and have been able to perform special memory feats such as memorising whole areas of knowledge perfectly, or remembering decks of cards in the order anyone chose to present them.

In most cases these individuals were using special Memorising Principles known as mnemonics. Traditionally these Principles have been scorned as mere tricks, but recently the attitude towards them has changed. It has been realised that the methods which initially enable minds to remember something more easily and quickly, and then to remember it for much longer afterwards, actually use the brain's natural ability.

Current knowledge about the ways in which our minds work shows that these principles are indeed closely connected to the basic ways in which the brain functions. The use of Mnemonic Principles has consequently gained respectability and popularity, and they are currently being taught in universities and schools as additional aids in the general learning process. The improvement of memory performances that can be achieved is quite remarkable, and the range of techniques is wide.

There is not enough space in the present chapter to give a complete coverage, but I shall introduce in the next few pages the basic theory behind the system, and a simple system for remembering up to ten items.

Assuming that the items to be remembered are:

1 **table**
2 **feather**
3 **cat**
4 **leaf**
5 **student**
6 **orange**
7 **car**
8 **pencil**
9 **shirt**
10 **poker**

In order to remember these it is necessary to have some system which enables us to use the **associative** and **linking** power of memory to connect them with their proper number.

The best system for this is the Number-Rhyme System, in which each number has a rhyming word connected to it.

The rhyming key words are:

1 **bun**
2 **shoe**
3 **tree**
4 **door**
5 **hive**
6 **sticks**
7 **heaven**
8 **skate**
9 **vine**
10 **hen**

In order to remember the first list of arbitrary words it is necessary to link them in some strong manner with the rhyming words connected to the numbers. If this is done successfully, the answer to a question such as 'what word was connected to number 3?' will be easy. The rhyming word for 5, 'hive', will be recalled automatically and with it will come the connected image of the word that has to be remembered. *See Colour Plate I.*

'SMASHIN' SCOPE' OF MEMORY

The important thing in this and all other memory systems is to make sure that the rhyming word and the word to be remembered are totally and securely linked together. In order to do this, the connecting images must be one or many of the following:

1 Synaesthesia/sensuality

Synaesthesia refers to the blending of the senses. The great 'natural' memorisers, and the great mnemonists, developed exceptional sensitivity in each of their senses, and then blended these senses to produce enhanced recall. In developing the memory it has been found to be essential to sensitise increasingly and train regularly your:

a) vision
b) hearing
c) sense of smell
d) taste
e) touch
f) kinaesthesia – your awareness of bodily position and movement in space.

2 Movement

In any mnemonic image, movement adds another giant range of possibilities for your brain to 'link in' and thus remember. As your images move, make them three-dimensional.

3 Association

Whatever you wish to memorise, make sure you associate or link it to something stable in your mental environment, i.e. Peg system: one = bun.

4 Sexuality

We all have a virtually perfect memory in this area. Use it!

5 Humour

Have fun with your memory. The more funny, ridiculous, absurd and surreal you make your images, the more outstandingly memorable they will be. Salvador Dali, the surrealist painter, said that, 'My paintings are photographs painted by hand of the irrational made concrete' and that in many instances they are the paintings of the perfectly held memories of his day and night dreams.

6 Imagination

Einstein said, 'Imagination is more important than knowledge. For knowledge is limited, whereas imagination embraces the entire world, stimulating progress, giving birth to evolution.' The more you apply your imagination to memory, the better your memory will be.

7 Number
Numbering adds specificity and efficiency to the principle of order and sequence.

8 Symbolism
Substituting a more meaningful image for a more normal or boring image increases the probability of recall. You may also use traditional symbols, e.g. stop sign or light bulb.

9 Colour
Where appropriate, and whenever possible, use the full range of the rainbow, to make your ideas more 'colourful' and therefore more memorable.

10 Order and/or sequence
In combination with the other principles, order and/or sequence allows for much more immediate reference, and increases the brain's possibilities for 'random access'. Expanded use of order and sequence allows you to develop Memory Matrices, such as the Self-Enhancing Memory Matrix, enabling you to memorise as many as 10,000 items of information and more (see *Master Your Memory*).

11 Positivity
In most instances positive and pleasant images are better for memory purposes, because they make the brain *want* to return to the images. Certain negative images, even though applying all the principles above, and though in and of themselves 'memorable', could be blocked by the brain because it finds the prospect of returning to such images unpleasant.

12 Exaggeration
In all your images, exaggerate size, shape, and sound.

These can easily be remembered by the mnemonic anagram **smashin' scope**.

THE NUMBER-RHYME SYSTEM

It is important, when forming the images, to have a very clear mental picture in front of your inner eye. To achieve this it is often best to close your eyes and to project the image on to the inside of your eyelid, or on to a screen inside your head, and to hear, feel, smell or experience it in the way that works best for you. (For example, think of what you ate for lunch yesterday: how does your brain recreate it for you? Use the same medium.)

To make all this clearer, let us try the ten items given.

1 bun   table

Imagine a giant bun on top of a fragile table which is in the process of crumbling from the weight. Smell the fresh cooked aroma, taste your favourite bun.

2 shoe   feather

Imagine your favourite shoe with an enormous feather growing out of the inside, preventing you from putting your shoe on, tickling and tickling your feet.

3 tree   cat

Imagine a large tree with either your own cat or a cat you know stuck in the very top branches frantically scrambling about and mewing loudly.

4 door   leaf

Imagine your bedroom door as one giant leaf, crunching and rustling as you open it.

5 hive   student

Imagine a student at his desk, dressed in black and yellow stripes, buzzing busily, or with honey dripping on his pages.

6 sticks   orange

Imagine large sticks puncturing the juicy surface of an orange that is as big as a beach ball. Feel and smell the juice of the orange squirting out.

7 heaven   car

Imagine all the angels sitting on cars rather than clouds; experience yourself driving the car you consider heavenly.

8 skate   pencil

Imagine yourself skating over the pavement, hearing the sound of the wheels on the ground, as you see the multi-coloured pencils attached to your skates creating fantastic art wherever you go.

9 vine   shirt

Imagine a vine as large as Jack and the Bean Stalk's bean stalk, and instead of leaves on the vine, hang it all over with brightly coloured shirts blowing in the wind.

10 hen   poker

Have fun!

Now fill in as many of the words as you can on the next page.

With a little practice it would be possible to remember ten out of ten each time, even though using the same system. The words to be remembered can, like the clothes they were compared to, be taken off the hook and other clothes substituted. The words which must remain constant and which in any case are almost impossible to forget are the rhyming key words.

As mentioned earlier there are many other systems which are equally as easy to remember as this simple one but would take (and already have done) another book to explain. Ones which are particularly useful include the Major System, which enables recall of more than a thousand items in the manner of the Number-Rhyme System, as well as giving a key for memorising numbers and dates, and the Face-Name System which helps prevent the embarrassing and wide-spread habit of not being able to recall either the names or faces of people you have met. For further information on these Systems, see *Use Your Memory* and *Master Your Memory*.

THE 'IMPOSSIBLE' TASK

As you will have gathered throughout the development of this chapter, memory is primarily an associative and linking process which depends in large part on **Key Words** and key concepts properly imagined. These memory/mnemonic techniques really *do* work – sometimes so well as to be considered by some unbelievable. A class of fourteen-year-old students in Sweden were set, by their teacher, what he described as an impossible task, stating that they should simply try to do as well as they could. The class was, in one evening, to memorise as many of the countries and capitals of the world as they could.

One of the children was a young boy who went home particularly oppressed and depressed by the task, and told his father of what he thought was an unfair assignment. His father had taken a Use Your Head Course, and enthusiastically set about teaching his son how to apply memory techniques to what was in reality not that difficult at all.

Two weeks later the father was phoned by the headmaster of the school, apologising for having to convey the bad news that his son had been cheating. Upon questioning by the father, the headmaster explained that in a recent geography test, the top mark in the school had been 123, and that his son had scored over 300, 'proving' that he had cheated!

The story ended happily, with the boy in question teaching his schoolmates how to use *their* memories.

Although the chapter entitled Memory is coming to an end the next three chapters on Mind Mapping are themselves very closely connected with remembering and recalling. The information in this chapter should be reviewed after the following chapters have been completed.

As a final *review*, check your improving memory once again. In the spaces below write the rhyming key word for the Number-Rhyme System, and next to it the words used earlier in the chapter to illustrate the system.

Rhyming key words   **word connected**

1 _____   _____

2 _____   _____

3 _____   _____

4 _____   _____

5 _____   _____

6 _____   _____

7 _____   _____

8 _____   _____

9 _____   _____

10 _____   _____

Personal notes and applications

6 Mind Maps – introduction

OVERVIEW

▶ **Exercise and discussion – Kusa-Hibari**

▶ **Key Words – Recall and creative**

▶ **Multi-ordinate nature of words**

▶ **Key Word versus standard notes**

EXERCISE AND DISCUSSION

Imagine that your hobby is reading short stories, that you read at least five a day, and that you keep notes so that you will not forget any of them. Imagine also that in order to ensure a proper recall of each story you use a card filing system. For each story you have one card for the title and author, and a card for every paragraph. On each of these paragraph cards you enter a main and a secondary key word or phrase. The key words/phrases you take either directly from the story or make up yourself because they summarise particularly well.

Imagine further that your ten thousandth story is *Kusa-Hibari* by Lafcadio Hearne, and that you have prepared the title-and-author card.

Now read the story on pages 78–80, and for the purpose of this exercise enter a key recall word or phrase for both the main and secondary idea for the first five paragraphs only, in the space provided on page 80.

KUSA-HIBARI   *Lafcadio Hearne*

1 His cage is exactly two Japanese inches high and one inch and a half wide: its tiny wooden door, turning upon a pivot, will scarcely admit the tip of my little finger. But he has plenty of room in that cage – room to walk, and jump, and fly, for he is so small that you must look very carefully through the brown-gauze sides of it in order to catch a glimpse of him. I have always to turn the cage round and round, several times, in a good light, before I can discover his whereabouts, and then I usually find him resting in one of the upper corners – clinging, upside down, to his ceiling of gauze.

2 Imagine a cricket about the size of an ordinary mosquito – with a pair of antennae much longer than his own body, and so fine that you can distinguish them only against the light. Kusa-Hibari, or 'Grass-Lark' is the Japanese name of him; and he is worth in the market exactly twelve cents: that is to say, very much more than his weight in gold. Twelve cents for such a gnat-like thing! . . . By day he sleeps or meditates, except while occupied with the slice of fresh egg-plant* or cucumber which must be poked into his cage every morning . . . to keep him clean and well fed is somewhat trouble-some: could you see him, you would think it absurd to take any pains for the sake of a creature so ridiculously small.

3 But always at sunset the infinitesimal soul of him awakens: then the room begins to fill with a delicate and ghostly music of indescri-bable sweetness – a thin, silvery rippling and trilling as of tiniest electric bells. As the darkness deepens, the sound becomes sweeter – sometimes swelling till the whole house seems to vibrate with the elfish resonance – sometimes thinning down into the faintest imaginable thread of a voice. But loud or low, it keeps a penetrating quality that is weird . . . All night the atom thus sings: he ceases only when the temple bell proclaims the hour of dawn.

4 Now this tiny song is a song of love – vague love of the unseen and unknown. It is quite impossible that he should ever have seen or known, in this present existence of his. Not even his ancestors, for many generations back, could have known anything of the night-life of the fields, or the amorous value of song.

5 They were born of eggs hatched in a jar of clay, in the shop of some insect-merchant: and they dwelt thereafter only in cages. But he sings the song of his race as it was sung a myriad years ago, and as faultlessly as if he understood the exact significance of every note. Of course he did not learn the song. It is a song of organic memory – deep, dim memory of other quintillions of lives, when the ghost of him shrilled at night from the dewy grasses of the hills.

* aubergine

Then that song brought him love – and death. He has forgotten all about death: but he remembers the love. And therefore he sings now – for the bride that will never come.

6 So that his longing is unconsciously retrospective: he cries to the dust of the past – he calls to the silence and the gods for the return of time . . . Human lovers do very much the same thing without knowing it. They call their illusion an Ideal: and their Ideal is, after all, a mere shadowing of race-experience, a phantom of organic memory. The living present has very little to do with it. . . . Perhaps his atom also has an ideal, or at least the rudiment of an ideal; but, in any event, the tiny desire must utter its plaint in vain.

7 The fault is not altogether mine. I had been warned that if the creature were mated, he would cease to sing and would speedily die. But, night after night, the plaintive, sweet, unanswered trilling touched me like a reproach – became at last an obsession, an affliction, a torment of conscience; and I tried to buy a female. It was too late in the season; there were no more kusa-hibari for sale, – either males or females. The insect-merchant laughed and said, 'He ought to have died about the twentieth day of the ninth month.' (It was already the second day of the ten month.) But the insect-merchant did not know that I have a good stove in my study, and keep the temperature at above 75°F. Wherefore my grass-lark still sings at the close of the eleventh month, and I hope to keep him alive until the Period of Greatest Cold. However, the rest of his generation are probably dead: neither for love nor money could I now find him a mate. And were I to set him free in order that he might make the search for himself, he could not possibly live through a single night, even if fortunate enough to escape by day the multitude of his natural enemies in the garden – ants, centipedes, and ghastly earth-spiders.

8 Last evening – the twenty-ninth of the eleventh month – an odd feeling came to me as I sat at my desk: a sense of emptiness in the room. Then I became aware that my grass-lark was silent, contrary to his wont. I went to the silent cage, and found him lying dead beside a dried-up lump of egg-plant as grey and hard as a stone. Evidently he had not been fed for three or four days; but only the night before his death he had been singing wonderfully – so that I foolishly imagined him to be more than usually contented. My student, Aki, who loves insects, used to feed him; but Aki had gone into the country for a week's holiday, and the duty of caring for the grass-lark had developed upon Hana, the housemaid. She is not sympathetic, Hana the housemaid. She says that she did not forget the mite – but there was no more egg-plant. And she had never thought of substituting a slice of onion or of cucumber! . . . I spoke words of reproof to Hana the housemaid and she dutifully expressed contrition. But

the fairy-music had stopped: and the stillness reproaches; and the room is cold, in spite of the stove.

9 Absurd! . . . I have made a good girl unhappy because of an insect half the size of a barley-grain! The quenching of that infinitesimal life troubled me more than I could have believed possible. . . . Of course, the mere habit of thinking about a creature's wants – even the wants of a cricket – may create, by insensible degrees, an imaginative interest, an attachment of which one becomes conscious only when the relation is broken. Besides, I had felt so much, in the hush of the night, the charm of the delicate voice – telling of one minute existence dependent upon my will and selfish pleasure, as upon the favour of a god – telling me also that the atom of ghost in the tiny cage, and the atom of ghost within myself, were forever but one and the same in the deeps of the Vast of being. . . . And then to think of the little creature hungering and thirsting, night after night and day after day, while the thoughts of his guardian deity were turned to the weaving of dreams! . . . How bravely, nevertheless, he sang on to the very end – an atrocious end, for he had eaten his own legs! . . . May the gods forgive us all – especially Hana the housemaid!

10 Yet, after all, to devour one's own legs for hunger is not the worst that can happen to a being cursed with the gift of song. There are human crickets who must eat their own hearts in order to sing.

Key words or phrases for main and secondary ideas from *Kusa-Hibari*

	main	**secondary**
paragraph 1	_____	_____
paragraph 2	_____	_____
paragraph 3	_____	_____
paragraph 4	_____	_____
paragraph 5	_____	_____

Opposite you will find sample key words and phrases from the notes of students who have previously done this exercise. Briefly compare and contrast these with your own ideas.

Students' suggested key words and phrases

	main	secondary
paragraph 1	his cage	two Japanese inches
	wooden door	wooden floor
	ceiling of gauze	plenty of room
	small insect	discover whereabouts
paragraph 2	cricket	Grass-Lark
	weight in gold	twelve cents
	antennae	market
	Kusa-Hibari	gnatlike
paragraph 3	sleep	fresh cucumber
	clean and well fed	pains
	occupied	meditation
	absurd	small
paragraph 4	penetrating	silvery rippling
	music	house vibrating
	electric bells	penetrating
	soul	hour of dawn
paragraph 5	love	night-life
	amorous	insect merchant
	the hills	significance
	death	love and death

In class situations instructors then circled one word from each section:

	main	secondary
paragraph 1	wooden door	discover whereabouts
2	weight in gold	market
3	occupied	pains
4	penetrating	hour of dawn
5	love	night-life

Students were then asked to explain why, in the context of the exercise, these words and phrases and not others had been selected. Answers usually included the following: 'good image words', 'imaginative', 'descriptive', 'appropriate', 'good for remembering', 'evocative', etc.

Only one student in fifty realised why the instructors had chosen these words: in the context of the exercise the series chosen was disastrous.

To understand why, it is necessary to imagine a time some years after the story has been read when you are going to look at the notes again for recall purposes. Imagine that some friends have played a prank, taking out the title cards of some of your stories and challenging you to remember the titles and authors. You would have no idea to start with to which story your cards referred, and would have to rely solely on them to give you back the correct images.

With the Key Words at the bottom of page 81, you would probably be forced to link them in the following way: 'wooden door', a general phrase, would gain a mystery-story air when you read 'discover whereabouts'. The next two keys 'weight in gold' and 'market' would confirm this, adding a further touch of intrigue suggesting a criminal activity. The next three key words, 'occupied', 'pains' and 'penetrating' might lead you to assume that one of the characters, perhaps the hero, was personally in difficulty, adding further tension to the ongoing plot as the 'hour of dawn', obviously an important and suspense-filled moment in the story, approached. The final two keys, 'love' and 'night-life' would add a romantic or risqué touch to the whole affair, encouraging you to thumb quickly through the remaining key words in search of further adventures and climaxes! You would have created an interesting new story, but would not remember the original one.

Words which seemed quite good at the time have not, for some reason, proved adequate for recall. To explain why, it is necessary to discuss the difference between Key Recall Words and key creative words, and the way in which they interact after a period of time has passed. Good recall words would have been the following:

	main	secondary
paragraph 1	cage	2 Japanese inches
2	cricket	Grass-lark
3	sleep	fresh cucumber
4	music	amorous value
5	song	organic memory

Understanding why these words are better for recall can be based on the way in which we realise the human brain processes information.

KEY WORDS – RECALL AND CREATIVE

A Key Recall Word or phrase is one which funnels into itself a wide range of special images, and which, when it is triggered, funnels back the same images. It will tend to be a strong noun or verb, on occasion being surrounded by additional Key adjectives or adverbs. *See fig 25.*

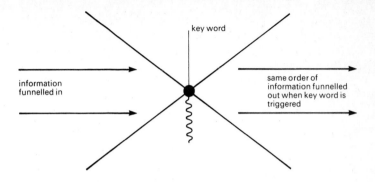

Fig 25 Diagram representing Key Recall Word. *See text on opposite page.*

A creative word is one which is particularly evocative and image-forming, but which is far more general than the more directed Key Recall Word. Words like 'ooze' and 'bizarre' are especially evocative but do not necessarily bring back a specific image. *See fig 26.*

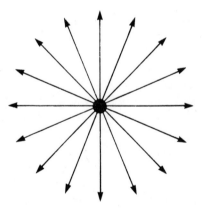

Fig 26 A creative word sprays out associations in all directions. *See text this page.*

Apart from understanding the difference between creative and recall words, it is also necessary to understand the nature of words themselves as well as the nature of the brain which uses them.

MULTI-ORDINATE NATURE OF WORDS

Every word is 'multi-ordinate', which simply means that each word is like a little centre on which there are many, many little hooks. Each hook can attach to other words to give both words in the new pair slightly different meanings. For example the word 'run' can be hooked quite differently in 'run like hell' and 'her stocking has a run in it'. *See Colour Plate II.*

In addition to the multi-ordinate nature of words, each brain is also different from each other brain. As shown in the first chapter, the number of connections a brain can make within itself is almost limitless. Each individual also experiences a very different life from each other individual (even if two people are enjoying the 'same experience' together they are in very different worlds: A is enjoying the experience with B as a major part of it, and B is enjoying the experience with A as a major part of it). Similarly the associations that each person will have for any word will be different from everybody else's. Even a simple word like 'leaf' will produce a different series of images for each person who reads or hears it. A person whose favourite colour is green might imagine the general greenness of leaves; someone whose favourite colour is brown, the beauty of autumn; a person who had been injured falling out of a tree, the feeling of fear; a gardener, the different emotions connected with the pleasure of seeing leaves grow and the thought of having to rake them all up when they had fallen, etc. One could go on for ever and still not satisfy the range of associations that you who are reading this book might have when *you* think of leaves.

As well as the unique way in which the mind sees its personal images, each brain is also, by nature, both creative and sense-organising. It will tend to 'tell itself interesting and entertaining stories' as it does for example when we day- or night-dream.

The reason for the failure of the recall and general words selected from *Kusa-Hibari* can now clearly be seen. When each of the multi-ordinate words or phrases was approached, the mind automatically picked the connecting hooks which were most obvious, most image-producing, or the most sense-making. The mind was consequently led down a path that was more creative than recall based, and a story was constructed that was interesting, but hardly useful for remembering. *See Plate II centre.*

Key Recall Words would have forced the mind to make the proper links in the right direction, enabling it to recreate the story even if for all other intentional purposes it had been forgotten. *See Plate II bottom.*

KEY WORD VERSUS STANDARD NOTES

The main body of a person's recalling is of this Key concept nature. It is not, as is often assumed, a word-for-word verbatim process. When people describe books they have read or places they have been to, they do not start to 're-read' from memory. They give Key concept overviews outlining the main characters, settings, events and add descriptive detail. Similarly the single Key word or phrase will bring back whole ranges of experience and sensation. Think for example of the range of images that enter your mind when you read the word 'child'.

How, then, does acceptance of these facts about Key Recall affect our attitude towards the structure of note taking?

Because we have become so used to speaking and writing words, we have mistakenly assumed that normal sentence structure is the best way to remember verbal images and ideas. Thus the majority of students and even graduates have taken notes in a normal literary fashion similar to the example of a university student whose notes were rated 'good' by his professor. *See next page.*

Our new knowledge of Key concepts and recall has shown that in this type of notes 90 per cent of the words are not necessary for recall purpose. This frighteningly high figure becomes even more frightening when a closer look is taken at what happens with standard sentence notes:

1 Time is wasted recording words which have no bearing on memory (estimated waste – 90%).

2 Time is wasted re-reading the same unnecessary words (estimated waste – 90%).

3 Time is wasted searching for the words which *are* Key Recall Words, for they are usually not distinguished by any marks and thus blend in with othe non-recall words.

4 The connections between Key Recall Words are interrupted by words that separate them. We know that memory works by association and any interference by non-recall words will make the connections less strong.

5 The Key Recall Words are separated in time by intervening words: after one Key word or phrase has been read it will take at least a few seconds to get to the next. The longer the time between connections, the less chance there will be of proper connection being made.

6 The Key Recall Words are separated in space by their distance from each other on the page. As with the point made about time,

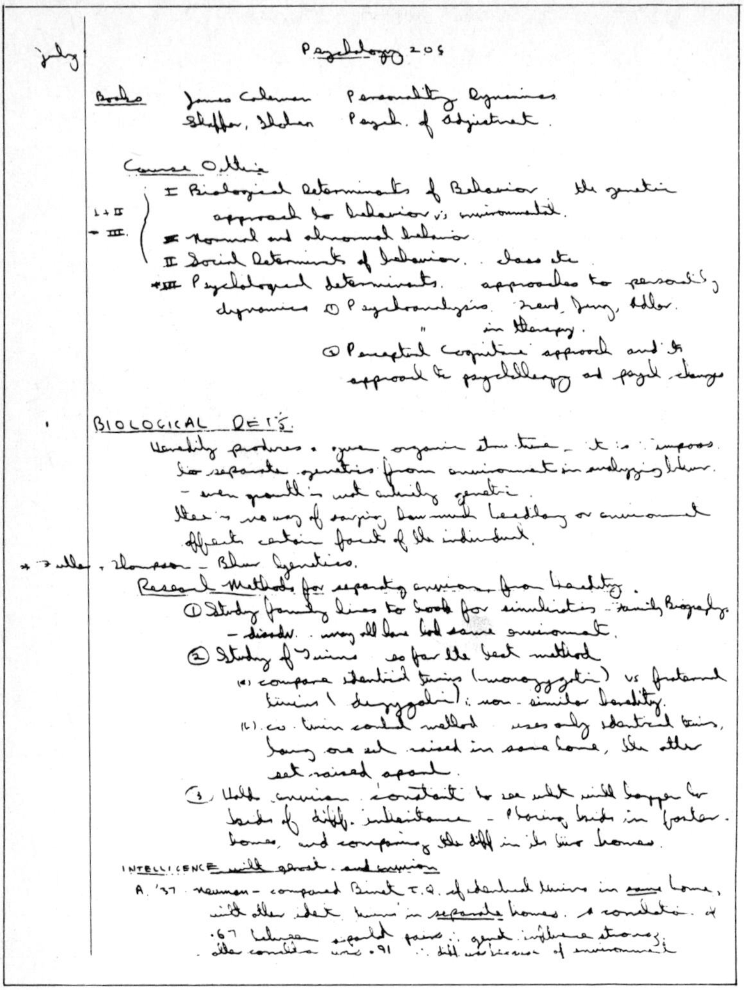

july

Psychology 205

Books James Coleman Personality Dynamics
Shaffer, Shoben Psych. of Adjustment.

Course Outline

I Biological determinants of Behavior the genetic approach to behavior v/s environmental.

I + II

→ III.

II Normal and abnormal behavior

II Social Determinants of behavior. class etc

*III Psychological determinants. approaches to personality dynamics (1) Psychoanalysis Freud, Jung, Adler.
" in therapy.
(2) Perceptual cognitive approach and its approach to psychology and psych. change

BIOLOGICAL DET'S.

Heredity produces a given organic structure - it is impossible to separate genetics from environment in analyzing behav.
- even growth is not entirely genetic
There is no way of saying how much heredity or environment affects certain facets of the individual.

* Fuller, Thompson - Behav. Genetics.

Research Methods for separating environ. from heredity.
(1) Study family lines to look for similarities - family Biography.
- disadv. [illegible] may all have had same environment.
(2) Study of Twins so far the best method
(a) compare identical twins (monozygotic) vs fraternal twins (dizygotic); non-similar heredity.
(b) co-twin control method uses only identical twins, having one set raised in same home, the other set raised apart.
(3) Hold environ. constant to see what will happen to kids of diff. inheritance - Placing kids in foster homes, and comparing the diff in the two homes.

INTELLIGENCE with growth and environ

A. '37 Newman - compared Binet I.Q. of identical twins in same home, with the ident. twins in separate homes. A correlation of .67 between separated pairs ∴ great influence strong; the correlation was .91 ∴ diff was because of environment

Fig 27 An example of a student's traditionally 'good' university notes. *See text on previous page.*

the greater the distance between the words, the less chance of there being a proper connection.

You are advised to practise Key Recall Word and phrase selection from any previous notes made during periods of study. It will also be helpful at this point for you to summarise this chapter in Key note form.

In addition, reconsider Key Recall and creative words in the light of the information in the chapter on Memory, especially the section dealing with Mnemonic Principles. Similarly the memory chapter itself can be reconsidered in the light of this chapter, with a similar emphasis on the relationship and similarities between Mnemonic systems and Key and creative concepts.

The review graph is another important consideration. Review is made much easier when notes are in Key form, because less time is expended, and because the recall itself will be superior and more complete. Any weak linkages will also be cemented more firmly in the early stages.

Finally, linkages between Key Recall words and concepts should always be emphasised and where possible simple lists and lines of Key words should be avoided. In the following chapter advanced methods of Key Recall Word linking and patterning will be explained in full, in the technique called Mind Mapping.

Personal notes and applications

7 Mind Maps – the laws

OVERVIEW

► **Exercise – space travel**

► **Linear history of speech and print**

► **Your brain and Mind Mapping**

► **Mind Mapping laws**

EXERCISE – SPACE TRAVEL

Prepare a half-hour speech on the topic of Space Travel on a piece of paper starting immediately after having reached the end of this paragraph. Allow no more than five minutes for the task, whether or not you have finished. This exercise will be referred to later in the chapter. Also any problems with thought organisation experienced in performing the task should be noted here.

Problems experienced

LINEAR HISTORY OF SPEECH AND PRINT

For the last few hundred years it has been popularly thought that man's mind worked in a linear or list-like manner. This belief was held primarily because of the increasing reliance on our two main methods of communication, speech and print.

In speech we are restricted, by the nature of time and space, to speaking and hearing one word at a time. Speech was thus seen as a linear or line-like process between people. *See fig 28.*

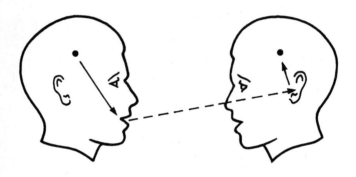

Fig 28 Speech has traditionally been seen as a list-like affair. *See text this page.*

Print was seen as even more linear. Not only was the individual forced to take in units of print in consecutive order, but print was laid out on the page in a series of lines or rows.

This linear emphasis overflowed into normal writing or notetaking procedures. Virtually everyone was (and still is) trained in school to take notes in sentences or vertical lists. (Most readers will probably have prepared their half-hour speech in one of these two ways, as shown in fig 29.) The acceptance of this way of thinking is so long-standing that little has been done to contradict it. However, recent evidence shows the brain to be far more multi-dimensional and pattern making, suggesting that in the speech/print arguments there must be fundamental flaws.

The argument which says that the brain functions linearly because of the speech patterns it has evolved fails to consider, as do the supporters of the absolute nature of IQ tests, the nature of the organism. It is easy to point out that when words travel from one

A Normal line structure – sentence-based

B Standard list structure – order-of-importance-based

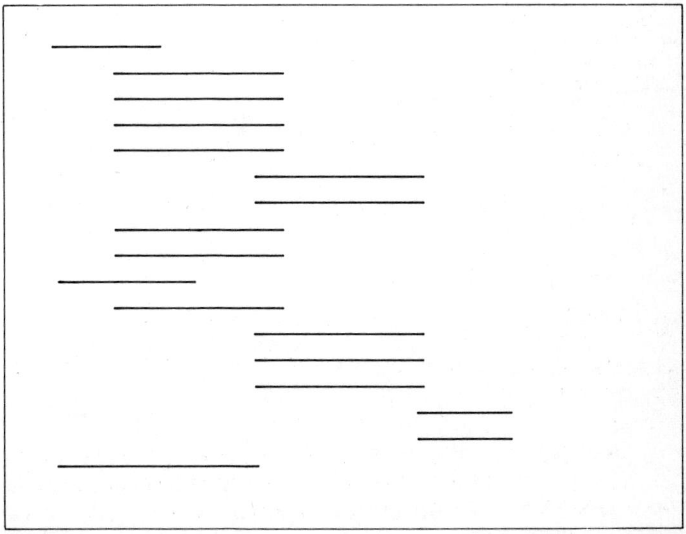

Fig 29 Standard forms of 'good' or 'neat' notes.

person to another they necessarily do so in a line, but this is not really the point. More to the point is the question: How does the brain which is speaking, and the brain which is receiving the words, deal with them *internally*?

The answer is that the brain is most certainly *not* dealing with them in simple lists and lines. You can verify this by thinking of the way in which your own thought processes work while you are speaking to someone else. You will observe that although a single line of words is coming out, a continuing and enormously complex process of sorting and selecting is taking place in your mind through-out the conversation. Whole networks of words and ideas are being juggled and interlinked in order to communicate a certain meaning to the listener.

Similarly the listener is not simply observing a long list of words like someone sucking up spaghetti. He is receiving each word in the context of the words that surround it. At the same time he is also giving the multi-ordinate nature of each word his own special inter-pretation as dictated by the structure of his personal information patterns and will be analysing, coding and criticising throughout the process.

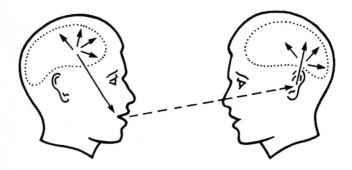

Fig 30 It is the network inside the mind, and not the simple order of word presentation, which is more important to an understanding of the way we relate to words. *See text pages 90–92.*

You may have noticed people suddenly reacting negatively to words you liked or thought were harmless. They react this way because the associations they have for these words are different from yours. Knowing this will help you understand more clearly the nature of conversations, disagreements and misunderstandings.

The argument for print is also weak. Despite the fact that we are trained to read units of information one after each other, that these are presented in lines and that we therefore write and note in lines, such linear presentation is not necessary for understanding, and in many instances is a disadvantage.

Your mind is perfectly capable of taking in information which is non-linear. In its day-to-day life it does this nearly all the time, observing all those things which surround it which include common *non*-linear forms of print: photographs, illustration, diagrams, etc. It is only our society's enormous reliance on linear information which has obscured the issue.

Your brain's non-linear character is further confirmed by recent biochemical, physiological and psychological research. Each area of research is discovering to its amazement and restrained delight that the brain is not only non-linear but is so complex and interlinked that it guarantees centuries of exhilarating research and exploration.

YOUR BRAIN AND MIND MAPPING

If the brain is to relate to information most efficiently the information must be structured in such a way as to 'slot in' as easily as possible. It follows that if the brain works primarily with Key concepts in an interlinked and integrated manner, our notes and our word relations should in many instances be structured in this way rather than in traditional 'lines'.

Rather than starting from the top and working down in sentences or lists, one should start from the centre with the main idea and branch out as dictated by the individual ideas and general form of the central theme.

A Mind Map such as that outlined in fig 31 has a number of advantages over the linear form of note taking.

1 The centre with the main idea is more clearly defined.

2 The relative importance of each idea is clearly indicated. More important ideas will be nearer the centre and less important ideas will be near the edge.

3 The links between the Key concepts will be immediately recognisable because of their proximity and connection.

4 As a result of the above, recall and review will be both more effective and more rapid.

5 The nature of the structure allows for the easy addition of new information without messy scratching out or squeezing in, etc.

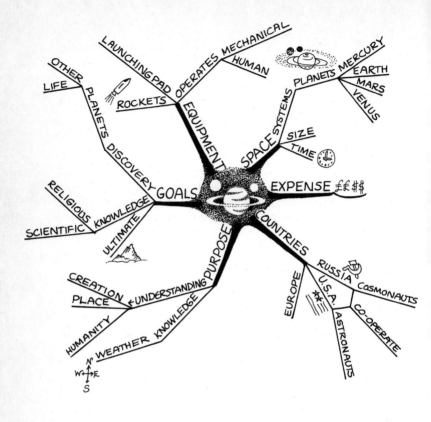

Fig 31 Initial ideas Mind Mapped around a central theme. *See text pages 93–95.*

6 Each map made will look and be different from each other map. This will aid recall.

7 In the more creative areas of note making, such as essay preparations etc, the open-ended nature of the map will enable the brain to make new connections far more readily.

In connection with these points, and especially with the last one, you should now do an exercise similar to your space travel speech at the beginning of this chapter, but this time using a Mind Map rather than the more linear methods. Follow the Mind Map laws given opposite.

MIND MAPPING LAWS

1 Start with a coloured image in the centre. An image often is 'worth a thousand words' and encourages creative thought while significantly increasing memory.

2 Images throughout your Mind Map. As No 1 and to stimulate all cortical processes.

3 Words should be printed. For reading-back purposes a printed map gives a more photographic, more immediate, and more comprehensive feed-back. The little extra time that it takes to print is amply made up for in the time saved when reading back.

4 The printed words should be on lines, and **each line should be connected to other lines.** This is to guarantee that the Mind Map has basic structure.

5 Words should be in 'units', i.e. **one word per line.** This leaves each word more free hooks and gives note taking more freedom and flexibility.

6 Use **colours** throughout the Mind Map as they enhance memory, delight the eye and stimulate the right cortical process.

7 In creative efforts of this nature **the mind should be left as 'free' as possible.** Any 'thinking' about where things should go or whether they should be included will simply slow down the process.

The idea is to recall everything your mind thinks of around the central idea. As your mind will generate ideas faster than you can write, there should be almost no pause – if you do pause you will probably notice your pen or pencil dithering over the page. The moment you notice this get it back down and carry on. Do not worry about order or organisation as this will in many cases take care of itself. If it does not, a final ordering can be completed at the end of the exercise.

The Mind Mapping as thus described can be seen to eliminate all of the disadvantages of standard note-taking as outlined on page 85.

Use the Mind-Mapping laws above and the space provided on page 96 to branch out in the manner indicated in figure 31 in a Mind Map preparation for a speech on 'Myself'.

Start the exercise now.

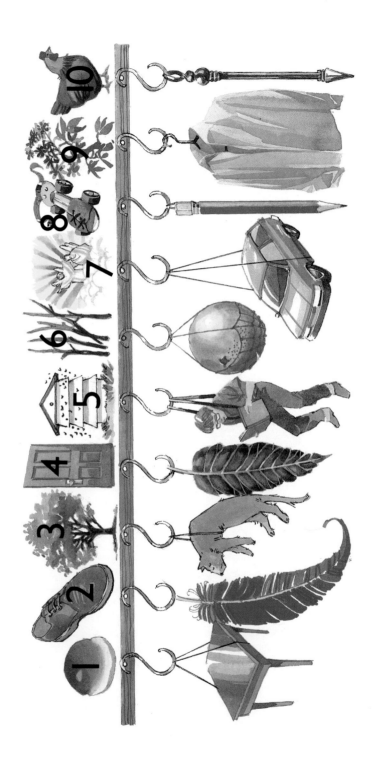

Plate I The Number Rhyme memory system. *See pages 70 to 73.*

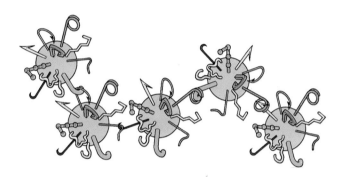

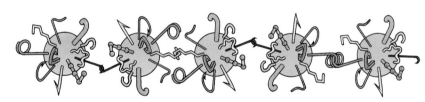

Plate II top Each word is multi-ordinate, which means that it has a large number of 'hooks'. Each hook, when it attaches to another word, changes the meaning of the word. Think, for example, of how the meaning of the word 'run' changes in different contexts. *See page 84.*

Centre Because words are multi-ordinate, the mind can easily follow the wrong connections, especially with creative words. *See pages 82 to 84.*

Bottom When proper Key Recall Words are used the mind will make the right connections. *See pages 82 to 84.*

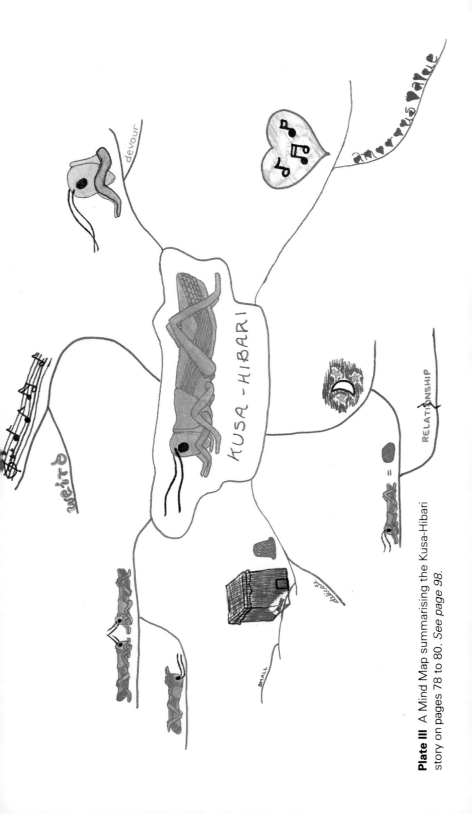

Plate II A Mind Map summarising the Kusa-Hibari story on pages 78 to 80. *See page 98.*

Plate IV Mind Map of Chapter 2. See pages 93 to 102.

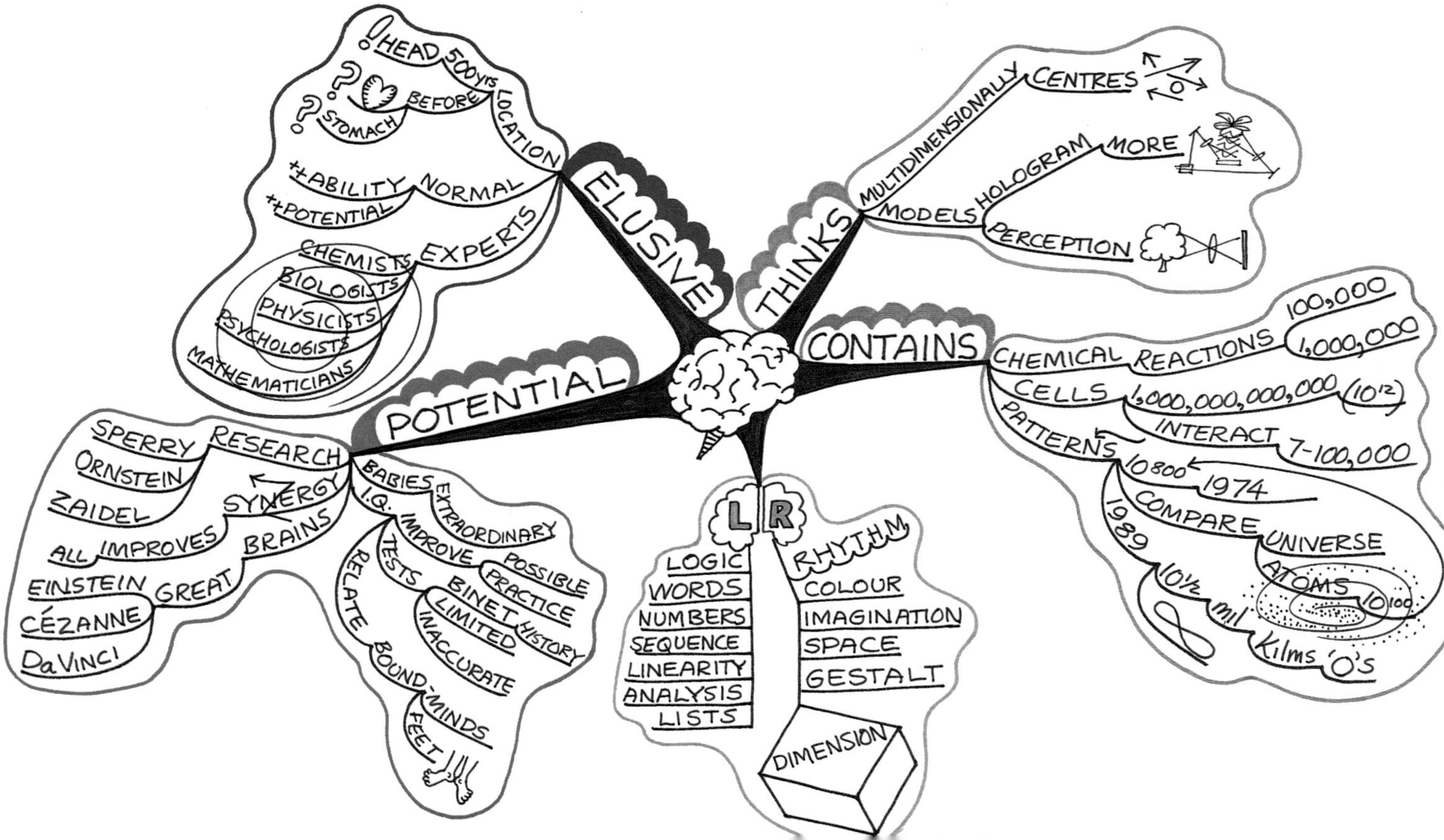

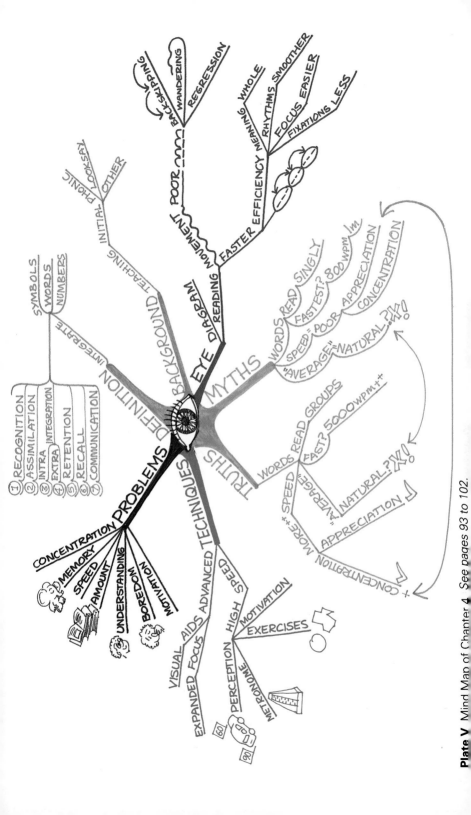

Plate V Mind Map of Chapter 4. See pages 93 to 102.

Plate VI Mind Map of Chapter 5. See pages 93 to 102.

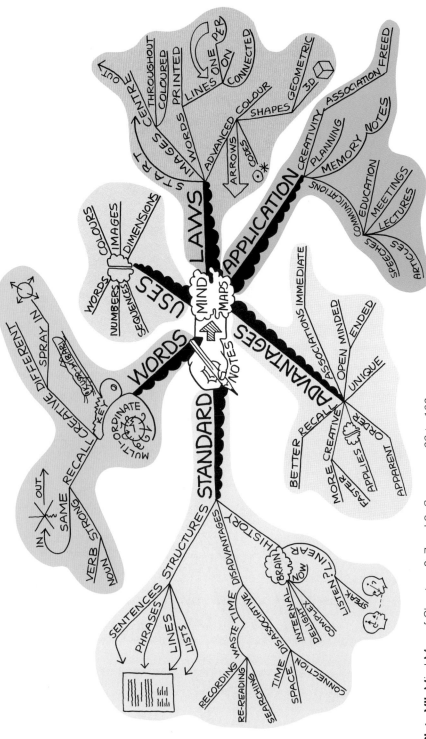

Plate VII Mind Map of Chapters 6, 7 and 8. See pages 93 to 102.

Plate VIII A Mind Map on the uses of Mind Maps. See Chapters 6 to 9.

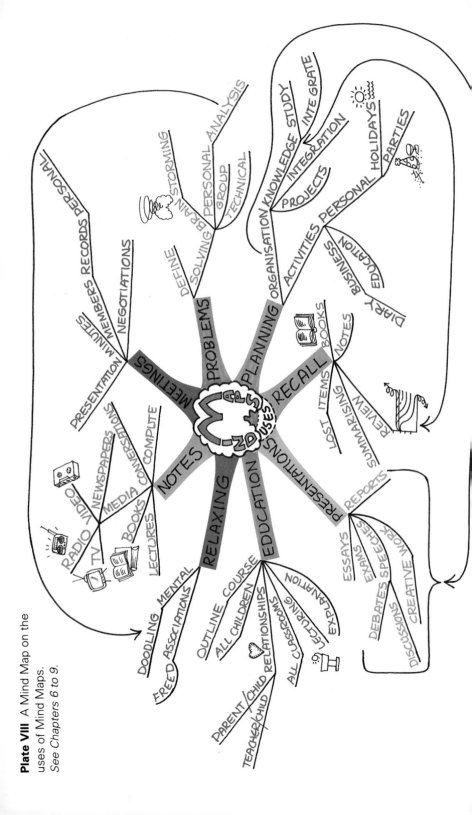

Although this first attempt at mapping may have been a little unusual, you will probably have noticed that the experience is quite different from that of the first exercise, and that the problems too may have been quite different.

Problems often noted in the first exercise include;

order	**organisation**
logical sequence	**time distribution**
beginning	**emphasis of ideas**
ending	**mental blocking**

These problems arise because people are attempting to select the main headings and ideas one after the other, and are attempting to put them into order as they go – they are trying to order a structure of speech without having considered all the information available. This will inevitably lead to confusion and the problems noted, for new information which turns up after the first few items might suddenly alter the whole outlook on the subject. With a linear approach this type of happening is disruptive, but with the Mind Map approach it is simply part of the overall process, and can be handled properly.

Another disadvantage of the list-like method is that it operates against the way in which the brain works. Each time an idea is thought of it is put on the list and forgotten while a new idea is searched for. This means that all the multi-ordinate and associative possibilities of each word are cut off and boxed away while the mind wanders around in search of another new idea.

With the Mind Map approach each idea is left as a totally open possibility so that the map grows organically and increasingly, rather than being stifled.

You might find it interesting to compare your efforts so far with the efforts of three school children. *See figs 32 to 34.*

Figure 32, page 99 shows the normal writing of a fourteen-year-old boy who was described as reasonably bright, but messy, confused, and mentally disorganised. The example of his linear writing represents his 'best notes' and explains clearly why he was described as he was. The Mind Map of English which he completed in five minutes shows almost completely the reverse, suggesting that we can often misjudge a child by the method by which we require him to express himself.

Figure 33, page 100 is the Mind Map of a boy who twice failed 'O' level Economics and who was described by the teacher as having enormous thinking and learning problems combined with an almost total lack of knowledge of his subject. The map, which also was completed in five minutes, shows quite the reverse.

Figure 34, page 101 is a Mind Map done by an 'A' Level grammar school girl on pure Mathematics. When this map was shown to a Professor of Mathematics he estimated that it was done by a University Honours student and that it probably took two days to complete. In fact it took the girl only twenty minutes. The map enabled her to display an extraordinary creativity in a subject which is normally considered dry, dull and oppressive. It could have been even better if each line had contained only 'units' of words instead of phrases. Her use of form and shape to augment the words will give an indication of the diversity possible in these structures. The following chapter extends this idea.

The Mind Map on Colour Plate III was done by a 13-year-old girl in California who, like Edward Hughes, was considered to be a 'normal' or 'average' student. The Mind Map, magnificently summarising both the content and also the feelings and emotions of the *Kusa-Hibari* story on pages 78–80, is a superb example of the way in which colour, code, form and image can be used to encapsulate an entire story.

The Mind Maps on Colour Plates IV–VII represent a new method for noting. They summarise chapters 2, 4, 5 and the chapters on Mind Mapping (6, 7, 8).

Page 102 has been left blank for you to create a Mind Map of chapter 7 for yourself.

In these Mind Maps, Key Recall Words and images are linked to each other around a main central image (in these cases, the overall theme of a chapter), and a mental picture is built up of an entire thought structure.

▶ The theory and method for making these Mind Maps are fully outlined in this chapter, starting on page 93.

▶ Use the Mind Map for each chapter as a **preview** of what is to come; they will make the reading of the chapter easier.

▶ After finishing a chapter, look at the Mind Map once again. This will serve as a **good review,** and will help you to remember what you have read. Continue to review in accordance with the Review Timetable if you wish the information to be committed to your Long Term Memory.

7) SETTING   Time + places in which the novel is situated

8) IMAGERY   the kind of images the author uses to describe (usually by simile or metaphor)

9) SYMBOLISM   one thing stands for another
The witches in Macbeth signifying evil

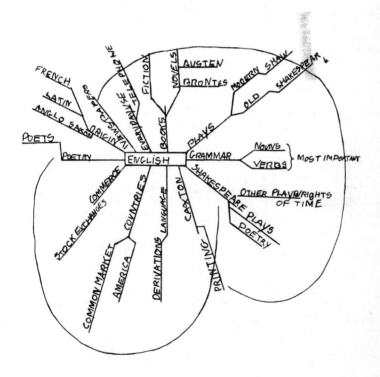

Fig 32 The 'best notes' in linear writing of a 14-year-old boy, and his Mind Map notes on English. *See text page 97.*

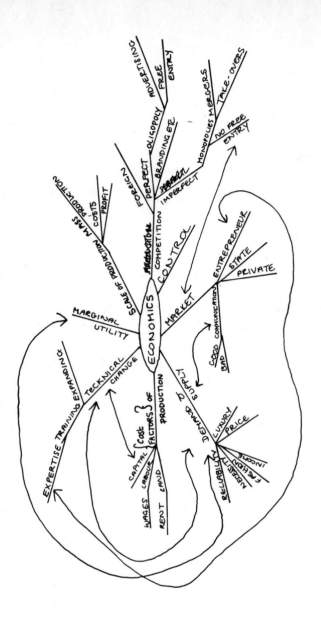

Fig 33 Mind Map by a boy who twice failed 'O' level Economics. *See text page 97.*

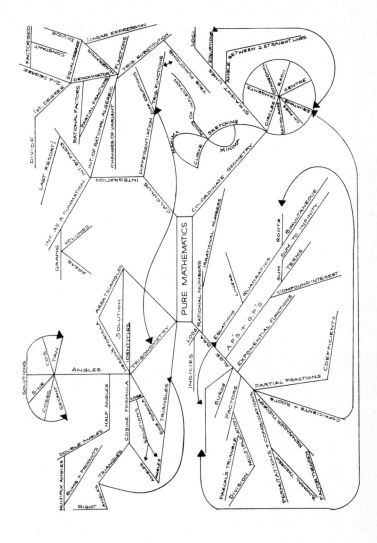

Fig 34 Mind Map by an 'A' level grammar school girl on pure Mathematics. *See text page 98.*

MAKE YOUR OWN MIND MAP OF CHAPTER SEVEN

Personal notes and applications

Mind Maps – advanced methods and uses

ADVANCED MIND MAPS

Combining the information from all previous chapters, and observing that the brain handles information better if the information is designed to 'slot in', and observing also the information from this chapter about the dimensional nature of the mind, it follows that notes which are themselves more 'holographic' and creative will be far more readily understood, appreciated and recalled.

There are many devices we can use to make such notes:

arrows

These can be used to show how concepts which appear on different parts of a pattern are connected. The arrow can be single or multi-headed and can show backward and forward directions.

codes

Asterisks, exclamation marks, crosses and question marks as well as many other indicators can be used next to words to show connections or other 'dimensions'.

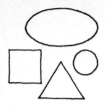

geometrical shapes

Squares, oblongs, circles, ellipses, etc. . . . can be used to mark areas or words which are similar in nature – for example triangles might be used to show areas of possible solution in a problem-solving pattern. Geometrical shapes can also be used to show order of importance. Some people, for example, prefer to use a square always for their main centre, oblongs for the ideas near the centre, triangles for ideas of next importance, and so on.

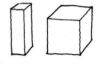

artistic three dimension

Each of the geometrical shapes mentioned, and many others, can be given perspective. For example, making a square into a cube. The ideas printed in these shapes will thus 'stand off' the page.

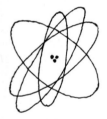

creativity images

Creativity can be combined with the use of dimension by making aspects of the pattern fit the topic. One man, for example, when doing a pattern on atomic physics, used the nucleus of an atom and the electrons that surrounded it, as the centre for his pattern.

colour

Colour is particularly useful as a memory and creative aid. It can be used, like arrows, to show how concepts which appear on different parts of the pattern are connected. It can also be used to mark off the boundaries between major areas of a pattern.

VBGYOR

MIND MAPS AND THE LEFT AND RIGHT CORTEX

At this point it is useful to consider how recent research into the brain adds strength to the points raised so far. In light of the fact, as already outlined, that the brain handles information better if the information is designed to 'slot in', consider the left and right cortex research of Roger Sperry, Robert Ornstein and Eran Zaidel.

This research alone *would lead you to conclude that a note-taking and thought-organisation technique designed to satisfy the needs of the whole brain would have to include not only words, numbers, order, sequence, and lines, but also colour, images, dimension, symbols, visual rhythms etc: in other words Mind Maps.*

From *whatever* perspective one approaches the question, be it from the nature of words and information, the function of recall, holographic models of the brain, or recent brain research, the conclusions in the end are identical – in order to fully utilise the brain's capacity, we need to consider each of the elements that add up to the whole, and integrate them in a unified way.

MIND MAPS – USES

The nature of Mind Maps is intimately connected with the function of the mind, and they can be used in nearly every activity where thought, recall, planning or creativity are involved. Colour Plate VIII is a Mind Map on the uses of Mind Maps, showing this wide variety of uses. In the remainder of this chapter I shall explain the application of Maps to the speech writing, essay writing, examination type of task; to meetings and communications, and to note taking.

MIND MAPPING FOR SPEECHES AND ARTICLES

Many people, when first shown Mind Maps, question if they can be used for any linear purpose, such as giving a talk or writing an article. If you refer to the Mind Map of this chapter on Plate VII, you will find how such a transformation took place:

Once the Mind Map has been completed, the required information is readily available. All that is necessary is to decide the final order in which to present the information. A good Mind Map will offer a number of possibilities. When the choice is being made, each area of the Mind Map can be encircled with a different colour, and numbered in the correct order. Putting this into written or verbal form is simply a matter of outlining the major areas to be covered, and then going through them point by point, following the logic of the branched connections. In this way the problem of redrafting and redrafting yet again is eliminated – all the gathering and organising will have been completed at the Mind Map stage.

It was using these techniques at Cambridge University that enabled Edward Hughes to complete his extraordinarily successful saga.

MIND MAPPING FOR LECTURES

It is advisable, when taking notes, to use a large (A3) blank page, to enable your brain to see 'the whole picture' of the information which your mind is investigating.

When taking notes, especially from lectures, it is important to remember that Key words and images are essentially all that is needed. It is also important to remember that the final structure will not become apparent till the end. Any notes made will therefore probably be semi-final rather than final copy. The first few words noted may be fairly disconnected until the theme of the lecture becomes apparent. It is necessary to understand clearly the value of so-called 'messy' as opposed to 'neat' notes, for many people feel apprehension at having a scrawly, arrowed, non-linear page of notes developing in front of them. 'Neat' notes are traditionally those which are organised in an orderly and linear manner. *See fig 31* in the previous chapter. 'Messy' notes are those which are 'untidy' and 'all over the page'. The word 'messy' used in this way refers to the *look* and not to the *content*.

In note taking it is primarily the content and not the look that is of importance. The notes which look 'neat' are, in information terms, messy. As explained on page 85, the key information is disguised, disconnected, and cluttered with many informationally irrelevant words. The notes which look 'messy' are informationally far neater. They show immediately the important concepts, the connections, and even in some cases the crossings-out and the objections.

Mind Mapped notes in their final form are usually neat in any case and it seldom takes more than ten minutes to finalise an hour's notes on a fresh sheet of paper. The final Mind Map reconstructing is a productive exercise, particularly if the learning period has been organised properly so as to fit in perfectly as the first review. *See pages 64–66.*

MIND MAPPING FOR MEETINGS

Meetings, notably those for planning or problem solving, often degenerate into situations where each person listens to the others only in order to make his own point as soon as the previous speaker has finished. In such meetings many excellent points are passed over or forgotten, and much time is wasted. A further aggravation is that points which are finally accepted are not necessarily the best, but those made by the most vociferous or important speakers.

These problems can be eliminated if the person who organises the meeting uses a Mind Map structure. On a board at the front of the room the central theme of the discussion, together with a couple of the sub themes, should be presented in basic map form. The members of the meeting will have pre-knowledge of what it is about, and will hopefully have come prepared. As each member finishes the point he is making, he can be asked to summarise it in Key form, and to indicate where on the overall Mind Map he thinks his point should be entered.

The following are the advantages of this approach:

1 The contribution of each person is registered and recorded properly.

2 No information is lost.

3 The importance given to ideas will pertain more to what was said than to who said it.

4 People will be speaking more to the point, thereby eliminating digressions and long wafflings.

5 After the meeting each individual will have a Mind Mapped record and will therefore not have lost most of what is said by the following morning.

One further advantage of Mind Maps, especially in note taking and communications, is that the individual is kept continually and actively involved in the complete structure of what is going on, rather than being concerned solely with 'getting down' the last point made. The more complete involvement will lead to a much greater critical and analytical facility, a much greater integration, a much greater ability to recall and a much greater overall understanding.

Mind Maps are an external 'photograph' of the complex inter-relationships of your thought at any given time. They enable your brain to 'see itself' more clearly, and will greatly enhance the full range of your thinking skills: they will add increasing competence, enjoyment, elegance and fun to your life.

Personal notes and applications

The Mind Map organic study technique (MMOST)

The subject of Study is divided into two sections: Preparation and Application. First, does this story seem familiar?

A: THE RELUCTANT LEARNER

OVERVIEW

▶ **The study book as a threat**

▶ **Old and new study techniques**

THE RELUCTANT LEARNER

The Six-o'clock-In-The-Evening-Enthusiastic-Determined-And-Well-Intentioned-Studier-Until-Midnight is a person with whom you are probably already familiar. At 6 o'clock he approaches his desk, and carefully organises everything in preparation for the study period to follow. Having everything in place he next carefully adjusts each item again, giving him time to complete the first excuse; he recalls that in the morning he did not have quite enough time to read all items of interest in the newspaper. He also realises that if he is going to study it is best to have such small items completely out of the way before settling down to the task at hand.

He therefore leaves his desk, browses through the newspaper and notices as he browses that there are more articles of interest than he had originally thought. He also notices, as he leafs through the pages, the entertainment section. At this point it will seem like a good idea to plan for the evening's first break — perhaps an interesting half-hour programme between 8 and 8.30 pm.

He finds the programme, and it inevitably starts at about 7 pm.

At this point, he thinks 'well, I've had a difficult day and it's not too long before the programme starts, and I need a rest anyway and the relaxation will really help me to get down to studying. . . .' He returns to his desk at 7.45 pm, because the beginning of the next programme was also a bit more interesting than he thought it would be.

At this stage, he still hovers over his desk tapping his book reassuringly as he remembers that phone call to a friend which, like the articles of interest in the newspaper, is best cleared out of the way before the serious studying begins.

The phone call, of course, is much more interesting and longer than originally planned, but eventually the intrepid studier finds himself back at his desk at about 8.30 pm.

At this point in the proceedings he actually sits down at the desk, opens the book with a display of physical determination and starts to read (usually page one) as he experiences the first pangs of hunger and thirst. This is disastrous because he realises that the longer he waits to satisfy the pangs, the worse they will get, and the more interrupted his study concentration will be.

The obvious and only solution is a light snack. This, in its preparation, grows like the associative structure of a Mind Map, as more and more tasty items are linked to the central core of hunger. The snack becomes a feast.

Having removed this final obstacle the desk is returned to with the certain knowledge that this time there is nothing that could possibly interfere with the dedication. The first couple of sentences on page one are looked at again . . . as the studier realises that his stomach is feeling decidedly heavy and a general drowsiness seems to have set in. Far better at this juncture to watch that other interesting half-hour programme at 10 o'clock, after which the digestion will be mostly completed and the rest will enable him to *really* get down to the task at hand.

At 12 o'clock we find him asleep in front of the TV.

Even at this point, when he has been woken up by whoever comes into the room, he will think that things have not gone too badly, for after all he had a good rest, a good meal, watched some interesting and relaxing programmes, fulfilled his social commitments to his friends, digested the day's information, and got everything completely out of the way so that tomorrow, at 6 o'clock. . . .

THE STUDY BOOK AS A THREAT

The above episode is amusing, but the implications of it are significant and serious.

On one level the story is encouraging because, by the very fact that it is a problem experienced by everybody it confirms what has long been suspected: that everyone is creative and inventive, and that the feelings that many have about being uncreative are not necessary. The creativity demonstrated in the example of the reluctant student is not applied very usefully. But the diversity and originality with which we all make up reasons for *not* doing things suggests that each person has a wealth of talent which could be applied in more positive directions!

Fig 35 At the present time information is being given more importance and emphasis than the individual. As a result he is being mentally swamped and almost literally 'weighed down' by it all. Both the information and publication explosions are still continuing at staggering rates, while the ability of the individual to handle and study it all remains neglected. If he is ever to cope with the situation he must learn not more 'hard facts' but new ways of handling and studying the information – new ways of using his natural abilities to learn, think, recall, create, and solve problems. *See also fig 37 and text pages 116–118.*

On another level the story is discouraging because it shows up the wide-spread and underlying fear that most of us experience when confronted with a study text.

This reluctance and fear arises from the examination-based school system in which the child is presented with books on the subjects he is 'taking' at school. He knows that text books are 'harder' than story books and novels; he also knows that they represent a lot of work; and he further knows that he will be tested on his knowledge of the information from the books.

The fact that the type of book is 'hard' is discouraging in itself. The fact that the book represents work is also discouraging, because the child instinctively knows that he is unable to read, note, and remember properly.

And the fact that he is going to be tested is often the most serious of the three difficulties. It is well known that this threat can completely disrupt the brain's ability to work in certain situations. The number of cases are enormous of people who literally cannot write anything in an exam situation despite the fact that they know their subject thoroughly – as are the number of cases of people who, even though they are able to write some form of answer, have gigantic mental blocks where whole areas of knowledge are completely forgotten during an exam period. And in even more extreme cases many people have been known to spend a whole two hour period writing frantically, assuming that they were answering the question, but in fact repeating over and over again either their own name or one word.

Faced with this kind of threat, which for many is truly terrifying, the child has one of two choices: he can either study and face one set of consequences, or not study and face a different set of consequences. If he studies and does badly, then he has proven himself 'incapable', 'unintelligent', 'stupid', a 'dunce' or whatever the appropriate negative expression is at the time. Of course this is not really the case, but he has no way of knowing that it is the system which is not testing him properly, and not his own ineptitude causing the 'failure'.

If he does *not* study, the situation is quite different. Confronted with having failed a test or exam, he can immediately say that of course he failed it because he 'didn't study and wasn't interested in that kind of stuff anyway.'

By doing this, he solves the problem in a number of ways:

1 He avoids both the test and the threat to his self-esteem that studying would involve;

2 He has a perfect excuse for failing;

3 He gets respect from the other children because he is daring to attack a situation which is frightening to them. It is interesting to note that such a child will often find himself in the position of a leader.

It is also interesting to note that even those who do make the decision to study will still reserve a little part of themselves for behaving like the non-studier. The person who gets scores as high as 80 or 90 per cent will also be found using exactly the same excuses for not getting 100 per cent, as the non-studier uses for failing.

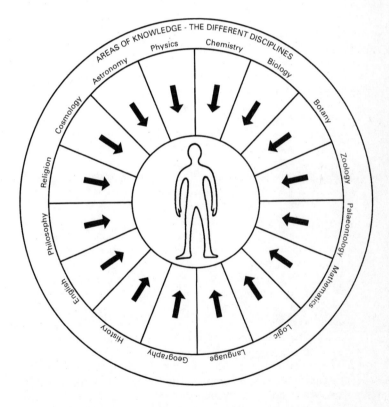

Fig 36 In traditional education information is given or 'taught' about the different areas of knowledge that surround the individual. The direction and flow is *from* the subject *to* the individual – he is simply given the information, and is expected to absorb, learn and remember as much as he possibly can. *See also fig 35 and text page 116.*

OLD AND NEW STUDY TECHNIQUES

The situations described above are unsatisfactory for everyone concerned, and have arisen for various reasons, many of them outlined in earlier parts of this book. One further and major reason for poor study results lies in the way we have approached both study techniques and the information we wanted people to study.

We have surrounded the person with a confusing mass of different subjects or 'disciplines' demanding that he learn, remember and understand a frightening array under headings such as Mathematics, Physics, Chemistry, Biology, Zoology, Botany, Anatomy, Physiology, Sociology, Psychology, Anthropology, Philosophy, History, Geography, Trigonometry, Palaeontology, etc. In each of these subject areas the individual has been and is still presented with series of dates, theories, facts, names, and general ideas. *See fig 36.* What this really means is that we have been taking a totally lopsided approach to study and to the way in which a person deals with and relates to the information and knowledge that surrounds him. *See figs 36 and 37.*

As can be seen from the figures, we are concentrating far too much on information about the 'separate' areas of knowledge. We are also laying too much stress on asking the individual to feed back facts in pre-digested order or in pre-set forms such as standard examination papers or formal essays.

This approach has also been reflected in the standard study techniques recommended in Schools, Universities, Institutes of Further Education and text books. These techniques have been 'grid' approaches in which it is recommended that a series of steps always be worked through on any book being studied. One common suggestion is that any reasonably difficult study book should always be read through three times in order to ensure a complete understanding. This is obviously a very simple example, but even the many more developed approaches tend to be comparatively rigid and inflexible – simply standard systems to be repeated on each studying occasion.

It is obvious that methods such as these cannot be applied with success to every study book. There is an enormous difference between studying a text on Literary Criticism and studying a text on Higher Mathematics. In order to study properly, a technique is needed which does not force the same approach to such different materials.

First, it is necessary to start working from the individual outwards. Rather than bombarding him with books, formulas and examinations we must begin to concentrate on teaching each person how he or she *can* study most efficiently. We must teach ourselves how our eyes work when we read, how we remember, how we think, how we can learn more effectively, how we can organise noting, how we can solve problems and in general how we can best use our abilities, whatever the subject matter.

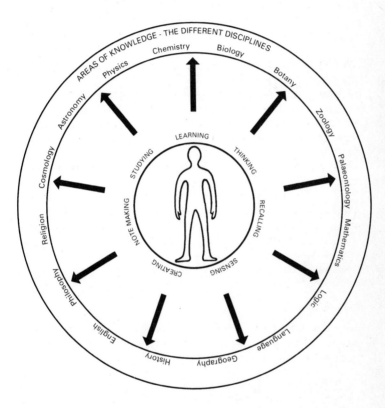

Fig 37 In the new forms of education, the previous emphases must be reversed. Instead of first teaching the individual facts about other things, we must first teach him facts about himself – facts about how he *can* learn, think, recall, create, solve problems etc. *See text opposite.*

One is tempted to note here that in our society we have Instruction Manuals and 'How To Do It' booklets on nearly everything, including the simplest of machines. But when it comes to the most compli- cated, complex, and important organism of all, ourselves, there has been practically no help. We need our own Owner's Manual on how to operate our own Super Bio Computer. Use Your Head is designed to be just that.

Most of the problems outlined in the first chapter will be eliminated when we finally do change the emphasis away from the subject toward the individual and how he can select and understand any information he wants to. People will be equipped to study and remember whatever area of knowledge is interesting or necessary. Things will not have to be 'taught to' or 'crammed in'. Each person will be able to range subjects at his own pace, going for help and personal supervision only when he realises it is necessary. *See fig 37.*

Yet another advantage of this approach is that it will make both teaching and learning much easier, more enjoyable and more pro- ductive. By concentrating on the individual and his abilities we will finally and sensibly have placed the learning situation in its proper perspective.

B: PREPARATION

The Mind Map Organic Study Technique is divided into two main sections: Preparation and Application. Each of these sections is divided into four sub-sections:

Preparation	Browse
	Time and Amount
	Knowledge Mind Map
	Questions and Goals
Application	Overview
	Preview
	Inview
	Review

It is important to note at the outset that although the main steps are presented in a certain order, this order is by no means essential and can be changed, subtracted from and added to as the study texts warrant.

This section will deal with the Preparation:

OVERVIEW

- ▶ **The browse**
- ▶ **Time and amount**
- ▶ **Mind Map of knowledge on the subject**
- ▶ **Asking questions and defining goals**

THE BROWSE

Before doing anything else, it is *essential* to 'browse' or look through the entire book or periodical you are about to study. The browse should be done in the way you would look through a book you were considering buying in a bookshop, or in the way you would look through a book you were considering taking out from the library. In other words casually, but rather rapidly, flipping through the pages, getting the general 'feel' of the book, observing the organisation and structure, the level of difficulty, the proportion of diagrams and illustrations to text, the location of any results, summaries and conclusions sections etc.

TIME AND AMOUNT

These two aspects can be dealt with simultaneously because the theory behind them both is similar.

The first thing to do when sitting down to study a text book is to decide on the period of time to be devoted to it. Having done this decide what amount to cover in the time allocated.

The reason for insisting on these two initial steps is not arbitrary, and is supported by the findings of the *Gestalt* Psychologists. (Before reading on, complete the activity on page 120, figure 38.)

The *Gestalt* Psychologists discovered that the human brain has a very strong tendency to complete things – thus most readers will find that they labelled the shapes in figure 38 straight line, cylinder, square, ellipse or oval, zig-zag line, circle, triangle, wavy or curved line, rectangle. In fact the 'circle' is not a circle but a 'broken circle'. Many actually see this broken circle as a circle. Others see it as a broken circle but assume that the artist intended to complete it.

A more abstract example of our general desire to complete things is our universal tendency as children to build up a language that

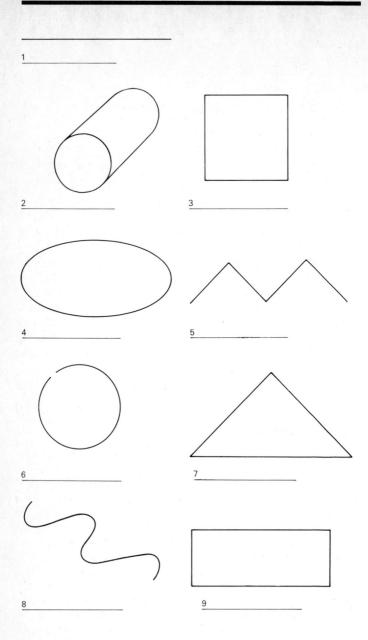

1 _____

2 _____   3 _____

4 _____   5 _____

6 _____   7 _____

8 _____   9 _____

Fig 38 Shape recognition.
Enter the name of the shape of each of the items above next to the appropriate number. *See text on page 119 after completion.*

helps us to make sense of, and form completed ideas of, our surroundings.

In study, making a decision about Time and Amount gives us immediate chronological and volume terrain, as well as an end point or goal. This has the added advantage of enabling the proper linkages to be made rather than encouraging a wandering off in more disconnected ways.

An excellent comparison is that of listening to a lecturer. A good lecturer who is attempting to expound a lot of difficult material will usually explain his starting and his ending points and will often indicate the amount of time he intends to spend on each area of his presentation. The audience will automatically find his lecture easier to follow because they have guide-lines within which to work.

It is advisable to define physically the amount to be read by placing reasonably large paper markers at the beginnings and end of the section chosen. This enables the reader to refer back and forward to the information in the amount chosen.

A further advantage of making these decisions at the outset is that the underlying fear of the unknown is avoided. If a large study book is plunged into with no planning, the reader will be continually oppressed by the number of pages he eventually has to complete. Each time he sits down he will be aware that he still has 'a few hundred pages to go' and will be studying with this as a constant and real background threat. If, on the other hand, he has selected a reasonable number of pages for the time he is going to study, he will be reading with the knowledge that the task he has set himself is easy and can certainly be completed. The difference in attitude and performance will be marked.

There are still further reasons for making these time and amount decisions which are concerned with the distribution of the reader's effort as time goes on.

Imagine that you have decided to study for two hours and that the first half-an-hour has been pretty difficult, although you have been making some progress. At this point in time you find that understanding begins to improve and that your progress seems to be getting better and faster.

Would you pat yourself on the back and take a break?

Or would you decide to keep the new and better rhythm going by studying on for a while until you began to lose the new impetus?

Ninety per cent of people asked those questions would carry on. Of those who would take a break, only a few would recommend the same thing to anyone else!

And yet surprisingly the best answer *is* to take a break. The reason for this can be seen by referring back to the discussion in the chapter on Memory and the amount that is recalled from a period of learning.

Despite the fact that understanding may be continually high, the recall of that understanding will be getting worse if the mind is not given a break, thus the graph, fig 20, is particularly relevant in the study situation. It is essential that any time period for studying be broken down into 20–50 minute sections with small rests in between. *See fig 21*. The common student practice of swotting five hours at a stretch for examination purposes should become a thing of the past, for understanding is *not* the same as remembering, as all too many failed examination papers give witness.

The breaks themselves are also important for a number of reasons:

1 They give the body a physical rest and a chance to relax. This is always useful in a learning situation, and releases the build-up of tension.

2 They enable recall and understanding to 'work together' to the best advantage.

3 They allow a brief period of time for the just-studied information completely to relate each part of itself to the other part – to intra-integrate. *See fig 23*.

This last point also relates to the Memory chapter and the graph on forgetting as time progresses. During each break the amount of knowledge that can immediately be recalled from the section just studied will increase and will be at a peak as the next section is commenced. This means that not only will more be recalled because the time period itself is best, but also that even more will be recalled because of the rest period.

To assist this even further, do a quick review of what you have read and a preview of what you are about to read at the beginning and end of each study period.

It has taken a number of pages to explain the necessity of deciding on a period of time and on an amount to be covered, but remember that the decisions themselves are extremely brief and will usually become automatic as you near completion of your browse. When these decisions have been made the next step can be taken:

MIND MAP OF KNOWLEDGE ON THE SUBJECT

Having decided on the amounts to be covered, next jot down as much as you know on the subject as fast as you can. No more than two minutes should be devoted to the exercise. Notes should be in Key words and in Mind Map form.

The purpose of this exercise is to improve concentration, to eliminate wandering, and to establish a good mental 'set'. This last term refers to getting the mind filled with important rather than unimportant information. If you have spent two minutes searching your memory for pertinent information, you will be far more attuned to the text material and far less likely to continue thinking about the strawberries and cream you are going to eat afterwards.

From the time limit of five minutes on this exercise it is obvious that a person's entire knowledge is not required on the pattern – the two minute exercise is intended purely to activate the storage system and to set the mind off in the right direction.

One question which will arise is 'what about the difference if I know almost nothing on the subject or if I know an enormous amount?' If knowledge in the area is great, the five minutes should be spent forming a pattern of the major divisions, theories, names etc. connected with the subject. As the mind can flash through information much faster than the hand can write it, all the minor associations will still be mentally 'seen' and the proper mental set and direction will be established.

If the knowledge of the subject is almost nothing, the two minutes should be spent patterning those few items which are known, as well as any other information which seems in any way at all to be connected. This will enable the reader to get as close as he possibly can to the new subject, and will prevent him from feeling totally lost as so many do in this situation.

Apart from being immediately useful in study, a continued practice with patterning information gives a number of more general advantages. First, the individual gains by gathering together his immediate and current state of knowledge on areas of interest. In this way he will be able to keep much more up to date with himself and will actually know what he knows, rather than being in a continually embarrassing position of not knowing what he knows – the 'I've got it on the tip of my tongue' syndrome.

In addition, this continued practice of recalling and integrating ideas gives enormous advantage in situations where such abilities are essential: examinations, impromptu speeches and answering on the spot questions, to name but a few.

Once the five-minute period is up, the next stage should be moved to immediately.

ASKING QUESTIONS AND DEFINING GOALS

Having established the current state of knowledge on the subject, it is next advisable to decide what you want from the book. This involves defining the questions you want answered during the reading. The questions should be asked in the context of goals aimed for and should, like noting of knowledge, be done in Key Word and Mind Map form. Many prefer to use a different coloured pen for this section, and rather than starting a new map they add their questions to the already existing map on current knowledge.

This exercise, again like that for noting knowledge, is based on the principle of establishing proper mental sets. It should also take not much more than five minutes at the outset, as questions can be redefined and added to as the reading progresses.

A standard experiment to confirm this approach takes two groups of people who are generally equal in terms of age, education, aptitude etc. Each group is given the same study text and is given enough time to complete the whole book.

Group A is told that they are going to be given a completely comprehensive test on everything in the book and that they must study accordingly.

Group B is told that they will be tested on two or three major themes which run through the book, and that they also must study accordingly.

Both groups are in fact tested on the entire text, a situation which one would immediately think unfair to the group that had been told they would be tested only on the main themes.

One might also think that in this situation the second group would do better on questions about the themes they had been given, the first group better on other questions and that both groups might have a similar final score.

To the surprise of many, the second group not only does better on questions about the themes, but they achieve higher total scores which include better marks on all parts of the test.

The reason for this is that the main themes act like great grappling hooks through the information, attaching everything else to them. In other words the main questions and goals acted as associative and linking centres to which all other information became easily attached.

The group instructed to get everything had no centres at all to connect new information to, and because of this was groping with no foundations through the information. It is much like a situation where a person is given so much choice that he ends up making no decision; the paradox where attempting to get everything gains nothing.

Asking questions and establishing goals can be seen, like the section preceding it, to become more and more important as the theory behind becomes better understood. It should be emphasised that the more accurately these questions and goals are established, the more able the reader will be to perform well in the Application section of the Mind Map Organic Study Technique.

C: APPLICATION

OVERVIEW

- ▶ **Study overview**
- ▶ **Preview**
- ▶ **Inview**
- ▶ **Review**
- ▶ **Text notes and Mind Mapping**
- ▶ **Continuing review**
- ▶ **Summary: the Mind Map Organic Study Technique**

STUDY OVERVIEW

One of the interesting facts about people using study books is that most, when given a new text, start reading on page one. It is *not* advisable to start reading a new study text on the first page. The following situation is a parallel illustration of this point:

Imagine that you are a fanatical jigsaw-puzzle-doer. A friend arrives on your doorstep with a gigantic box wrapped in paper and tied with string, and tells you that it's a present: 'the most beautiful and complex jigsaw puzzle yet devised by man!'. You thank her, and as you watch her walk away down the front path, you decide that from that moment on you are going to devote yourself *entirely* to the completion of the puzzle.

Before continuing, note in *precise detail* the steps you would take from that point on in order to complete the task.

Now check your own answers with the following list compiled from my students:

1 Go back inside the house.
2 Take the string off the box.
3 Take off the paper.
4 Dispose of string and paper.
5 Look at the picture on the outside of the box.
6 Read the instructions, concentrating on number of pieces and overall dimensions of the puzzle.
7 Estimate and organise amount of time necessary for completion.
8 Plan breaks and meals!
9 Find surface of appropriate dimensions for puzzle.
10 Open box.
11 Empty contents of box onto surface or separate tray.
12 If pessimistic, check number of pieces!
13 Turn all pieces right side up.
14 Find edge and corner pieces.
15 Sort out colour areas.
16 Fit 'obvious' bits and pieces together.
17 Continue to fill in.
18 Leave 'difficult' pieces to end (for reason that as the overall picture becomes more clear, and the number of pieces used increases, so does the probability increase that the difficult pieces will fit in much more easily when there is greater context into which they *can* fit).
19 Continue process until completion.
20 Celebrate!

This jigsaw analogy can be applied directly to study, in the first instance making it clearer why it is so important not to commence studying on page one, as doing so would be like finding the bottom left-hand corner, and insisting to yourself that the entire picture be built up step by step from the corner only.

What is essential in a reasonable approach to study texts, especially difficult ones, is to get a good idea of what's in them before plodding on into a learning catastrophe. The overview is designed to perform this task, and may be likened to looking at the picture, reading the instructions, and finding the edge and corner pieces of the puzzle. What this means in the study context is that you should scour the book for all material not included in the regular body of the print, using your visual guide as you do so. Areas of the book to be covered in your overview include:

results	tables	subheadings
summaries	table of contents	dates
conclusions	marginal notes	italics
indents	illustrations	graphs
glossaries	capitalised words	footnotes
back cover	photographs	statistics

The function of this is to provide you with a good knowledge of the graphic sections of the book, not skimming the whole thing, but selecting specific areas for relatively comprehensive coverage. *See fig 39.* At this time complete the central image and main branches of your Mind Map.

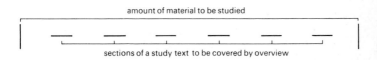

Fig 39 Sections of a study text to be covered by overview. *See text above.*

It is extremely important to note again that throughout the overview a pen, pencil, or other form of visual guide should always be used.

The reason for this can best be explained by reference to a graph. If the eye is unaided, it will simply fixate briefly on general areas of the graph, then move off, leaving only a vague visual memory and an interference to that memory because the eye movement will not have 'registered' the same pattern as the graph.

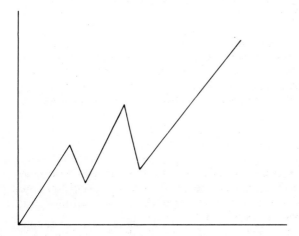

Fig 40 Example pattern of graph to be studied.

If a visual aid is used, the eye will more nearly approximate the flow of the graph and the memory will be strengthened by each of the following inputs:

1 The visual memory itself.
2 The remembered eye movement approximating the graph shape.
3 The memory of the movement of the arm or hand in tracing the graph (Kinaesthetic memory).
4 The visual memory of the rhythm and movement of the tracer.

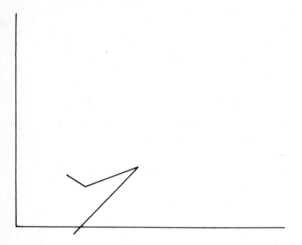

Fig 41 Standard pattern of unguided eye movement on graph causing conflicting memory of shape of graph.

The overall recall resulting from this practice is far superior to that of a person who reads without any visual guide. It is interesting to note that accountants often use their pens to guide their eyes across and down columns and rows of figures. They do this naturally because any very rigid linear eye movement is difficult to maintain with the unaided eye.

PREVIEW

The second section of study application is the preview – covering all that material not covered in the overview. In other words the paragraphed, language content of the book. This can be likened to organising the colour areas of your puzzle.

During the preview, concentration should be directed to the beginnings and ends of paragraphs, sections, chapters, and even whole texts, because information tends to be concentrated at the beginnings and ends of written material.

If you are studying a short academic paper or a complex study book, the Summary Results and Conclusion sections should always be read first. These sections often include exactly those essences of information that you are searching for, enabling you to grasp that essence without having to wade through a lot of time-wasting material.

Having gained the essence from these sections, simply check that they do indeed summarise the main body of the text.

In the preview, as with the overview, you are not fully reading all the material, but simply concentrating once again on special areas. *See fig 42*.

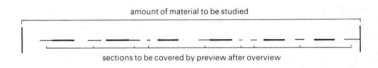

amount of material to be studied

sections to be covered by preview after overview

Fig 42 Sections to be covered by preview after overview. *Again add any appropriate information or references to your Mind Map. See text this page.*

The value of this section cannot be overemphasised. A case in point is that of a student taught at Oxford who had spent four months struggling through a 500-page tome on psychology. By the time he had reached page 450 he was beginning to despair because the amount of information he was 'holding on to' as he tried to get to the end was becoming too much – he was literally beginning to drown in the information just before reaching his goal.

It transpired that he had been reading straight through the book, and even though he was nearing the end, did not know what the last chapter was about. It was a complete summary of the book! He read the section and estimated that had he done so at the beginning he would have saved himself approximately 70 hours in reading time, 20 hours in note-taking time and a few hundred hours of worrying.

In both the overview and preview you should very actively select and reject. Many people still feel obliged to read everything in a book even though they know it is not necessarily relevant to them. It is far better to treat a book in the way most people treat lecturers. In other words, if the lecturer is boring skip what he says, and if he is giving too many examples, is missing the point or is making errors, select, criticise, correct, and disregard as appropriate.

INVIEW

After the overview and preview, and providing that still more information is required, inview the material. This involves 'filling in' those areas still left, and can be compared with the filling in process of the jigsaw puzzle, once the boundaries and colour areas have been established. It is *not* necessarily the major reading, as in some cases most of the important material will have been covered in the previous stages.

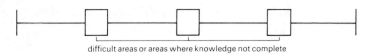

difficult areas or areas where knowledge not complete

Fig 43 Sections covered after inview has been completed. As you proceed, add the relevant information to your Mind Map. *See text this page.*

It should be noted from fig 43 that there are still certain sections which have been left incomplete even at the inview stage. This is because it is far better to move *over* particularly difficult points than to batter away at them immediately from one side only.

Once again the comparison with the jigsaw puzzle becomes clear: racking your brains to find the pieces that connect to your 'difficult bit' is a tension-producing waste of time, and jamming the piece in, or cutting it with a pair of scissors so that it *does* fit (assuming or pretending you understand in context when *really* you don't) is similarly futile. The difficult sections of a study text are seldom essential to that which follows them, and the advantages of leaving them are manifold:

1 If they are not immediately struggled with, the brain is given that most important brief period in which it can work on them subconsciously. (Most readers will have experienced the examination question which they 'can't possibly answer' only to find on returning to the question later that the answer pops out and often seems ridiculously simple.)
2 If the difficult areas are returned to later, they can be approached from both sides. Apart from its obvious advantages, considering the difficult area in context (as with the difficult bit in the jigsaw) also enables the brain's automatic tendency to fill in gaps to work to greater advantage.
3 Moving on from a difficult area releases the tension and mental floundering that often accompanies the traditional approach.

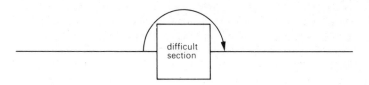

Fig 44 'Jumping over' a stumbling block usually enables the reader to go back to it later on with more information from 'the other side'. The block itself is seldom essential for the understanding of that which follows it. *See text opposite.*

An adjunct to this last point is that it tends to make studying a more creative process.

Looking at the normal historical development of any discipline, it is found that a fairly regular series of small and logically connected steps are interrupted by great leaps forward.

The propounders of these giant new steps have in many cases 'intuited' them (combining left and right cortex functions, as outlined in chapter 2), and afterwards been met with scorn. Galileo and Einstein are examples. As they then explained their ideas step by step, others gradually and progressively understood, some early in the explanation, and others as the innovator neared his conclusion.

In the same manner in which the innovator jumps over an enormous number of sequential steps, and in the same manner in which those who first realised his conclusions did so, the studier who leaves out small sections of study will be giving a greater range to his natural creative and understanding abilities. *See fig 45.*

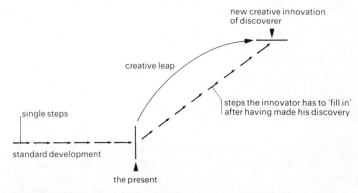

Fig 45 Historical development of ideas and creative innovations. *See text this page.*

REVIEW

Having completed the overview, preview and inview, and if further information is still required to complete goals, answer questions or solve problem areas, a review stage is necessary.

In this stage simply fill in all those areas as yet incomplete, and reconsider those sections marked as noteworthy. In most cases it will be found that not much more than 70 per cent of that initially considered relevant will finally be used. Then complete your Mind Map notes.

TEXT NOTES AND MIND MAPPING

Noting while studying takes two main forms:
1 Notes made on the text itself.
2 A growing Mind Map.

1 Notes you make in the book itself can include:

1 Underlining.
2 Personal thoughts generated by the text.
3 Critical comments.
4 Marginal straight lines for important or note-worthy material.
5 Curved or wavy marginal lines to indicate unclear or difficult material.
6 Question marks for areas that you wish to question or that you find questionable.
7 Exclamation marks for outstanding items.
8 Your own symbol code for items and areas that relate to your own specific and general objectives.
9 Mini Mind Maps in the margins.

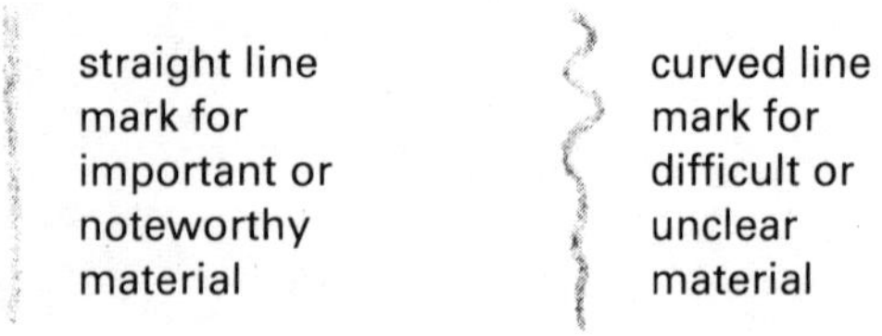

| straight line mark for important or noteworthy material | curved line mark for difficult or unclear material |

Fig 46 Techniques for marking text.

If the book is not valuable, markings can be made in colour codes. If the book is a cherished volume, then markings can be made with a very soft pencil. If the pencil is soft enough, and if a *very* soft eraser is used, the damage to the book will be less than that caused by the finger and thumb as they turn a page.

2 The growing Mind Map

You will find that Mind Mapping the structure of the text as you progress through it is very similar to building up the picture of the jigsaw puzzle as you fit in bit by bit. Ideally the bulk of Mind Map noting should take place during the latter stages of study, as in the earlier stages it is very difficult to know what is *definitely* note-worthy, and subsequently unnecessary noting can be avoided.

It is best to start with a central image that captures the essence of that which you are studying, and from that central image, to branch out with the major sub-subject headings or chapter headings forming the central arms from which the secondary and tertiary levels of your note taking will emanate. *Re-read now chapter 7, 'Mind Mapping laws', starting on page 95.*

The advantage of building up a Mind Map as you progress through the study text is that you externalise and integrate a lot of information that would otherwise be 'up-in-the-air'. The growing Mind Map also allows you to refer back quickly to areas you have previously covered, rather than having to thumb through pages already read.

It will enable you after a reasonable amount of basic study, to see just where the areas of confusion in your subject are, and to see also where your subject connects with other subjects. As such it will place you in the creative situation of being able to: integrate the known; realise the relevance to other areas; and to make appropriate comment where confusion and debate still exist. The final stage of your study will include the completion and integration of any notes from your text with the Mind Map, which will act as your basis for ongoing study and review.

When you have completed this final stage, you should, as did our imaginary jigsaw puzzle fanatic, celebrate! This may sound humorous, but it is also serious: if you associate the completion of study tasks with personal celebration, the context of your study will become increasingly more pleasant, and thus the probability of your studying far greater.

Once your study programme is well under way, it is advisable to keep enormous 'Master' Mind Maps which summarise and overview the main branches and structures of your subject areas.

CONTINUING REVIEW

Apart from the immediate review, a continuing review programme is essential, and should be constructed in the light of the knowledge we have concerning memory as discussed in the chapter on Memory.

It was seen that memory did not decline immediately after a learning situation, but actually rose before levelling off and then plummeting.

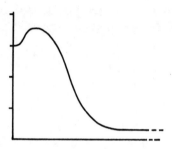

Fig 47 Graph showing that memory actually rises after learning, before declining sharply. *See text this page.*

This graph can be warped to your advantage by reviewing just at that point where the memory starts to fall. A review here, at the point of highest memory and integration, will keep the high point up for another one or two days and so on as explained on page 64. *See also fig 24.*

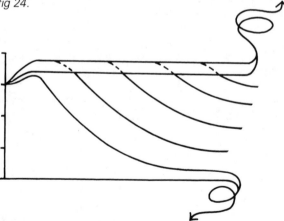

Fig 48 This graph shows how quickly forgetting takes place after something has been learned. It also shows how review can 'warp' this graph to enormous advantage. *See text this page.*

SUMMARY: THE MIND MAP ORGANIC STUDY TECHNIQUE

The entire Mind Map Organic Study Technique must be seen not as a step by step progression, but as a series of inter-related aspects of approaching study material. It is quite possible to switch and change the order from the one given here. The amount to be covered may be decided upon before the period of time; the subject matter may be known before the time and amount are decided upon and consequently the knowledge Mind Map could be completed first; the questions can be asked at the preparation stage or after any one of the latter stages; the overview can be eliminated in books where it is inappropriate, or repeated a number of times if the subjects were mathematics or physics. (One student found that it was easier to read four chapters of post-degree mathematics 25 times per week for four weeks quickly using the survey technique, than to struggle through one formula at a time. He was of course applying to its extreme, but very effectively, the point made about skipping over difficult areas.) Preview can be eliminated or broken down into separate sections; and the inview and review can be variously extended or eliminated.

In other words each subject, and each book of each subject, can be confidently approached in the manner best suited to it. To each book you will bring the knowledge that whatever the difficulties, you possess the fundamental understanding to choose the appropriate and necessarily unique approach.

Study is consequently made a personal, interactive, continually changing and stimulating experience, rather than a rigid, impersonal and tiresomely onerous task.

It should also be noted that despite the apparently greater number of 'times the book is being read' this is *not* the case. By using the Mind Map Organic Study Technique you will be on average reading most sections once only and will then be effectively reviewing those sections considered important. A pictorial representation can be seen in fig 49.

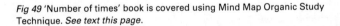

Fig 49 'Number of times' book is covered using Mind Map Organic Study Technique. *See text this page.*

By contrast, the 'once through' reader is *not* reading it once through but is reading it an enormous number of times. He thinks he is reading it through once only because he takes in once piece of information after another. He does not realise that his regressions, back-skipping, re-reading of difficult sentences, general disorganisation and forgetting because of inadequate review, result in an actual reading of the book or chapter as many as ten times.

Fig 50 'Number of times' book is covered using traditional 'once through' reading techniques. *See text this page.*

The Mind Map Organic Study Technique will allow you easy and delightful access to the world of knowledge in a manner that will encourage your brain to learn more and more easily as it learns more, and will turn you from a reluctant learner to one who will, like Edward Hughes, avidly devour books by the hundred!

Personal notes and application

10 Directions

WHAT A DIFFERENCE FIFTEEN YEARS CAN MAKE

As the twentieth century ends, the human race, with many members still not realising it, has entered what will probably be considered by future historians as the beginning of the greatest Renaissance ever, and one which will arguably become a permanent feature of human evolution.

In the fifteen years since I first wrote *Use Your Head*, there has been a worldwide explosion of interest in art, theatre, music, the sciences, general knowledge, the exploration of our terrestrial, extra-terrestrial and Universal environments, and, perhaps most of all, our fascination with and accelerating investigation of our own intelligence.

Old myths are disintegrating in the glare of our knowledge about ourselves. Take, for example, ideas about the way human mental ability declines with age.

REVIEW, MENTAL ABILITY AND AGE

The way in which a person reviews has an interesting connection with popular ideas about the way human mental ability declines with age. It is normally assumed that IQ scores, recall ability, ability to see special relationships, perceptual speed, speed of judgement, induction, figural relations, associative memory, intellectual level, intellectual speed, semantic relations, formal and general reasoning etc., decline after reaching a peak at the age of 18 to 25 (*see fig 51*). Valid as the figure produced may be, two important factors must be noted:

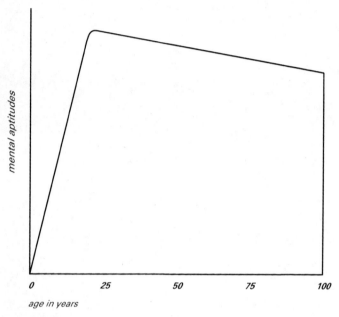

mental aptitudes

0   25   50   75   100

age in years

Fig 51 Graph showing standard results of measuring mental aptitudes as a person gets older. It is assumed that after reaching a peak at approximately 18–25, decline is thereafter slow but steady. *See text on previous page.*

1 The decline over the life-time is little more than 5 to 10 per cent. When considered in relation to the brain's enormous inherent capacity, this is insignificant.

2 The people who took part in the experiments which arrived at these discouraging figures had been educated traditionally, and therefore in most cases would not have been practising proper learning, reviewing and remembering techniques.

Looking at figure 51 it can be easily seen that such a person's mental 'conditioning' would have been at a very low level for an increasing number of years. In other words his real intellectual capacities would have been in 'cold storage'. It is not surprising that such an unused mind would do slightly worse after 20 to 40 years of mis- or no use – it is surprising that it still manages to do as well as it does!

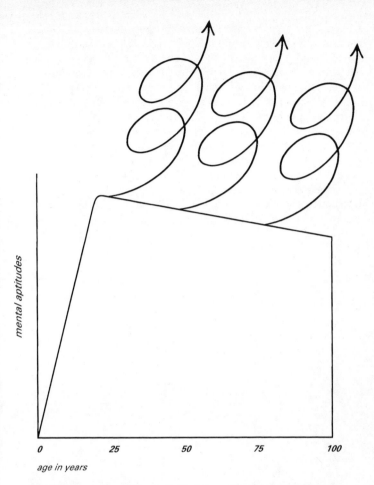

Fig 52 Graphs such as shown in fig 51 are based on statistics from people taught traditionally. A human being would naturally tend to improve these capacities with age if taught in a manner that complemented and nourished the brain's natural functioning.

If, on the other hand, the mind were continually used, and its capacities expanded, the effect on the graph for age would be dramatic. This can be seen by taking note of those older people who have remained active and explorative rather than assuming that they were going to get worse as the years passed. Very often their recall is almost total, and their ability to understand and learn new areas of knowledge far surpasses that of equally enthusiastic but younger and less experienced minds. *See fig 52.*

In studying human mental performance it has been mistakenly assumed that the decline found with age is 'natural' and unavoidable. Instead a closer look should be taken at the people being studied, and then experiments should be performed to find out how abilities can be maximised rather than minimised.

Increasingly we are finding positive **'Renegades from the Norm':** people over the age of 70 whose defining characteristics are: vitality, optimism, humour, physical strength, persistence, mischievousness, enthusiasm, interest, expanding knowledge, curiosity, kindness, exhaustive memory and sensuality. The very characteristics that one would ascribe to children.

We are finding that if we understand, care for and 'use our heads' in the way they were designed, the Edward Hughes Story will become the Every Child Story.

Afterword

As you approach the end of *Use Your Head* I hope that you will be realising that it is not the end, but the real beginning. With the physical beauty and complexity of your brain, and its enormous intellectual and emotional powers, with your ability to absorb information and to manage the memorisation of that information, and with the new techniques for allowing your brain to express and organise itself in matters which are more comprehensibly attuned to the way you function, reading, studying, learning, and life in general should become what they can be: delightful and flowing processes that bring not pain and frustration, but pleasure and fulfilment.

Anyone interested in further reading or in courses dealing with the subject covered in *Use Your Head* can contact the author c/o:

The Buzan Centre
Suite 2
Cardigan House
37 Waterloo Road
Winton
Dorset BH9 1BD.

Appendix

THE BRAIN CLUB

The Brain Club is an international organisation designed to help you increase your mental, physical and spiritual awareness. This is done by waking that sleeping giant, your Brain, and teaching you how to access its vast intelligences, first by Learning How to Learn and then by developing specific skills in areas that you choose.

You can do this by studying in your own home, or meeting regularly with others who also wish to expand their vast range of mental skills as outlined in *Use Your Head*.

Join these 'mental gymnasiums' and improve the following skills:

a Memorising
b Range/Speed Reading
c Mind Mapping and Creative Thinking
d Learning and Studying
e IQ
f Mathematics
g The Arts
h Physical performance
i Vocabulary Building/Language Learning
j Communicating
k Personality Development
l Games skills
m Specialist skills

Each area within The Brain Club will be graded and certificates awarded as you reach advancing levels of competence. For details of the nearest Cell of The Brain Club, contact:

The Buzan Centre
Suite 2, Cardigan House, 37 Waterloo Road, Winton,
Dorset BH9 1BD. Telephone: 0202 533593 Fax: 0202 534572

PRODUCTS

Audiotapes

Learning and Memory – produced for *Psychology Today* magazine.

The Intelligence Revolution (set of 3 tapes)
Tony Buzan on Memory and Advanced Mind Mapping.

Make the Most of Your Mind – based on the book of the same name, and *Use Your Head*.

Supercreativity and Mind Mapping – a comprehensive introduction to the workings of your brain, and the theory and use of Mind Mapping (with mini-manual).

Videotapes

Use Your Head – the original nine-part BBC TV series attractively presented with updated facilitator's manual and *Use Your Head* and *Use Your Memory* books.

The Enchanted Loom – documentary on the brain featuring interviews with the world's major contributors to the field, devised and presented by Tony Buzan.

Buzan Business Training – complete business training course emphasising the application of Mind Mapping, Memory and Information Management to business.

Family Genius Training – complete video series based on *Use Your Head* and *Make the Most of Your Mind*, which guides the family through the latest information on the brain and brain training.

Posters

'Body and Soul' Master Mind Map poster – a limited edition poster depicting, in a surrealist manner, all the principles taught by Tony Buzan. This beautiful picture is called 'Body and Soul' and each numbered copy is signed by the Swedish artist, Ulf Ekberg.

'Brain' Cartoons by Pecub.

Thinking Cap by Lorraine Gill.

Mind Map Kits

Specially designed A3 & A4 pads and pens.

Master Your Memory Matrix 0–10,000

Laminated 0–99 and 100 to 10,000 Matrix plus full instructions to assist the *Master Your Memory Reader*.

To order, contact:

The Buzan Centre
Suite 2, Cardigan House, 37 Waterloo Road, Winton,
Dorset BH9 1BD. Telephone: 0202 533593 Fax: 0202 534572

THE UNIVERSAL PERSONAL ORGANISER (UPO)

This *new* and *unique* approach to time and self management is a diary system, based on the techniques created and taught by Tony Buzan.

The Universal Personal Organiser is a living system that grows with you, and that provides a comprehensive perspective on your life, your desires, and your business and family functions.

The Universal Personal Organiser is the first diary system to use the principles that Leonardo da Vinci discovered in the Italian Renaissance: that images and colour enhance both *creativity* and *memory*, as well as being more *enjoyable* and *easier* than regular diary systems.

The Universal Personal Organiser *reflects you*, and gives you the *freedom* to perform at your Highest Potential. The Universal Personal Organiser is made of materials that are to the *highest quality*, using the best leathers and paper available.

The Universal Personal Organiser is designed to help you manage the four main areas of life: *health* (mental, physical and emotional); *happiness (family); creativity;* and *wealth*.

The Universal Personal Organiser, in so doing, allows you to *organise* your past, present and future in a manner that is both *enjoyable* and *fun*.

The Universal Personal Organiser's pages and partitions have been designed to enable you to get a comprehensive perspective on your *yearly plan*, your *monthly* and *weekly plans*, and your *daily plan*, using the new *24 hour diary clock, Mind Mapping*, and *Use Your Head* systems.

BUZAN TRAINING COURSES

Courses are prepared for:
► Governments
► Corporations
► Schools and universities
► Private groups and organisations
► Foundations
► Children
► Families
► Senior citizens

The courses are based on the following books by Tony Buzan:
► *Use Your Head*
► *Use Your Memory*
► *Make the Most of Your Mind*
► *Master Your Memory*
► *Speed (and Range) Reading*
► *The Brain User's Guide*
► *Harnessing the ParaBrain*
► *Universal Personal Organiser*

The courses emphasise:
► Mind Mapping
► Memory skills – advanced
► Speed reading – advanced
► Learning to learn
► Creativity
► Presentation skills
► Work/study skills
► Corporate and family brain training
► The ageing brain
► Managing change
► Personal and time management
► Especially tailored courses

For enquiries, contact:

The Buzan Centre
Suite 2, Cardigan House, 37 Waterloo Road, Winton,
Dorset BH9 1BD.
Telephone: 0202 533593 Fax: 0202 534572

FOR FURTHER INFORMATION ON:

- ► Training courses based on Tony Buzan's methods
- ► Co-ordination of The Brain Club
- ► Supportive books, tapes and educational products

contact:

The Buzan Centre
Suite 2, Cardigan House, 37 Waterloo Road, Winton,
Dorset BH9 1BD.
Telephone: 0202 533593 Fax: 0202 534572

Please send a stamped, self-addressed envelope for
your reply.

ACKNOWLEDGEMENTS

The illustration on page 16 is from *The Organisation of the Brain* by
Walle J. H. Nauta and Michael Feirtag, copyright © September 1979 by
SCIENTIFIC AMERICAN Inc. All rights reserved.

Black and white illustrations: Al Creative Services; Lorraine Gill; Mike Gilkes;
Pep Reiff; Robert Walster
Colour plates: Bob Harvey (Plate I), Robert Walster (Plate II),
Pep Reiff (Plates IV–VIII)

Bibliography

Atkinson, Richard C., and Shiffrin, Richard M. 'The Control of Short-term Memory.' *Scientific American*, August 1971.

Baddeley, Alan D. *The Psychology of Memory*. New York: Harper & Row, 1976.

Borges, Jorge L. *Fictions* (especially *Funes, the Memorious*). London: J. Calder, 1985.

Brown, Mark. *Memory Matters*. Newton Abbot: David & Charles, 1977.

Brown, R., and McNeil, D. 'The "Tip-of-the-Tongue" Phenomenon.' *Journal of Verbal Learning and Verbal Behavior* **5,** 325–37.

Buzan, Tony. *The Brain User's Guide*. New York: E. P. Dutton, 1983.

Buzan, Tony. *Make the Most of Your Mind*. London: Pan, 1988.

Buzan, Tony. *Master Your Memory*. Newton Abbot: David & Charles, 1988.

Buzan, Tony. *Memory Visions*. Newton Abbot: David & Charles, 1989.

Buzan, Tony. *Use Your Memory*. London: BBC Books, 1989.

Buzan, Tony. *Speed (and Range) Reading*. Newton Abbott: David & Charles, 1988.

Ebbinghaus, H. *Über das Gedächtnis*. Leipzig: Duncker, 1885. op.

Gelb, Michael. *Present Yourself*. London: Aurum Press, 1988.

Haber, Ralph N. 'How We Remember What We See.' *Scientific American*, May 1970, 105.

Howe, J. A., and Godfrey, J. *Student Note-Taking as an Aid to Learning*. Exeter: Exeter University Teaching Services, 1977. op.

Howe, M. J. A. 'Using Students' Notes to Examine the Role of the Individual Learner in Acquiring Meaningful Subject Matter.' *Journal of Educational Research* **64,** 61–3.

Hunt, E., and Love, T. 'How Good Can Memory Be?' in *Coding Processes in Human Memory*, pp. 237–60, edited by A. W. Melton and E. Martin. Washington, DC: Winston/Wiley, 1972. op.

Hunter, I. M. L. 'An exceptional memory.' *British Journal of Psychology* **68,** 155–64, 1977.

Keves, Daniel. *The Minds of Billy Milligan.* New York: Random House, 1981; London: Bantam, 1982.

Loftus, E. F. *Eyewitness Testimony.* Cambridge, Mass.: Harvard University Press, 1980.

Luria, A. R. *The Mind of a Mnemonist.* Cambridge, Mass.: Harvard University Press, 1987.

Penfield, W., and Perot, P. 'The Brain's Record of Auditory and Visual Experience: A Final Summary and Discussion.' *Brain* **86,** 595–702.

Penfield, W., and Roberts, L. *Speech and Brain-Mechanisms.* Princeton, NJ: Princeton University Press, 1959. op.

Penry, J. *Looking at Faces and Remembering Them: A Guide to Facial Identification.* London: Elek Books, 1971. op.

Ruger, H. A., and Bussenius, C. E. *Memory.* New York: Teachers College Press, 1913. op.

Russell, Peter. *The Brain Book.* London: Routledge & Kegan Paul, 1966; Ark, 1984.

Standing, Lionel. 'Learning 10,000 Pictures.' *Quarterly Journal of Experimental Psychology* **25,** 207–22.

Stratton, George M. 'The Mnemonic Feat of the "Shass Pollak".' *Physiological Review* **24,** 244–7.

Suzuki, S. *Nurtured by love: a new approach to education.* New York: Exposition Press, 1969.

Thomas, E. J. 'The Variation of Memory with Time for Information Appearing During a Lecture.' *Studies in Adult Education,* April 1972, 57–62.

Tulving, E. 'The Effects of Presentation and Recall of Materials in Free-Recall Learning.' *Journal of Verbal Learning and Verbal Behaviour* **6,** 175–84.

von Restorff, H. 'Über die Wirkung von Bereichsbildungen im Spurenfeld.' *Psychologische Forschung* **18,** 299–342.

Wagner, D. 'Memories of Morocco: the influence of age, schooling and environment on memory.' *Cognitive Psychology* **10,** 1–28. 1978.

Yates, F. A. *The Art of Memory.* London: Routledge & Kegan Paul, 1966; Ark, 1984.

Index